T0084760

American Heresies and Higher Education

Other works of interest from St. Augustine's Press

Peter Augustine Lawler, *Homeless and at Home in America:*
Evidence for the Dignity of the Human Soul in Our Time and Place

Peter Lawler, *Allergic to Crazy:*
Quick Thoughts on Politics, Education, and Culture, Rightly Understood

Philippe Bénéton, *The Kingdom Suffereth Violence:*
The Machiavelli / Erasmus / More Correspondence

Albert Camus, *Christian Metaphysics and Neoplatonism*

Rémi Brague, *On the God of the Christians (and on one or two others)*

Rémi Brague, *Eccentric Culture: A Theory of Western Civilization*

Edward Feser, *The Last Superstition: A Refutation of the New Atheism*

H.S. Gerdil, *The Anti-Emile: Reflections on the Theory and Practice of*
Education against the Principles of Rousseau

Gerhard Niemeyer, *The Loss and Recovery of Truth*

James V. Schall, *The Regensburg Lecture*

James V. Schall, *The Modern Age*

Pierre Manent, *Seeing Things Politically*

Josef Kleutgen, s.j., *Pre-Modern Philosophy Defended*

Marc D. Guerra, *Liberating Logos:*
Pope Benedict XVI's September Speeches

Peter Kreeft, *Summa Philosophica*

Ellis Sandoz, *Give Me Liberty:*
Studies on Constitutionalism and Philosophy

Roger Kimball, *The Fortunes of Permanence:*
Culture and Anarchy in an Age of Amnesia

Stanley Rosen, *Essays in Philosophy* (2 vols., *Ancient* and *Modern*)

Roger Scruton, *The Meaning of Conservatism*

René Girard, *The Theater of Envy: William Shakespeare*

Joseph Cropsey, *On Humanity's Intensive Introspection*

American Heresies and Higher Education

Peter Augustine Lawler

Dissident American Thought Today Series

ST. AUGUSTINE'S PRESS
South Bend, Indiana

Copyright © 2016 by Peter Augustine Lawler

All rights reserved. No part of this book may be reproduced, stored in a retrieval system, or transmitted, in any form or by any means, electronic, mechanical, photocopying, recording, or otherwise, without the prior permission of St. Augustine's Press.

Manufactured in the United States of America.

1 2 3 4 5 6   23 22 21 20 19 18 17 16

Library of Congress Cataloging in Publication Data
Lawler, Peter Augustine, author.
American heresies and higher education / Peter Augustine Lawler.
South Bend, Indiana: St. Augustine's Press, 2016
Series: Dissident American thought today series
Includes index.
LCCN 2016012555
ISBN 9781587310393 (pbk: alk. paper)
LCSH: Education, Higher – United States.
LCC LA227.4 .L37 2016
DDC 378.73 – dc23
LC record available at https://lccn.loc.gov/2016012555

∞ The paper used in this publication meets the minimum requirements of the American National Standard for Information Sciences - Permanence of Paper for Printed Materials, ANSI Z39.48-1984.

St. Augustine's Press
www.staugustine.net

Contents

Introduction:
True Diversity and Being a
Dissident Postmodern Conservative

These closely interrelated essays explore who we think we are and what we believe we are supposed to do as free and relational persons these days. They were all written for particular occasions, and each is meant to stand alone.

Our country is rife with heresies, a situation which shouldn't be regarded as all that negative. Heresies are always partly true, and they highlight part of the truth we might otherwise ignore. Our insistent efforts to maximize our autonomy is based upon the truth that each one of us, as a free person, is more than merely part of a species or part of a country. Our libertarians—who are typically our most savvy futurologists—constantly celebrate the freedom we've won for ourselves through our technological capabilities. They typically fail to remind us, as Alexandre Solzhenitsyn does, that those same achievements and capabilities are now a particularly intricate challenge to our free wills. Technology is only good if limited and directed by our relational responsibilities, as well as by each of us authentically living in the truth.

Similarly, our evolutionary psychology is a heresy. It highlights the fact that we're irreducibly relational beings, and that most of our happiness comes from carrying out our natural responsibilities as members of a highly social species. An excessive concern with autonomy produces loneliness and disorientation, and it is surely the main cause of the birth dearth that threatens the future of our basic entitlements and may even become a national security issue. But evolutionary psychology can't even begin to account for the greatness and misery of our irreducible freedom, for, among other things, our self-conscious existence for a moment between two abysses. It also has little to say about what really animates priests, philosophers, poets, presidents, physicists, and so forth, because it can't capture anywhere near the whole range of polymorphous human eros.

Our Lockean pretensions about autonomy need to be chastened by what the Darwinians know about the "eusocial" animal, just as the Darwinians stand in need of guidance by the Lockean insight that each of us is not determined by some impersonal, species-driven biological destiny. And there's more. The Christians, at their best, teach us the whole truth about who we are as unique and irreplaceable creatures with singular personal destinies made in the image of a loving, creative, and rational God. It's the Christians, as our philosopher-pope emeritus reminds us, who discovered that the logos that governs the world must be personal, because, in our experience, logos is only present in persons.

Reform in higher education these days, the concern of roughly half the essays in this collection, is driven by the truth that each of us is a free being who works, and therefore it is irresponsible not to prepare students for the techno-vocational imperatives of the 21st century's global marketplace. Efforts at "disruptive innovation," however, are often at the expense of who we are as more than middle-class beings, as beings capable of both needing and loving genuinely higher education.

My purpose here is not to reject the blessings of technological progress, but to understand our various new births of freedom in light of the one true progress toward wisdom and virtue that occurs over the course of a particular human life. These essays are all about creating a "safe space" for liberal education in our increasingly one-dimensional educational system by deploying all means necessary to defend our genuine moral and intellectual diversity. The only way to create a safe space for diverse heresies is to form a point of view that grasps what is true and what is not true about each of them.

Because each of these essays is some kind of friendly criticism of the excesses of our time, it's not surprising that they draw often from the best friendly criticisms of democracy ever written: Alexis de Tocqueville's *Democracy in America*, book 8 of Plato's *Republic*, and Aleksandr Solzhenitsyn's "We have ceased to see the purpose," the speech he delivered at the International Academy of Philosophy in Liechtenstein

on September 14, 1993. It's rather stunning how much these three leading experts agree, and so all I have to do, in many cases, is join the cho-
rus. I can only hope that American democrats today will feel our tough
love.

The True Diversity Found in American Views of Education

That's not to say I'm confident that I possess the single comprehensive
view of who each of us is that can, in fact, inform our deliberations about
the content and mode of delivery of genuinely higher education. If you
look closely, it's not hard to see at least seven partial views of the purposes of higher education in our country, and each deserves its place.
My modest goal is to curb each partial view insofar as it mistakes itself
for a comprehensive view that excludes the others. If the proponents of
each view, however, are appropriately modest about their claims, it would
not even be true that they are heretical. I offer this list with the hope that
someone, somewhere will found an institution of higher education that
fits them all together in an institutional mission that incorporates all of
the diverse learning outcomes that correspond to the whole strange and
wonderful truth about who each of us is.

Aristocratic Platonism. Leisurely contemplation is for the few and
work is for the many. The few live outside the "cave," while the many
are completely formed by the city's (country's) process of socialization.
For the many, education is vocational and civic-minded. For the few, education consists of seeking the truth, and the truth is discovered primarily
by attending to the words of the philosophers in their "great books," although it also includes the latest breakthroughs in theoretical physics.
The highest form of higher education is for the philosophers of the future, who may or may not, as Senator Marco Rubio observes, find gain-
ful employment. Socrates, of course, lived in ten-thousand-fold poverty
because he had no leisure for what most people would call work, and he
wasn't even properly grateful for his rich friends who so often picked
up his tab.

Aristotelianism or Stoicism. Education should be directed toward
the cultivation of the souls of all rational men and women, but especially
future leaders. It fosters the pleasurable practice of the moral virtues,

the spirited virtue of courage, the classy virtues of generosity and magnanimity, and the more graceful social virtues having to do with manners and wittiness. A rational man has an appreciation for cultivated leisure, but he also knows that his life is for more than that. He lives by an honor code shared by rational men and women everywhere that allows him to know who he is and what he's supposed to do, even in the most difficult and lonely situations. So the point of classical education is to produce men like the fictional Atticus Finch or the POW Admiral Stockdale or, most of all, the irreproachably generous and magnanimous George Washington.

Middle-Class or Techno-Vocational Education. Higher education should be preparing free beings for work. The goal is for students to acquire flexible skills and competencies that allow men and women to flourish in the global marketplace. Education for contemplation or "knowing oneself," in this view, is a self-indulgent luxury. We should privilege the STEM majors not out of love of theoretical physics and mathematics but for their techno-productivity. If the traditional subjects, such as literature or philosophy, are to be taught, it's only because they offer students indispensable competencies such as critical thinking or effective communication; their actual content is of little interest or relevance. Traditional liberal education was once needed to breed gentlemen. As higher education becomes more democratic yet more costly, we need to ensure that students today waste neither time nor money on what they don't need. As Senator Rubio says, there hasn't been a market for "Greek philosophers" for over 2,000 years, but we're still pretty short on welders, who can be trained for a life of dignified productivity in a lot less than four years.

Political Correctness. The point of higher education is to eradicate racism, sexism, classism, and heterosexism. Educators and students should enlighten society and actively criticize the literary and artistic productions of our benighted past. Even academic freedom should give way to academic justice, and higher education should dispense with complacent serenity of privileged detachment and focus on activist engagement in pursuit of social justice. The most enlightened educational programs tend to be organized around diverse forms of personal identity and end in "studies," such as women's studies, African American studies, queer studies and so forth. Remember that American's aren't really pro-choice when it comes to the protection of rights, due to the high principles that inform our founding and our political development over time. We should celebrate the progress made by women, African Americans, gays, and so forth in the direction of justice, and part of higher education for us all should be an activist determination to do even better.

Literary Liberal Education. It is particularly important for those pursuing literary careers to read the classical Greek and Roman authors in their original languages. Advocates of this approach don't believe that the classical authors are right about everything. They're strong where techno-democracy is weak. Our writers should think of themselves as sustaining distinctions that correspond to the higher parts of the soul or the greatness of human individuality in a hostile, leveling environment. Those distinctions otherwise become trivialized in a society where metaphysics, theology, and poetry lose ground, and where all language tends to get flattened out in a techno-direction. It's unreasonable to expect most middle-class Americans to have the time or inclination to elevate democratic discourse through classical study, but they can be elevated as the audience for those who do.

Democratic Civic Education. Higher education should be primarily about "civic literacy." The premise of democracy is that each of us is not only a free being who works but a free citizen who has the responsibility of sharing in ruling. To that end, higher education must teach the "self-evident" principles of the *Declaration of Independence* and how they've been explained and applied by our leading statesmen. Because our Declaration is philosophic, even civic education can't just be about our "cave." It has to balance our devotion both to universal principles and to our particular country.

Christian Education. The basic insight, found in St. Augustine, is that both work and contemplation are for all of us made in the image of God. None of us sinners are too good not to work, and all of us are made to know God as well as the good for ourselves. Tocqueville reminds us of the Puritans, who made a rather high level of public education available to everyone. Their intention was partly technical, but it was also driven by the belief that every creature should be able to understand the Bible for himself or herself. And we should remember the great achievement that was the American system of secondary and higher Catholic education, where ordinary working-class men and women (including, of course, lots of recent immigrants) were given a rather classical, text-based liberal education to become Christian ladies and gentlemen able to understand and defend their faith. It's the Christians that allow us get beyond our silly dispute over whether higher education should be vocational or "liberal. None of us is too good to work, and we're all called to "contemplate" or think deeply and gratefully about who each of us is as a creature born for more than a merely biological destiny. Jesus himself was a carpenter (and might today be one of Rubio's welders), but he made it clear that nothing is more important for each of us than taking the time to listen to what he had to say about who we are and what we're supposed to do.

Think of the above as a kind of multiple choice test in response to the question "what is higher education?" If you're looking for the choice "all of the above," then you are a true defender of our country's moral and intellectual diversity. If you instantly want to rank or prioritize those choices, keep in mind that our large and wonderful array of public and private institutions allows for different rankings for different places. Remembering *that* should lead us all to become sworn enemies of all the tendencies toward leveling uniformity facilitated by our foundations, government, and accrediting associations.

Postmodern Conservatism as Dissident Political Thought

Because this book is one of the first in a series on American dissident political thought, let me add a bit to what I have said above about the postmodern and conservative approach that animates my writing. This approach deserves to be called dissident political thought. The idea of being postmodern and conservative can be found in the work of John Courtney Murray, Walker Percy, Aleksandr Solzhenitsyn and Václav Havel. It is a characteristic feature of both indigenous American Thomism and anti-Communist dissident thought.

To be postmodern and conservative is to deconstruct other uses of "postmodern" by beginning with the obvious. To be postmodern means to be about conserving what is true and good about the modern world, as well sustaining and restoring what is true and good about various pre-modern forms of thought and life. It is, as Solzhenitsyn explained, about criticizing the modern world for its excessive materialism and its replacement of God and virtue with therapeutic techno-comforts and legalism. It is also about criticizing the medieval world for its excessively single-minded focus on spiritual life, or the soul, at the expense of the body.

One of our conservative criticisms of purely modern thought is its prejudice in favor of endless innovation, which can be seen, for example, in its overly technological view of science. Maybe the purest source of modern thought these days is the hyper-libertarianism of some economists and Silicon Valley technologists which points in the direction of transhumanism. The false hope is that through techno-innovation we can become better or more free than merely humans, a hope that depends on ungratefully misunderstanding how stuck with—and how blessed—we are to be beings born to know, love, and die. That is not to say that we believe, as do those existentialists, that biological death is the final word about who each of us is.

To be postmodern and conservative is to take a stand somewhere between the traditionalists and the libertarians. The traditionalists focus on who each of us is as a relational being with duties and loyalties to particular persons and places. The libertarians—or, to be more clear, the individualists—focus on who each of us is as an irreducibly free person with inalienable rights. For the individualists, a person can't be reduced to a part of some whole greater than himself or herself.

A postmodern conservative is about showing how a free person privileged by nature and God with rights is also a rational and relational person with invincible responsibilities. All the progress we can imagine can't free us from being stuck with virtue. Still, we don't agree with some traditionalists that the cure for what ails us is somehow a return to a way of life that corresponds to a different or previous form of the division of labor. We're not for going back to Wendell Berry's farm or Alasdair MacIntyre's medieval village (or polis).

There's no reason that modern technology can't serve dignified human ends, and we should, as Solzhenitsyn said, embrace it as a challenging and so potentially ennobling gift. We even can talk up what's good about shopping at Walmart (a godsend for a large family in which both parents earn modest incomes) or eating at Waffle House. We can also see, however, that the progress of the division of labor in our time might be at the expense of opportunities for worthwhile work that supports a dignified relational life for many or most Americans. And the libertarians are wrong to think that there are techno-deregulatory fixes for all the negative effects of the global competitive marketplace on ordinary lives. The progressives, of course, are also wrong that any effective fix can come from a better and more omnicompetent government. We can have a kind of selective nostalgia for the days when some Americans had good wages, benefits, and pensions through unions, but that doesn't mean that there's any way to bring those unions back.

The libertarians are also right that things are getting better in many ways. There's much to be said for our meritocracy based on productivity, for our thinking of persons less than ever as members of races, sexes, classes, religions and sexual orientations. There's a lot to be said for the view of justice that has allowed women to become as free and equal economic actors as men. People these days don't ask who you are, but only what you can do. People are living longer than ever, especially those with the sense to prudently attend to what we now know about the various risk factors that imperil one's very being.

There are also the democratizing effects of the various screens that surround us, which are smarter and cheaper than ever. Everyone now has access, it seems, to all the information, wisdom, and entertainment that the world has produced. Globalization in many ways has expanded each person's menu of choice. Meanwhile, the family lives of very sophisticated and prosperous Americans are getting more stable and even somewhat more child-centered.

The traditionalists focus, however, on the many relational ways that things are getting worse. The families of ordinary Americans are getting pathological; the number of both single moms and lonely old people is rapidly growing. Add jobless recoveries, our failing schools, and the decline of the work ethic and we have lots of reasons why the increased dependence on government has made our welfare state unsustainable these days. Men have no idea how to treat women (and vice versa), and more and more people actually believe that being safe and consensual is the whole of sexual morality. We are more death-haunted than ever, and the result is that we're becoming ominously Puritanical and prohibitionist when it comes to health and safety. We have a birth dearth that would be worse if it weren't for the fruitful and multiplying procreative habits of our observant religious believers. And as our population ages, we've lost all sense of what old people are for, and so we feverishly try to look and act young as long as we can to remain productive. Unproductive caregiving is less valued or honored, and it seems less possible than ever to detach personal dignity from productivity. Our excessive concern with personal autonomy has been at the expense of the relational contexts in which it's possible to find real personal significance.

Language is becoming more vulgar or technologically one-dimensional, and we often lack the words that correspond to being moved by love, death, and God or his absence. The omnipresence of the screen diverts us from who we really are and robs us of the pleasures of both being alone in our rooms and being in love with real persons in the present. Liberal education in both its Christian and Stoic-classical dimensions is withering away, and in the name of the administrative project of "diversity" we are surrendering the real diversity that has been the saving grace of our educational system. As technology makes us more powerful, we personally get smaller. As courage declines, loyalty and gratitude become countercultural, leisure becomes indistinguishable from recreation, enduring friendship is displaced by convenient networking, and honor becomes merely a word.

We are wrong to, out of envy, criticize our meritocrats for their money; money is what they have earned. Our real problem is that we lack common standards of merit or virtue that show us what our money and power are for; members of our "cognitive elite" are often pathetically weak in connecting privileges with the responsibilities of being magnanimous, generous, and charitable. Liberty is too often understood as freedom from the relational responsibilities we have in common as creatures and citizens.

Well I could go on, but you get the picture. Postmodern conservatives dissent with rigorous selectivity from the dominant modes of complacently fashionable thought.

In getting this book together for publication, I'm especially indebted to the meticulous and industrious Berry College students Daniel Boddie

Andrew Hubbard, Matthew Klein, and Nathan Womack, as well as to the unfailing competence of the amazing Diane Land. For the tough love of needed criticism, I thank Adam Keiper, Daniel Boddie, and Richard Reinsch. My more enduring debts are three. My generous publisher Bruce Fingerhut. My students over 37 years at Berry College. And last and most, my family—Rita, Sara, Cat, Patrick, Molly, and Henry.

The chapters included here were originally found, sometimes in earlier versions, in *The New Atlantis*, *The Weekly Standard*, *Perspectives on Political Science*, *Claremont Review of Books*, *The City*, *Law and Liberty*, *Minding the Campus*, *Ethika Politika*, *National Affairs*, *The American Interest*, *Academic Questions*, and books published by SUNY Press, Fermentation Press, and Penn Press.

Part 1
American Heresies and Higher Education:
The Foundations

Chapter 1
Modernity and Our American Heresies

America, according to some of its critics, has less grounding in tradition than any other nation in history. The German philosopher Martin Heidegger said that the United States and the Soviet Union were metaphysically indistinguishable in their technological orientation, in their understanding of nature as nothing but resources to be exploited. The Canadian philosopher George Grant, influenced by Heidegger, claimed that the United States has wholly given itself over to technology, defining human purpose as nothing more than the acquisition of power. All genuinely political life, and all philosophy, theology, and other forms of contemplation, have disappeared from America. For these not entirely friendly foreign critics, the United States is the country mostly wholly in the thrall of the technological "how" at the expense of any reflection on the "why" of humanly worthy purposes.

If, as Alexandre Solzhenitsyn claimed, it is characteristic of the modern West to have "ceased to see the purpose" that should be the foundation of human life, it is perhaps in America that the individualized and demoralizing consequences of modern emptiness are most advanced. Beneath our therapeutic happy-talk and technologically optimistic pragmatism, a critic like Solzhenitsyn can hear the howl of existentialism. Americans have "nothing," nothing but inarticulate anxiety, with which to resist the "something," the measurable effects, of technological progress.

Fortunately, we have technological remedies for our anxiety. There are, of course, those of the pharmacological variety. But there are also the diversion of the screen, from the smartphone to the laptop, from social media to video games to Internet porn. The complacently honest libertarian Tyler Cowen points to the dark side of our hyper-meritocratic future, where those individuals not clever and competent enough to succeed will lead marginally productive lives, contented by screen-based entertainment and other cheap high-tech diversions made by those at the top. But neither class, in this vision of the future, will include many who will be distinguished by the heart-enlarging traditional virtues of generosity or charity.

The genuinely countercultural philosopher-comedian Louis C.K. denies his daughters smartphones so that they might not find an easy way out of the anxious sadness that overwhelms us all from time to time for no good reason. We are more and more satisfied with the predictable, minimalist emotion that comes from being diverted both from one's own solitary emptiness, one's misery without God or without the communal and intimate attachments of a rich relational life, and from the empathy that comes from closeness to others.

The wasteland of emptiness grows in America, most of all, because of our lack of a culture or tradition to keep it in check. Certainly there never was a pre-modern America. Americans have little experience of living in close-knit communities like the medieval village or the classical polis that Alasdair MacIntyre finds indispensable for human flourishing. Although the agrarian localist Wendell Berry sometimes writes about the unsettling of America, he has also written that America, the country or project, was born unsettled; the Europeans were already modern when they moved to the New World and imposed their liberated will upon the indigenous people.

It is characteristically American not to be able to resist progress, even in order to preserve the way of life, the manners, morals, and virtues, of a particular place. From its foundation, America has existed, in MacIntyre's memorable phrase, "after virtue." It is, as Carey McWilliams put it, a "technological republic" in which republican virtue is replaced by the enlightened management of self-interest. McWilliams argued that it was the philosopher John Locke who provided enlightened Americans with the "educational technology" that was "the mirror of the framers' political principles." To be a Lockean American is to be distrustful of authority and attachment and "driven by the desire for freedom and mastery." For these critics, Locke's theory of the inventive conquest of nature for human convenience is America. Maybe more precisely, it is America's theory, and it increasingly is becoming American practice. What we say, especially if we have the Lockean opinion that words are basically weapons that we use to achieve our practical or technical goals, cannot help but transform what we do. Much of the history of America has been defined by our inability to limit Locke's individualistic and technological understanding of who each of us is. That is why, for Heidegger, America represented the way "the wasteland grows" in our technological era.

The wasteland grows, ironically, on the basis of Locke's technological understanding of what waste is. Prior to the invention of money, according to Locke, wastefulness meant picking more apples than you can eat before they spoil. The injunction not to waste was nothing more or less than a sensible recognition of a natural limit on effective human labor; it kept people from sweating for no good reason, from picking for the sake of picking. But after the invention of money, no apples picked need spoil; they could be traded for little pieces of yellow metal that never do. Given the Lockean technology-friendly view that just about all real "value" comes from human labor, from improving upon what we are given by nature, "thou shalt not waste" comes to mean that any uncultivated land is wasted. All of nature is to be treated as a resource to be technologically transformed for our convenience.

In light of that technological imperative not to waste, it is ironic that the wasteland grows. As America's critics would put it, everything we are given is degraded or despoiled by the infinite imperatives of our material needs. Nothing in America exists "according to nature" anymore. And everything, as our traditionalist critics argue (following Marx), has a cash value. But what Marx views in positive ways—he admires the ardor with which capitalism mobilized human labor to overcome natural scarcity—critics like MacIntyre and Heidegger view negatively. They believe, after all, that nature gives us more than fearful misery and the freedom to do something about it; nature, properly understood, is the source of the purposes that make life worth living. For these critics of the American technological way of life, the fundamental fact is not natural scarcity but natural order, and our truthful understanding of that order is embedded in traditions and customs of particular places that are laid waste by promiscuous technological innovation.

Technological Virtues

So critics such as Heidegger, MacIntyre, and Grant see that American liberalism is really a kind of technological nihilism. It is freedom for nothing in particular beyond power and control. Sometimes they turn to Alexis de Tocqueville to remind us that this nihilism is really a feature of American democracy, although Tocqueville is really not quite as pessimistic as they are. Tocqueville explains that Americans follow the Cartesian method without having ever read a word of Descartes. That modern method, the foundation of the technological view of the world, is doubt. All I really know is that I am, and so the only point of life, the only reasonable use of my freedom, is to keep me from not not-being for as long as possible. The only kind of science that survives methodical doubt is that which improves the comfort and security of particular individuals, of me in particular. The proud desire to know for its own sake is less worthwhile because it is unproductive and as such would be a waste of our productive potential.

The Cartesian method is the democratic method, which is why the modern Americans could have discovered it without reading Descartes. It is all about doubting personal authority. If I defer to your word, then I let you rule me. That is true of all personal authority, from princes to priests to parents and even or especially the personal God. Nobody is better than me, and so nobody knows better than me. I methodically doubt my way to that democratic opinion. I have no reason to privilege anyone's opinion over my own.

Of course, this Cartesian position of doubt is not quite the nihilism that America's critics decry. But it does pose some problems for our democracy. According to this Cartesian-democratic doubt, nobody is better than me, but I am no better than anyone else. So I have no personal content, no point of view by which to privilege my opinion over the opinions of others. As Tocqueville observes, I especially have no point of view by which to resist public opinion, which appears to be determined by no one in particular. It is undemocratic to defer to some person, but it seems perfectly democratic, in a way, for all persons to defer equally to some impersonal force. That goes not only for public opinion, but also for other impersonal forces such as "History," and of course "technology." I know

I'm not nothing, but I lack what it takes, all by myself, to fill myself up with something. And so I'm carried along by impersonal forces I have no right to resist, especially if, as in the case of technology, the impersonal forces aim to keep me, as a person, around as long as possible.

Technology is both impersonal, insofar as it cannot distinguish one person from other, and highly personal, insofar as it is about sustaining the lives of people by controlling the impersonal nature that would otherwise be a constant threat to us. But seeing personal life as nothing more than gaining the power and control necessary to sustain life against an indifferent and hostile nature is what leads to America's technological and democratic nihilism. It is nihilistic because it empties personal life of the relational context, which includes dogmatic personal authority, in which it can find real content, a point of view, or spirit of resistance. That's why it makes good sense to say American democracy is, in principle, "after virtue." The democrat does not know who he is (beyond not not-being) or what he is supposed to do.

If there is any kind of American virtue, it is nothing more than being as attentive as possible to health and safety. The traditional virtues of chastity and gentlemanliness, with all their complex demands governing and shaping the relationships between the sexes, are replaced with the much simpler virtue of "safe sex," which means not only sensibly avoiding the infectious diseases that might cut short our lives, but also avoiding the babies that might cut short our lives as free individuals, unfettered by relationships with noisy little dependants. But while sex has become much simpler, the worries we have about avoiding "risk factors" have been multiplying every day, as scientists tell us more and more about how everything from cheeseburgers to spending too much time in the sun (or too little!) could threaten our health and even end up killing us years down the road. At least in principle, most Americans are likely sympathetic to the transhumanist dream of a world in which all the risk factors have gone away, in which all sex is safe, and in which we would not have to be concerned with generating replacements because no one would need to be replaced.

The emotional result of the American's interpersonal isolation is what Tocqueville named individualism, the indifference that flows from the mistaken judgment that love and hate are more trouble than they're worth. If you want to see a display of contemporary American individualism, watch a rerun of *Seinfeld* or *Curb Your Enthusiasm* or even the Charlie Sheen version of *Two and a Half Men*. Healthy men have hearts so contracted that they don't have what it takes emotionally (they're fine physically) to reproduce. We also recognize American men and women described as emptied of content by democratic or anti-relational doubt in Allan Bloom's classic *The Closing of the American Mind*. Those "flat souled" or erotically lame sophisticated Americans are unmoved by either love or death; they are nothing more, it seems, than technological beings: clever and competent, specialists and survivalists.

Religion to the Rescue

If all these gloomy ideas about the sorry state of our souls in America sound almost too bad to be true, that's because they are. For Tocqueville, the worst evils of individualism and technological obsessiveness were more of an inherent possibility for America than a description of how most Americans really lived. Americans combat individualism through various heart-enlarging activities, the most important among them being religion. Tocqueville was astonished by the way Americans exempted their religious faith from their habitual doubt. Today, much more than in Tocqueville's time, Americans are actually less individualistic, less selfishly withdrawn and more concerned about their responsibility to their country and their fellow creatures than Europeans. And the reason is the nation's exceptional religiosity. It is Americans' religion that gets their minds off their own material wellbeing and points them in the direction of their personal, relational duties. It is their religious authorities, their preachers, ministers and rabbis and priests, who persuade them that the truth is more than technological, that they were born to contemplate both who God is and their own singular personal destinies as beings with souls. It is this religious knowledge and cultivation that give Americans the confidence to think and act freely, to rule themselves and others as free and relational beings.

But, our traditionalist critics respond, we should look at the reality of American religion, and not Tocqueville's idealized version of it. Well, most of it has been Christian, that is, various forms of Christian heresy.

Consider the ridiculous and tyrannical Puritans who wanted to turn every sin into a crime; the hyper-enthusiastic and at times semi-literate evangelicals; the incomprehensible tongue-speaking Pentecostals and holiness snake-handlers; and the Mormons, that uniquely American Christian heresy that even has another whole book of Scripture. Meanwhile, our mainstream Protestants have made, from the beginning, too many compromises with modern individualism to have served effectively as counterweights to the extremes of self-expressive pantheism and unhinged enthusiasm that have characterized our beliefs. What about the more orthodox and traditional religions of our immigrants, such as the Catholics and Jews? Traditionalists can complain that America has changed Catholicism a lot more than Catholicism has changed America. And the practicing Orthodox Jews say the same thing about most American Jews.

These heretical deviations from religious tradition and orthodoxy are hardly new in America. As Tocqueville observed, the Americans, having rejected the intellectual and emotional resources of tradition and deference to personal authority, find it hard to think and act reasonably about God and the soul. The Americans are characterized less by reason than by will, and so they are full of exaggerations—at one moment vainly overestimating the significance of who they are and what they do, and in another paralyzed by the perception of the puny insignificance of any particular being.

Capitalist Christianity

Even when we admit that American religion is full of heresies, we have to remember heresies aren't all bad. They often highlight something that has been neglected by orthodox tradition. When I watch a low-church movie starring Robert Duvall, *Tender Mercies* or *The Apostle*, I know that I'm seeing a truthful portrayal of Christian truth, if far from the whole truth. The murderer-on-the-run preacher in *The Apostle* who founds a church where class and status make no difference, a congregation of displaced misfits who are poor and poorer, dumb and dumber, black and white, male and female, fat and fatter still, is telling people who need to hear (because they can't read) what they most need to know to turn their lives around; they can be saved, despite it all, if they believe in Jesus and "Holy Ghost power." There is something exceptional about a country that carries the truth about amazing grace in its popular culture and its country music.

Traditionalists often exaggerate what a technological wasteland America is by denying that evangelicals and Pentecostals are really Christian. Sure, no other country is plagued so much by warehouse churches, touchy-feely platitudes posing as theology, and the soul-challenged music that's called Christian contemporary. But none of those criticisms gets to the question of whether the evangelicals really believe or whether they really practice the virtues, beginning with charity, that flow from love of the personal God. Where would Americans be without the exceptional fact of their belief? Certainly there has to be room for that free, egalitarian, and virtuous belief, and the whole Christ-haunted South, in an account of who we are as a nation.

American Protestantism is not simply or even mainly the individualistic negation of relational life. Marx said that for Americans even religion is just another whimsical private preference like any other commodity and is a sign of our alienation from community. Americans "church shop," and lots of them switch churches as often as they switch cars. American Protestant ministers are often paid what amounts to a percentage of the Sunday collection. So they have every incentive to be consumer-sensitive, and one result is all the technological amenities that we can find in our mega-churches. Economists might say that the reason religion flourishes in America is that government does nothing to sustain it, and so our preachers and churches are wonderfully entrepreneurial. The idea of selecting the religion that's "right for you" the same way we shop around for the right car is, of course, ridiculous, and in a country that is full of conflicting theological views, individuals choosing among them can't help but wonder if any of them could really be true.

This Marxist understanding of American religion, in which Americans turn to church to free themselves from the competitive rigors of the dog-eat-dog world of capitalism, only to find their churches destabilized as much as any other American institution by the logic of the market, is, of course, distorted by the "historicist" conviction that the success of capitalism had authoritatively and permanently discredited every "spiritual" claim for truth. We find a similar kind of distortion in Bloom's conviction that modern theory had transformed every feature of American practice, just as we find it in Grant's or Heidegger's conviction that to be American is to regard nature and other persons as nothing more than resources to be exploited.

Many American preachers, certainly most of those we see on TV, have to some extent confused being entrepreneurial with being evangelical. It is also true, however, that the best way to be a successful religion entrepreneur is to be evangelical, to be all about the good news that we all have a friend in the Jesus who sees and loves us just as we are. American Christianity is relatively anti-institutional and surely seems to pit emotion against reason, the heart against the head, and the "Biblical worldview" against "the secular, rationalist worldview." Tocqueville, by describing the characteristically American religious form of the revivalist camp meeting, called attention to its excessive displacement and its over-reliance on raw enthusiasm. But he also saw it as evidence that the soul has and will always have needs that can be denied or distorted but not eradicated. And he compared the enthusiasm of the Americans to that of the original Christians in reaction against Roman Epicureanism. It is a reaction against the technological and political project to make each of us totally at home in this world. The good news is that the pedestrian claim that middle-class Americans have reasonably organized their lives according to the principles of self-interest is contradicted by the wondrous love that animates American faith.

Building Better Than They Knew

Not only are heresies not all bad, but American heresies have had the tendency to balance each other out. America's first and most wonderful and effective theological balancing act was our Declaration of Independence, the greatness of which lies in its compromise between the Deistic and Lockean and the more Calvinist or residually Puritan members of the Continental Congress. Congress amended Thomas Jefferson's more Deistic draft, "mangling" it in Jefferson's own opinion, but actually improving it. A key compromise was between the unrelational, past-tense God of nature (held by the modern philosophers, including especially

John Locke) and the personal, judgmental, providential Creator (held by the Puritans). By reconciling the God of nature with the God of the Bible, our Declaration can be called a kind of accidental Thomism, an accidental affirmation of the personal natural law of St. Thomas Aquinas. That result was intended by neither the Calvinist nor Lockean parties to the compromise.

Our Declaration suggests that we are free and relational beings by nature, natural persons, without referring at all, of course, to Biblical revelation. Our natural longings as free persons point toward a certain kind of Creator, and we know who we are in that respect even if we do not have particular knowledge of or faith in who that God is. Our transcendence is not merely our Cartesian or Lockean freedom from nature for self-determination. Nor is our transcendence merely the elitist, selfish, and fundamentally amoral "freedom of the mind," that philosophers, including Jefferson's private letters, claim. We are free from political determination for, as Madison wrote, doing our conscientious duties to our Creator, duties that even Madison did not sufficiently recognize are not lonely and inward but social and relational. For Americans, freedom of religion, properly understood, is freedom for churches, of personal authority embodied in organized religion.

The greatest American Catholic political thinker, Orestes Brownson, claimed that our written Constitution (and, of course, our Declaration) depended on our "providential constitution," on the intellectual and cultural resources that shaped the American people. Brownson also claimed that our Founders, as statesmen, took into account what Americans were given when building their political institutions, which is why their particular political accomplishments are better than their abstract or Lockean political theory, which is why they built "better than they knew," in the phrase that Catholic thinker John Courtney Murray popularized.

The lucid dogma of equality that distinguished our Declaration seems to have more than one source, and its emergence from various forms of Christian heresy allowed its insistent and truthful claim for the unique and irreplaceable dignity of every free and equal human person to be preserved in the form of a compromise. By being really very personal, the truth the Declaration teaches about "all men" reconciles particularity with universality. As Tocqueville explains, the difference between the egalitarian universalism of Christianity and that of, say pantheism, Buddhism, or Darwinism, is that only Christianity shields the truth about the person from absorption by the homogeneous forces that surround an American.

Puritan Contributions

The thing that might have amazed Tocqueville the most about our country is the determination that every person should be educated to exercise his freedom. No person exists by nature to be dominated by another, and slavery is contrary to the truth about who each of us is. That truth should not be hidden from anyone, because nobody should be suckered by lies—either the Puritans who emphasize the lies of Satanic deceivers who distort what the Bible says in the service of their own pride, or the Lockeans who emphasize the lies of aristocrats who vainly try to persuade us that the point of your life is to be in their service. From our Lockean Deists, we get the truth that every human being has interests. Nobody is above and nobody is below being a being with interests. We are all free beings who work, we are free to work, and we are stuck with working. The result, Tocqueville observed, is universal literacy and universal technical education. But that Lockean view comes at the expense of the cultivation of the soul, which is dismissed as a waste of one's valuable time. That is why when our libertarians criticize American colleges today, it is for charging so much money for all kinds of nonsense, such as philosophy and theology, which just won't help students get a job.

The Puritans, as the neo-Puritanical novelist Marilynne Robinson explains, are a key source of our devotion to liberal education, to education for civilization. From them we get the idea that education can be for the sake of more than mere work or productivity. Every person has a soul, and so everyone should be able to read what the Bible says about one's personal destiny and one's charitable, moral responsibilities for oneself. Most of our best colleges have had a religious inspiration, and they suffer in the most important respects when they lose confidence in what they can do for the souls of their students. Robinson calls attention to the neo-Puritanical Oberlin College in the 1830s. This college offered everyone, including African Americans and women, a liberal education and insisted that everyone on campus, including professors, both take part in manual labor and have time for leisurely study. To see how Oberlin has changed, watch the brilliant HBO series *Girls*, which is about a graduate of that school who is absolutely clueless about who she is as a person, that she is made to love, work, and know. She has no idea what she is supposed to do, and college did not help her out at all in answering the questions of her soul.

Of course, sophisticated Americans have always resisted the Puritanical correction to their enlightened individualism. One reason that this correction is indispensable is that the devotion to individual rights, by itself, does not justify the personal sacrifice required to achieve egalitarian political reform. The philosophical and theoretical language about the equality of man was also indispensable, but it was the neo-Puritanical abolitionists who produced the relentless egalitarian agitation that made the Civil War inevitable. The Civil Rights movement would likewise not have succeeded without the social reformism based on a kind of residually Puritanical or Biblical conception of citizenship which is one that did not shrink from the sacrifice of one's own blood for justice.

Then there is the American Puritanical personal morality so criticized by the rest of the highly civilized world. When a European says "The trouble with Americans such as you is that you're too Puritanical," your response should be, "I'm Puritanical and proud of it. You should be too. Look at you!" The typical European criticism of Americans is actually that they are both Puritanical repressive moralists and Lockean workaholic capitalists. The proper response is "there is nothing wrong with that." It is civilized to be moral and both necessary and fulfilling to be productive. We are the people who know how to balance love and work. About much of the Old World and its seemingly decayed-beyond-repair Christianity, Americans can say there is both a shortage of work and a shortage of love. Thanks to our observant Christians, Mormons, and Jews, we can add, the birth dearth, the demographic crisis that threatens the very future of free government and "Western culture" in Europe, is a very manageable problem in America.

Tocqueville notices, of course, that the virtues of chastity and marital fidelity are on display in America like they had never been before. And even today, we can say that Americans, because of their Christianity, take those virtues more seriously than people in many other developed countries. To be Puritanical, remember, is to be concerned with the souls of your fellow citizens and fellow creatures. It is easy to overdo that concern, as we Americans did with the piece of Puritanical fanaticism called Prohibition. But don't forget that the opposite of excessively intrusive concern is the yawn of indifference, which could hardly be a virtue. A Puritanical residue Tocqueville praises in America was Sunday closing laws, which gave everyone a leisurely respite from the busyness of commerce to focus through sermons and reading on one's own singular immortal destiny, on one's own soul and its relational needs and duties.

Lockean Contributions

I have probably overdone my praise of the Puritans, and so to restore the balance that is our Declaration, I will go on to explain some of the ways in which our country has benefited from the Deism of John Locke, starting with a few words about what Deism is.

Lockean Deists speak of God, but in the past tense. He's on a permanent vacation. He's not actively engaged in our lives. God made us free or somewhat unnatural persons who have to institute government to free ourselves from our fearful discontent with our natural existence. The teaching of the source of our freedom is that you are on your own to escape from nature to secure our inalienable rights. Deists believe that we must provide for ourselves because neither God, the author of each of our beings, nor nature cares about any of us in particular. The Deists are monotheists, but they deny that each of us has a personal relationship with God.

Locke and Jefferson viewed us all both as free persons and as simply a part of nature. The mystery of the personal identity each of us experiences makes room in Locke for belief in a real Creator, and it certainly is a personal refutation of those self-forgetting thinkers who claim that all is necessity. "Nature's God," the phrase used in the Declaration, is not the God of Aristotle, who is not a person but a principle, not a "who" but a "what," like a giant magnet.

The mystery of Christianity, rejected by most philosophers and scientists, is personal, relational monotheism. The most aggressive part of Locke's heresy is the rejection of that mystery, the mystery of the Trinity.

For Locke, God is personal, but not relational, just as we are personal, but not deep down relational. God, like each of us, is finally on his own.

Locke's personal, Christian heresy is actually more mysterious than the doctrine of the Trinity. How can God be both personal and not relational and loving? How can each of us be personal but not relational and loving? Can such a lonely and isolated personal identity really be possible? We can say for certain that Locke separates "personal" from "relational" in order to make it clear enough that personal identity and security is the bottom line, the point of all being. Locke, remember, is most justly famous for mocking out of existence the hyper-relational traditional arguments for tyranny, such as Filmer's divine right of kings, which portrayed us as all one big family under the personal paternalistic monarch ruling in God's image.

The shared personal focus explains why American Lockeans and more orthodox Christians have allied against every modern effort to reduce particular persons to expendable parts of some civic, natural, or Historical whole. It led the Americans to defeat every form of progressive ideology that would sacrifice real persons living today for some vague perfect tomorrow, for some historically created paradise right here on earth. It is that personal focus, whether found in orthodox believers or feminist autonomy fanatics, which has kept Americans from really believing for a moment that Darwin teaches the whole truth about who we are.

We also see the influence of this Lockean and Christian understanding in the determination of James Madison that religion in America should not be reduced to a civil theology, to degrading lies about our divine significance as a nation of beings who are citizens and nothing more. Our Constitution is silent on God precisely because it presupposes the person's freedom from political domination to discover his or her conscientious duties to the Creator. The separation of church and state only makes sense in terms of the Christian understanding of who each of us is. That is why the Italian theorist and politician Marcello Pera, for one, is wrong to say that a kind of "cultural" Christianity can be Europe's civil theology. If what the Christians teach about the person is true, then civil theology is a degrading lie. If it is not true, then there is no barrier to the state using religion as a vehicle of popular control.

We can say that the relative impersonality of the modern state is a radical improvement, on a Christian foundation, over the ancient polis and personal monarchies. The authority of the king is different in kind from that of the personal God. The relatively impersonal authority of the state is circumscribed by the more personal and relational authority of religion as an organized community of thought and action. It goes without saying that a pure Lockean cannot do justice to the purpose of the church in addressing our deepest longings as social and relational persons. But, thanks to our Puritanism or Calvinism, our Lockeanism has not been that pure.

Technology and Our Homelessness

The American, then, will not be martyred by civil or ecclesiastical authorities for either refusing to swear allegiance to the state or refusing to swear allegiance to Christ the King. American Christians can be dutifully loyal to both state and church, because neither claims competence over the sphere of the other. Americans resist both political domination of religion and religious domination of politics.

Even the progress of science, liberated in a technological direction by the modern emphasis on serving the needs of the free person, has really been progress from a Christian view. It is surely Christian to demand that science, politics, and economics have to be justified through the elevation of ordinary lives.

Modern science is also a revelation of who we are as free beings, although not, of course, a complete revelation. Modern science overemphasizes our "homelessness," our personal contingency, in a sometimes heroic effort to make this world a better home for us. It, of course, fails to abolish our homelessness, because it cannot address its deepest cause. Nonetheless, there is something Christian in acknowledging our inability to be fully at home in either nature or "the city." We are right to be concerned that the personal obsessions that fuel the transhumanist aspirations of modern science will come at the cost of living well as relational beings; that is yet another reason why our Deistic (or unrelational) heresy has to be balanced by our Puritanical (or intrusively un-relational) one.

Our admirable and friendly critic Solzhenitsyn, remember, called modern technology, with its dislocating effects on, for example, the relations between the generations, another trial of free will. There is no reason not to believe that technological progress can be guided by the one true progress that can occur in each personal life. As Walker Percy noted, technology can make us more alive than ever to the truth that this life is a pilgrimage, rooted in existential dislocation, for each of us.

Is Balance Sustainable?

Today, the balance of heresies that is the genius of our Declaration is threatened. On such issues as abortion, gay rights, and entitlements, our courts and bureaucracies are making decisions without deferring to the legislatures that are better equipped to strike the appropriate balance. The clash of reasons that produces democratic compromise can chasten the autonomy freaks and elevate some Christians from their fundamentalism, making it possible to balance free personal identity with the imperatives of relationality. But legislative compromise has been too largely displaced by the high principle that animates judges and bureaucrats.

Our courts seem to understand the word liberty to be nothing more than a weapon to be used by each generation of Americans to expand the realm of individual autonomy over time. That means that purely Lockean theory is to trump what we know through science, especially through Darwin and his successors, about who we are as social animals. It surpasses, in other words, realistic compromises by relational persons oriented by God and nature toward the truth about who humans are.

In recent decades our judges, liberal elites, and bureaucrats have claimed that their judicial decisions are more "final" than they conceivably can be. Their efforts to stifle civic and political deliberation might produce a kind of coherence, but almost never a genuinely decisive and enduring result. The most obvious example here is abortion, where *Roe v. Wade* has not settled the constitutional or moral issue for Americans, but has made real discussion of the issue, and the compromise of reasonable contending claims, all but impossible.

It is too easy to claim that our culture wars are between dogmatic secularists and dogmatic Christians. My friendlier interpretation is that they are mainly between two forms of Christian heresy. Lockean and Protestant Trinitarian. These two heretical forms, working together, have produced a country in which almost everyone "thinks personally" now. But it is also easy to see that thinking too personally can come at the expense of the relational context in which persons can think clearly, act confidently, find status or significance, find both love and duties, and be happy.

As our Founders discovered in the compromise of the Declaration, understanding God to be both personal and relational, and both the God of nature and the God of the Bible, comes closer to the whole truth about who we are than the understanding that governed either party to the compromise. Privileging legislative compromise over high principle need not be at the expense of the truth. It is just a realistic recognition that American heresies or American factions all come short of capturing the whole truth about who we are as persons "hardwired," so to speak, to be free and relational, willing and loving, and open to the truth.

Chapter 2
Truly Higher Education

Education is a perennial human good, and its decadence today comes, most of all, from neglecting its proper purposes. One of those purposes, of course, is to prepare free persons to compete effectively in the global competitive marketplace, and the evidence is abundant that our colleges and universities are failing us on that front. But another purpose, especially associated with higher education, is to help us understand who we are as more than free and productive beings. And on that front, most of our institutions of higher education seem even more inept.

Our political and economic freedoms are properly understood as mainly ministerial to what gives particular lives personal significance, as helping us in being good friends, parents, children, citizens, creatures, and so forth. Likewise, individual freedom must be a central goal of good government, but it must not be the only goal. The good of liberty to a person is most evident and true when it is practiced through roles that require responsibility to others. So let's begin by remembering that having freedom is not necessarily always a good in itself; politically speaking, libertarian means should be used for non-libertarian ends. Those Republicans who want to make real reforms in public policy should therefore be interested in more than cutting taxes for "job creators" and achieving maximum conceivable deregulation and personal autonomy. While economic growth is certainly good for everyone, growth alone cannot obliterate all the relational issues connected with our struggling, broken families and sinking middle class.

Some of the dependency facilitating institutions of the welfare state have surely contributed to personal irresponsibility in a world with too many feckless men and lonely single moms. But it's also true that the progress of the division of labor itself makes it more difficult for ordinary Americans to find jobs that afford them the wherewithal to live a life of relational dignity. Candid libertarian futurists, such as Tyler Cowen, explain that the future will be about the division of our country into a cognitive elite and those who work off the scripts devised through the intellectual labor of those elite. Once work becomes reliably scripted, of course, the worker can be replaced by a machine, a computer, or a robot, so that the top and bottom spread even further apart. "Average," Cowen tells us, "is over."

It's easy to get wrapped up in a (consciously selective) nostalgia for industrial unions, as the foundation for the "family wage" earned by so many workers. At one time, the largest non-governmental employer in the country was General Motors, where the average pay was around $40 an hour in today's money with excellent benefits. Today, it's Walmart, at about $10, and no benefits. Conservatives know that the day of the union is over and to proceed otherwise is literally counterproductive given the realities of the global marketplace. Genuinely conservative, or genuinely progressive or non-reactionary, reform today must be market-based and decentralizing.

Any attempt at educational reform has to come to terms with this changing reality. That means, for one thing, that higher education has to be oriented toward preparing people to be independent operators with flexible skills, in a world where employer and employee loyalty are withering away and "what you know" is more completely displacing "who you know." Colleges are frequently failing to prepare students for that future and not only in the ways that our economically obsessed political discussions tend to emphasize.

The College Bubbles

The elite model of American higher education used to be the most reliable path to a successful future. A privileged person could move from the fairly leisurely, cultivated, and comfortable environment of the liberal arts college to the enveloping institutional arms of the professional school, law, medicine, or business, and then on to a fairly secure "career" in a firm, practice or corporation. All along, a certain level of literacy and analytical ability was required, but the whole system was filled with "safety nets" that cushioned the person from the unmediated pressures of the market. And all along, the loans required to fund all this education were more than justified by the prospect of the high and secure income to come.

But the whole elite model of American higher education may soon be outmoded. Today, borrowing big to go to law or medical school is an extremely risky move. Physicians may soon be largely displaced by diagnostic computers, which know more and make many fewer errors. The personal touch and personal judgment can be provided by nurses, who will refer the rare case they and the computer can't handle to a specialist. Much of what lawyers do will also increasingly be done by machines. We see that the supply of lawyers already considerably exceeds the demand, and their average compensation and perks, like those of ordinary physicians, are dropping quickly. Enrollment in law school is also dropping, as is the quality of law students, and even good schools are being forced to discount their rates to fill seats. If you still love the law or medicine, you should still, of course, "follow your passion," but in a much more entrepreneurial spirit; just like everyone else, you'll likely spend your career functioning as an independent contractor, selling your skillful labor piecemeal for a price. From this skillful-labor point of view, higher education as "liberal education" seems like an ill-considered choice, not worth the cost in time and treasure.

Everyone agrees that higher education should be more responsive to the market and that graduates often are ill-prepared for a world in which many traditionally middle-class jobs are becoming harder and harder to find. Employers who complain about unprepared college graduates, however, often don't mean that students lack specific technical skills; the problem is that new workers don't have the general literacy, capacity for thought, and personal discipline necessary for life in the workplace. What employers often mean, in other words, is that graduates don't have the manners, morals, and confident literacy of ladies and gentlemen. They don't have what a college or even high-school diploma used to fairly reliably signify.

The blame for this failure is often placed on the artificial and infantilizing environment of the residential college, which is typically described as a "bubble." Though the form of the liberal arts college remains (in many cases), there is little trace of its old animating discipline. Students allegedly frolic freely in luxury while doing very little work. Little is required of them either in the classroom or the dorms. They are not only allowed but encouraged to express themselves as they please, as long as it's safe and consensual. This socially engineered environment often yields an unpleasant sense of entitlement. Students can end up altogether unfit to enter the competitive market upon graduation. This might be especially true if they've coasted through with one of the notoriously "easy" majors; colleges have not given these students any intellectual "value added" and perhaps the opposite of professional manners and morals.

Critics of the bubble often describe this way of life as the result of a corrupt bargain among professors and students. The "tenured radicals" of the professorial class also luxuriate with a rich sense of entitlement while doing very little work. They can teach all sorts of envious and malicious nonsense without being held accountable. Tenure allows them to do what they please, as long as students like them and continue to take their courses. All they have to do is give students good grades for very little effort; in return, students will give them good evaluations, whether or not these evaluations are deserved.

But the bubble of campus life is not the only troubling college bubble. Tuition and other costs continue to rise far faster than the rate of inflation. As with the housing bubble that peaked in 2006, easy credit facilitated by misguided government policy has artificially inflated prices. When the housing bubble popped, equity disappeared and foreclosures became commonplace. Some critics think the same thing will happen to many of our residential colleges; in fact, two small liberal arts colleges recently announced they will be closing their doors. Surely paying more and more for less and less, that is, for degrees that have less and less value in the marketplace, can't sustain universities much longer.

Critics on the right say that colleges have little incentive to be efficient and productive because, thanks to the government, it is too easy for students to borrow to cover bloated tuition and other costs. Young people with short mental time horizons are being seduced into a privileged, irresponsible way of life. When the party ends, their careers and other life choices are hobbled and even crippled by sometimes six-figure debt. The total amount of student debt in America now exceeds a trillion dollars, and not surprisingly, the rate of default is on the rise.

Conservatives and libertarians agree that the only solution is to wean our institutions of higher education off the government dole and force them to adjust educational costs to the realities of the marketplace. To the extent they remain on the dole, conservatives and libertarians agree that they should be disciplined by public policy that forces them to demonstrate that they actually give students their money's worth by getting them ready to compete in the marketplace. To this end, colleges should be held accountable for how many students graduate, how many of their graduates and non-graduates default on loans, how many graduates get well-paying jobs, and how many measurable learning outcomes each student has mastered.

But these related lines of criticism, being pushed primarily by conservative politicians, underestimate the ways in which American higher education is already submitting to the discipline of the marketplace and to the imperatives of technology and progress in the division of labor. Many institutions are following the lead of the corporate world by concentrating "mental labor" in the administration and reducing, as far as possible, instruction to working off a script devised by experts. The number of tenured and tenure-track or careerist professors is in free-fall; they now "deliver" a surprisingly small minority of the credit hours generated. Meanwhile, the number of temporary and adjunct faculty soars. Faculty governance, which is increasingly viewed as rule by those cluelessly out-of-touch with the market realities, is being displaced by strategic plans generated by administrators and their expert consultants.

Meanwhile, the top administrators, the self-appointed cognitive elite, have compensation, benefits, and even "golden parachutes" increasingly comparable to those found in the for-profit corporate sector. An administrative class with its own class consciousness is evolving, and members of that class speak (with conviction) in jargon borrowed from the world of corporations and schools of business.

The transfer of governance from the faculty to administrators is, of course, partly the fault of tenured faculty. Like members of any of the unions that are withering away, they don't see clearly enough that their perks are being dissolved by the market. More importantly, they are also often so wrapped up in their areas of scholarly specialization that they fail to take an interest in the development of their institution as a whole, which leads them to be complacent with introductory or "general education" courses being taught by temporary employees. Administrators are typically cagey enough not to go after professors' tenure, and the professors themselves are fatalistic enough to think the future of tenure is not a cause worthy of defense. Everyone really knows that safety nets like tenure, which cushion employees from being rigorously evaluated according to standards of measurable productivity, don't have much of a future. But a professor can reasonably imagine that tenure's future extends at least to the end of his own career.

The administrators now in charge are typically techno-enthusiasts, embracing without much reflection the various ways to make classrooms "smarter," create courses that are "blended" and "flipped," and profit from the rampant and loosely monitored proliferation of lucrative online learning. The general thought is that the use of machines and screens aids in scripting instruction according to "best practices," or empirically validated methods of most efficiently delivering skills and competencies, is the future of higher education. The spontaneity of faculty behavior occasionally leads to brilliant teachable moments, but those can't be relied upon and are a time-consuming indulgence. And administrators have found it easier to discipline insecure or temporary faculty working at subsistence (or even less); such instructors are far more open to the imposition of instructional rubrics. Joel Kotkin writes of the proletarianization of the middle class, and the general tendency is, as Marx suggests, to rip the halos off the cherished professors and reduce them to laborers being paid piecemeal. And once instruction has been mechanized or scripted, the instructor can be replaced by a machine.

Libertarian futurists see that most instruction in the future will be delivered by "genius machines" or astutely interactive computers. Cowen, Glenn Reynolds and others criticize colleges for not going down this road fast enough. They foresee that the popping of the bubble will dispel their remaining illusions and speed schools down the road they are already traveling. The libertarians talk up the new birth of equality in freedom that will come with a screen to which virtually everyone has access, and there is already plenty of evidence that this technology might have the power to burst both of the educational bubbles (economic and utopian) by delivering "good enough" education to everyone in the privacy of their own rooms.

But this future is not as close as some libertarians think. Our elite schools, because of their endowments and assured enrollments, are relatively insulated from these market pressures. Harvard professor Michael Sandel markets his celebrated justice MOOC (Massive Open Online Course) only to less prestigious places, and the techno-instructional initiatives coming out of Stanford and MIT aren't meant for the students at Stanford and MIT.

Some of our less selective and more precarious colleges are making a virtue out of necessity by branding themselves as exceptional in student-faculty engagement or personal service. But on those campuses, the pressure is on faculty to display how engaged they are in ways that pay off. Cowen remarks that, even once we've mechanized instruction, a place for faculty will remain as coaches who encourage slow and unmotivated students, and some of our small colleges are already making that kind of appeal to worried parents. The question for the future is whether engagement alone is worth taking out a big loan, when "good enough" is available online for almost nothing. If this kind of thinking were to become common, the tuition bubble would quickly pop.

The Scourge of Administration

So why is tuition so high? Although it's not true everywhere, the general trend indicates that the cost of instruction is dropping. Certainly, when most college faculty see tuition rising at double or more the rate of inflation, they, as much as anyone, wonder what the money is for, because it is not coming to them in compensation or other perks. As the size and status of faculty decline overall, there has been what almost seems to be a corresponding increase in the proliferation and status of administrators.

The most important cause of administrative proliferation appears to be the new division of labor. Administration has in many ways become more "cognitive" as "enrollment management" and "advancement" have become both more challenging and more expert-driven, as have their enhanced roles in determining curricular priorities and modes of instructional "delivery." It is generally conceded, for example, that as higher education moves online and becomes more widely and cheaply available, the on-campus product needs to be more carefully regulated; faculty can no longer be allowed the freedom to determine either the content or mode of delivery of their courses.

Administrators themselves often prefer to call attention to their new responsibilities in complying with increasingly intrusive governmental and accreditation regulations. Those responsibilities do, in fact, require an unprecedented deployment of time and resources. Consider, for example, the recent mandate from the Department of Education's Office of Civil Rights requiring that, to deal with accusations of sexual assault and rape, colleges develop their own internal processes that are meant to operate outside the realm of legal due process.

More generally, many institutions have a dean just for "diversity" and another to worry about hate speech, safe spaces, trigger warnings, microaggressions, and the like. These roles have arisen in response to external bureaucratic pressure; such initiatives have little or nothing to do with improving the quality of instruction. They are, in fact, generally perceived to make instruction worse, as faculty members are harassed by regulations and regulators, as well as by students, invigorated by the politically correct environment, that privilege "academic justice" over "academic freedom."

More and more administrative time is also spent on accreditation. The regional accrediting associations are always upping the ante when it comes to lengthy and data-laden reports. Every moment of instruction has to be validated by measurable acquisition of skills and competencies.

Lots of time is dedicated to determining what counts as a competency. The faculty who justify their courses in terms of competency acquisition, especially in the humanities, often do so ironically, reassured that their courses can (and should) be about a lot more than being competent. But some faculty members, having attended conferences dominated by administrators, buy into "the culture of assessment." Administrators charge these cooperative faculty members with leading the revision of curriculum and especially "general education" with the competencies in mind, typically truncating or emptying out its distinctive content. Competencies, after all, are content neutral.

This unfortunate process is a general trend that, as I've suggested, has had less effect on both elite institutions and on countercultural institutions secure in their missions. It does, however, explain why college administrators so readily submit to the discipline of accreditation: It is actually *their* discipline. It is imposed by the class of administrators as such on recalcitrant faculty at particular institutions. Accreditation is just one factor among many that is flattening the rhetoric of higher education, causing the class of administrators increasingly to deploy, with unironic enthusiasm, assorted buzzwords concerning competency, techno-disruption, diversity, assessment, and engagement. Those words aren't intrinsically bad, but it's becoming difficult to find administrators who can rise above them in the direction of genuine educational mission or content.

Benjamin Ginsberg, who teaches political science at Johns Hopkins, has ironically put forward a modest proposal for a MOOA (Massive Online Open Administration). Given that a large part of the increase in costs in higher education comes from administrative growth, and given "that a 'best practices' philosophy already leads administrators to blindly follow one another's lead in such realms as planning, staffing personnel issues, campus diversity, branding and curriculum planning," why not take the "best practices" idea to its logical conclusion and have a single, expert provost making decisions for hundreds of campuses? After all, it seems as if one size really does fit all, given that the strategic plans of our colleges and universities are becoming increasingly identical. Content, tradition or genuinely distinctive (for example, religious) missions are being replaced by feel-good gimmicks thought up by the marketing department.

As the president of my college has remarked, "the liberal arts don't sell anymore," so even they have to be rebranded with the current market in mind. Sometimes, colleges aim to keep the general ambiance of liberal education; so they attempt to keep the brand while emptying their curriculum of much of the traditional substance. A college with a traditional environment but techno-vocational content is an appealing combination.

As curriculum become more alike and academic missions morph into brands, residential colleges in particular aim to distinguish themselves by offering "lifestyle" amenities that make the "college experience" seem worth the money. As a result, higher education is in the midst of what amounts to an amenities arms race. One measurable outcome is the increase in staff and costs that have little to nothing to do with instruction, but everything to do with recruitment and retention. These unproductive and expensive features of college life are the result of accepting (not without reason) that market discipline is indispensable for the institution's self-preservation and flourishing.

The features of this rapid and often stunning improvement in the quality of campus life include cafeterias with gourmet food, health-club gyms, a proliferation of non-revenue-producing intercollegiate athletic teams, hotel-quality dorms, student-affairs staffs (that function like concierges to save students from boredom) and user-friendly and otherwise attractive study-abroad programs. According to recent surveys, the self-esteem of college students is on the rise, even as actual student achievement declines. One reason is that colleges, more than ever, treat students like consumers, maximizing health, safety, comfort and choice in every feature of campus life. Colleges do this for good reason; studies actually do show most students who choose a residential college usually do so more with the general lifestyle than the excellence or value of academic programs in mind. Colleges in many cases can be justly charged with emptying student pockets and indenturing their futures with debt in order to give them what they really want.

The Competence Gap

There is a great deal of justifiable outrage about crushing college loans that aren't worth the cost. These cases usually involve under-qualified and ill-informed students borrowing massive amounts of money to go to bad private colleges. Sometimes they drop out; other times, their college of choice doesn't give them what they need for their desired career. The real problem is almost always that they didn't have the advice they needed. Students who don't qualify for lots of financial aid should choose non-residential public institutions, and our country is full of decent ones. It is an abuse of the marketplace when the admissions representatives of expensive private colleges convince them otherwise. Those representatives are of course driven by the imperatives of the marketplace, and they are doing what's required to keep their schools in business. The student is a scarce resource, and there are more private residential colleges than we can really use.

It is a disservice to students to allow those schools to prop themselves up indefinitely on loans guaranteed by the government; the education they offer is not worth the burden of a five or six figure student loan. If the marketplace wasn't distorted in such a seductive way, young people would typically make safer and better choices. Colleges are failing young people by offering them choices they're not really competent to make.

Many of the criticisms of higher education in America today are related to a national crisis in competence or, more precisely, a competence gap. Some Americans, members of our cognitive elite, seem in some ways more competent than ever. The best secondary schools are better than ever, and their graduates are often so well prepared that they could go to Ivy League colleges and slouch through with minimal effort in grade-inflated, politically correct humanities courses and still be perfectly ready for the more cognitive parts of the workforce. And employers know that the SAT scores and fabulous résumés of teenage accomplishment that got them into their elite colleges are typically evidence enough that they have the brains and skills to learn on the job. Still, few question whether the Ivies and the other elite schools are worth the money, for a couple of reasons. For one thing, their huge endowments allow them to offer most students steep discounts. For another, there is little doubt (less, actually, than there should be) that their degrees, as well as the contacts students make on their campuses, are a reliable ticket to lucrative employment.

Elite schools aren't completely immune to competition. They don't have to worry about filling their desks with warm bodies, but their "brand" depends on getting the students with the best measurable credentials. One way the Ivies and other elite schools secure their students' highly marketable brand of excellence is through shameless grade inflation. The typical grade is some form of an A.

A few years ago, Princeton attempted to buck this trend and develop a reputation for rigor by enacting grading reform that reduced the number of A's to around 35%. It seemed to be a brilliant move; Princeton could boast that it was a little bit more demanding, and its students would have the benefit of having the reputation of surviving the "tough" Ivy. But the reform backfired. The admissions folks at the other Ivies started to warn the best and the brightest that they might be tarred with the stigma of B's if they went to Princeton, and Princeton, as a result, started to struggle in the competitive marketplace. So Princeton rather quickly caved and has since gone the other direction. The administration recently announced that it may well do away with or radically deemphasize grades, at least for freshmen, as a way to reduce student stress.

Grade inflation is a sensitive subject among Ivy League students. They argue that they are exceptionally good students and so deserve exceptionally high grades. Few of the highly competent people at such schools want to be rigorously compared with one another; the result might be an unfair reputation for mediocrity. In the end, despite or because of the well-known grade inflation, graduates can still enter the global competitive marketplace quite successfully with the impression of excellence maintained.

For elite schools, grades don't measure the basic competence required for the marketplace, although they might distinguish between ordinary and soaring excellence. But their grade-inflation scam affects almost all other colleges and universities, and similar grade inflation in less selective colleges has a far more insidious effect. Nobody really believes that being admitted to these colleges is a sure sign of competence, so earning inflated grades there really isn't either. But if professors deviate too much from the Harvard grading pattern, then their competent, accomplished students will be doubly disadvantaged. It might actually be harder to get an A at, say, Hampden-Sydney than it is at Harvard, but nobody is likely to believe that. So it becomes increasingly difficult to show that graduates from less selective colleges are competent. The fact that they often are not makes it even harder.

Just as troubling, while elite high schools continue to improve, most high schools are getting worse. The intention of the controversial Common Core project is to ensure that all high schools turn out students with a basic level of competence. There are valid criticisms of the Common Core as a form of techno-leveling that replaces a quest for genuinely humane learning, cultural acquisition, and civic literacy with a "good enough to be a cog in a machine" minimalist approach to competencies. Those are the same criticisms, after all, that are directed against the techno-confidence of competency-based higher education. But there is much more to criticize in the technocratic optimism reflected in Bill Gates's comparison of education delivery to standardized electrical outlets. With such misplaced confidence at its foundation, the Common Core will probably work about as well as "No Child Left Behind."

What's really wrong with most schools, however, may be less of the "method of delivery" than the social and economic context in which they operate. The failure of our schools is closely connected with our increasingly pathological families, the gradual disappearance of the middle class, and all the other trends that are dividing our country into two more clearly distinct classes. Members of our "cognitive elite" are herding together in particular zip codes and dominating our best schools, both public and private. Meanwhile our other schools are increasingly deprived of the genuine socioeconomic diversity that, until fairly recently, led to rich kids dating their poor classmates and to talented poor kids being raised up by the general excellence of the school. Social mobility is on the decline, and the composition of our schools reflects that fact.

Ordinary graduates of most of our secondary schools lack the basic competence required to enter the world of work. Schools now claim victory if they manage to successfully warehouse most of their students until they graduate. It wasn't that long ago that a high school diploma was regarded as a reliable measure of basic competence. Now high school graduates often aren't prepared in terms of skills or habituation for even entry-level manual labor or service-sector jobs. And those jobs, in any case, are getting rarer, less lucrative, and increasingly short on both benefits and security.

As a result, we now expect college to provide the basic levels of competence that used to be the fairly reliable result of a high school education. That's the main reason why jobs that used to be open to high school graduates now require a college degree, and it's why more of what our non-selective colleges do now is oriented toward teaching fairly low-level techno-vocational skills.

Some reformers think that the key to increasing American social mobility is to make sure that as many people as possible get college degrees. To ensure those degrees continue to mean something, foundations, bureaucrats, and others are working to enforce standards so that the college-degree credential is evidence of workforce competence. These reformers insist that every feature of "the undergraduate experience" be reconfigured with "demonstrated competence" in mind. What the Lumina Foundation, Gates and their compatriots really want is a Common Core for college to supplement the one for secondary school, so colleges can guarantee the competence that failing secondary schools no longer can.

Some may wonder why reformers are merely aiming for competency, instead of excellence. But "good enough" is a reasonably democratic goal, and it is still quite a challenge, as too many students leave the college bubble no better prepared for the world of work than when they entered. Given that college is now charged with accomplishing what public education used to do for most Americans for free, it's really a matter of justice that the college experience be as efficient and productive as possible. Degrees should be cheap, and a student should be able to get one quickly. Going beyond competence, in most cases, is a waste of time and money. In truth, it's outrageous that struggling young people have to borrow to get a credential required for a very modest job, and that "disruptive innovation" has come to mean getting them the skills they really need and nothing more. It is sad to think that the colleges that "disrupt" themselves with cheap and quick competence in mind may well be the institutions that have real futures.

A Liberal Education

The truth is that the parts of higher education known as the liberal arts or the humanities haven't ever been about competence but have rather presupposed it. And despite the current environment, they retain some of the mission they received from their aristocratic and religious heritage to raise students above middle-class vocationalism. Charles Murray has called attention to the inconvenient truth that a college student at the typical skill level will not only be unable to readily absorb this or that "great book," but he will be unable to absorb the average textbook in, say, world history class.

That doesn't mean the students don't have the brains to overcome their educational deficiencies. But it does mean that if institutions want to fix this situation, they need to both have the mission-based dedication to teach students the skills they lack that are indispensable for more than basic literacy and, more importantly, convince students that the effort will improve their lives. In most cases, however, this is a hard sell. The case for dedicating the time and money to achieving historical literacy or nurturing the ability to attentively absorb a difficult book seems weak.

Still, the truth is that the case for the higher competence in the liberal arts is quite strong. E. D. Hirsch has provided the strongest argument for the humanities, or the attentive reading of real books that are more than technical manuals or sources of information. There's a strong correlation between high-level success in life and the size of one's active vocabulary. This may seem implausible at first, but the more words a person really knows, the more he knows about the real world around him. To know what a word means is to really grasp the (always imperfect, of course) correspondence between the word and a part of reality. It is also to understand the limitations of words, when they are vaguely or incorrectly used. With that kind of knowledge comes a good deal of self-discipline and control. For example, there's a clear distinction between those who use today's expert techno-babble (about disruptive innovation and the like) seriously and those who are able to deploy such jargon ironically. The latter have both a better grasp of what's really going on and the ability to use what they know to their own advantage. Leaders, we notice, typically express themselves both precisely and ironically, and they are very adept at both description and deception. And there are, of course, obvious connections between being deeply literate and being innovative and creative in most areas of life.

The best way to acquire this kind of literacy is to be blessed with a bookish environment from the beginning. Kids whose parents read to them have a tremendous advantage, as do kids who grow up in a home full of books that is infused by the joy of reading. Our schools, for the most part, aren't capable of doing much to help students who haven't had this kind of upbringing overcome their disadvantage. So most students come to college without the capacity to revel in the process of discovery that accompanies being able to treat literature as a form of knowledge. And, even given the best possible environment, the capacity to be liberally educated in this sense is given only to relatively few.

All in all, most college students do not choose for themselves to read with this kind of wondrous enjoyment in mind, and not many of them even read whole books as a form of recreation. That's not to say they don't read at all; their literacy is fueled in a minimalist sense by the pleasures and opportunities available online. And in many cases, that's all they need to function well in the marketplace if usually not as leaders or part of the cognitive elite.

The model for leaders in America remains the undergraduate degree in the traditional areas of the liberal arts, combined with an advanced, more technical degree in law, public policy, public health, business, or medicine. Say what you will about the content of the 2012 presidential campaign; each of the candidates was uncommonly precise in speech and grammar. Both were able to deploy clichés with irony, and so with the suggestion of deeper meaning. Both Obama and Romney, of course, focused on the humanities at elite colleges and went on to professional graduate programs.

The same goes for leaders in other fields. The most astute and reflective of the Silicon Valley billionaires, Peter Thiel, majored in philosophy and then went on to law school. It's true that his education has not immunized him to the transhumanist technophilia characteristic of his chosen industry, but he has a far greater capacity for irony about both political correctness and technocratic educational engineering than, say, Gates. He has reflected broadly about the social responsibility given to the genius founders of start-ups, as well as on the conformist pseudo-science that disfigures business as an academic discipline.

In evolutionary psychology, the foundational field of today's social science, the outstanding scholar who has escaped the confines of the discipline is Jonathan Haidt, who has an undergraduate degree in philosophy. That means his science is rooted in the deeper and less time-bound, world-forming, soul-based concerns of Plato and Descartes.

Haidt is able to use selectively and with some irony the somewhat reductionist language of his discipline, especially regarding the members of the "eusocial" species with really big brains.

Given these advantages, there is a strong argument that liberal education should be for everyone, but especially for those destined to rise to positions of leadership in the various professions and in political life. But a reasonable goal is to do what we can to sustain it as a lifestyle option on as many campuses as possible.

We can see, to begin with, that liberal education most securely flourishes on campuses with missions that are more than a brand. Some of our elite institutions have the right environment, but it is more reliably found at good schools with a basically religious understanding of who we are and what we're supposed to do. It's possible to include on this list those colleges that retain a genuinely classical or Stoic understanding, one concerned with a rational self-confidence when it comes to manners and morals such as Hampden-Sydney or Morehouse.

The Morehouse man, as President Obama reminded us a few years ago, is so proud that nobody can tell him what to do. And it was at Morehouse that Martin Luther King, Jr., learned both to be absolutely fearless and to have magnanimous concern for doing what he could to elevate the people he championed.

Saving Diversity

Despite all its problems and shortcomings, the American system of higher education has one saving grace: not a uniform excellence or greatness but genuine moral and intellectual diversity. Many of our best colleges and universities have unique strengths, which ensures the higher education marketplace offers diversity of thought and approaches to teaching and learning. This diversity ensures a space for true liberal education.

If we look closely, we can see some of that diversity even on our large urban campuses, such as the genuinely distinguished Honors College at the University of Houston, which flourishes at a place mainly known for training top-flight engineers. Houston's achievement has been possible thanks to a group of faculty with a vision for their school, who appealed above the administrators to the trustees. (In fairness, the administrators at Houston also seem to be a lot less technocratic than at most places.)

This diversity is threatened by increasingly intrusive bureaucrats, education experts, accreditors, and administrators who, by insisting on weak "standards of competence," standardize higher education. And colleges and universities are dangerously vulnerable to such pressure because they depend on government money

That is why conservative educational reform should be about libertarian means for non-libertarian ends. That means working to reduce the footprint of accreditors, bureaucrats, technocratic administrators, and other interlopers, often including state governments. It means disagreeing with Scott Walker and other Republican governors who argue that the main driver of educational cost these days is tenured faculty not teaching enough, and that the remedy is to empower administrators to whip the faculty into line with their agendas. It means that, if we want a genuinely flexible and literate workforce that can adapt to our rapidly changing economy, we need to stop thinking of college only in terms of technology-driven workforce development.

For their part, our diverse array of private schools and colleges should work to do what they can to reduce their dependence on government funding. That means cutting back as much as possible on expensive and irrelevant amenities and taking the noble risk of putting the focus almost entirely on excellence in educating particular persons.

That there is a market for institutions that follow this advice is undeniable, and it may well increase rather rapidly in size. There are growing numbers of parents who home school as well as parents who value the religious and classical foundations of education for all sorts of reasons, and the charter school movement is surging. In focusing on liberal education and shunning bureaucrats and accreditors, the only thing to be lost by good colleges is government money; no one believes that being accredited is any sign of educational excellence or even reliable educational competence. Properly educated students will build the reputation for excellence that schools need without official outside validation. American colleges just need to have the courage to do what's right for their students.

Appendix:
How to Think about Accreditation

Professors, administrators, and potential founders of institutions of higher education convinced by what I've said in this chapter probably need a bit more encouragement on the issue of how to think about, reform, and perhaps dispense with accreditation.

Here was my reaction when I saw the title, "The Great Accreditation Farce," of Peter Conn's article in *The Chronicle of Higher Education*: finally, someone's telling the truth. Our system of accreditation of colleges is indeed a farce, a waste of "millions of dollars and tens of thousands of hours." To please external examiners, faculty and administration do work they would never do otherwise and is of no obvious benefit to students. For instance, they prepare reports "often hundreds of pages in length and chock full of data" that will do nothing to improve their institutions.

Our system of accreditation by regional agencies is one reason among many for administrative bloat and the transfer of institutional power from faculty to administrators. Most dedicated and competent teachers—especially in my field of political philosophy—have no respect for the process at all. They comply because they must, coming up with rubrics they don't believe in, expanding and fine-tuning syllabi with language that means little to them, and quantifying all sorts of stuff that doesn't need or is amenable to quantification. None of the good professors—often, award-winning professors—that I know think that the accreditation process has helped them do their jobs better. It's mainly a time-suck that falls just short of a serious threat to their sanity. So they approach the accreditation tasks delegated to them with a sense of ironic resignation—without spirit or enthusiasm. It is one of the duties for which they are paid, and not one of the joys that seduced them into choosing a profession that doesn't pay much.

Doesn't everyone know that "a culture of assessment" is a culture of intrusive boredom? And although its accreditation bureaucrats tend to talk up "diversity" as some kind of competency, the standardization supported by their pages and pages of standards that must be met by every institution—many of which have amazingly little to do with education in the precise sense—actually undermines the genuine moral and intellectual diversity that is the saving grace of American higher education. It has, in fact, devalued the language of missions and the ends of education, making the increasingly vacuous mission statements and educational outcomes of our colleges more similar and more content-light.

A Waste of Time and Treasure

The accreditation process is worse than a farce because it is a waste of time and treasure. And everyone agrees that college education has become way too expensive. One small but real way of reducing the size of the tuition bubble is to eliminate or radically streamline this process. My question has always been, "why do colleges with unimpeachable reputations put up with this degrading process, one that drags down excellence in the direction of measurable mediocrity?" The answer is that unaccredited colleges don't qualify for federal financial aid money, including federally subsidized student loans and Federal Work-Study. Of course, that means that being accredited qualifies colleges for money and students for debt, some not insignificant amount of which has to be used for staying accredited.

In the end, nobody is really going to deny Rhodes or Swarthmore or Kenyon accreditation. That would be an outrage. Even undeniably outstanding colleges, however, routinely get tortured by the accreditation folks, being forced into "redos" on their insufficiently quantitative reports and so forth. Why do they put up with that? Getting accredited doesn't add to their reputations; many inferior schools can boast of the same credential.

It's not that the accreditation standards are genuinely tough. Everyone knows that some really marginal and underperforming colleges get accredited, and accreditation isn't addressing the real causes of the declining quality of higher education. The reasons for ultimate denial have to do with egregious educational malpractice and financial meltdowns. So all accreditation really proves is that you're "good enough"—or not a fraud.

You're probably objecting that nothing I've said has anything to do with Conn's article. Well, that's because he doesn't really think accreditation is a farce. He's "the man," part of the educational establishment, not a true dissident at all. The only thing he thinks makes the present accreditation process a farce is "awarding accreditation to religious colleges." So he wants accreditation to become infinitely more intrusive by becoming highly judgmental when it comes to our colleges' missions. He wants to up the ante on accreditation's attack on our colleges' moral and intellectual diversity.

A Proposal for Reform

Here's a quick proposal for reform. In my state of Georgia, the health inspection of restaurants is conducted rather quickly but thoroughly by an inspector or team of inspectors who show up unannounced. They get the job done, and restaurants have to remain on their toes. A bad day could get a place shut down.

So let's have the accreditation team swarm on a college unannounced. It would go over the books, examine degree requirements, attend some classes, review the qualifications of the faculty, check out the syllabi, and talk to some students. Colleges would be required to have these records up-to-date at all times. The "inspectors" would, in most cases, quickly pronounce the college "good enough" for government purposes. The marginal cases would be put on warning and revisited, but in real life that list of losers isn't going to be all that long. Colleges could still have self-studies, strategic plans, and develop all kinds of metrics to satisfy themselves and their external constituencies. But they wouldn't have to undertake that optional (although doubtlessly valuable) work just to get accredited.

According to my scheme, America's adequately functioning colleges wouldn't have to do anything much they wouldn't do anyway—the various kinds of record-keeping are a must for any institution for all kinds of reasons—and accreditation would not be time-consuming, expensive, or a cause of tightening administrative and bureaucratic control over what good professors do. Now the scrutiny of a college, I admit, has to be more detailed and rigorous the first time it is accredited, but even then the review should be of what the college has to do anyway to get itself established.

The best argument I've heard for the present accreditation process is that, without its bureaucratically impressive deluge of paperwork and numbers, government would take over certifying colleges for funding, loans, and such. And the government would be more insistent and intrusive in imposing its random and ephemeral priorities on our institutions of higher education. Well, that might be true. Still, the argument amounts to this: please endure our senseless, demoralizing, and expensive torture to spare yourself even worse torture. Surely our best colleges should take the lead in being more confident and principled than that!

Now, if and when I start a college, I would make it as amenity-free and administrator-free as possible. I also would not get in the residential, food service, or intercollegiate athletics businesses, and I would, in the name of cutting costs to the bone, make our point of distinction small, techno-lite classes based solely on great or at least good books and huge amounts of writing. My faculty would work cheap, with demanding teaching loads, and without tenure for the joy of it. I think I could get tuition low enough that we could dispense with government funding of all kinds.

We would dispense with accreditation too. That might be hard at first, but only at first. The reputation of our highly literate and otherwise civilized graduates would soon be more than enough. After all, who could deny that they're superior to the sketchily educated graduates of most of our accredited schools? Of course, eschewing accreditation—and, by extension, federal financial aid—will require me to raise significant outside funds. But I suspect that private donors will flock to an institution that cares more about educating students than satisfying accreditors.

Part 2
Issues in Higher Education

Chapter 3
Liberal Education as Respecting Who We Are

I teach in a small, residential college in semi-rural Georgia. It's not really a liberal arts college in the mode of Pomona or Centre. There are lots of students who major in business, education, animal science, exercise science, and communication. And the college, in truth, is not oriented toward "enhancing" its "traditional" majors. The traditional majors we have—such as political science, English, psychology, French, history, philosophy, and religion—are holding their own in the face of benign institutional indifference. Benign indifference is, of course, punctuated by periodic enthusiasm for educational fads—both "politically correct" and techno-vocational, but those episodes are usually pretty episodic. Still, our administrators remain entranced by what the latest studies and the foundations are saying, and they want to do better in bringing Berry in line with the experts' "best practices." Thank God that common sense, blessed inertia, tradition, devotion to disciplines, and protecting "turf" often win out over various strategic initiatives to make our college distinctive in becoming like all the others.

Over the last year, I've been paying more attention to what the educational experts are claiming. I am, to a point, all about what political correctness—what diversity, multiculturalism, and all that has done to trivialize American higher education, producing, for example, identity politics majors such as gender studies that manage to be neither liberal education nor vocational education. I don't think, however, that the "social justice" of political correctness is the great danger liberal education faces. It's the so-called disruptive innovation that wants to hold higher education completely accountable to the logic of the market and measurable productivity. In this sense, the 1960s have lost and capitalism—or at the least the form of capitalism we find in Silicon Valley and other havens of our proudly meritocratic "cognitive elite"—has won. If there's a connection between political correctness and techno-vocational competence, it is that morality redefined as "diversity" is no barrier to the transformation of excellence for its own sake into marketable skills.

Listening to our administrators, it was impossible to miss a telling contradiction. There's anxiety about each college having a distinctive mission that easily morphs into a "brand." Liberal arts colleges have to explain why they're different from and even better than their rivals in order to flourish in the increasingly competitive educational marketplace. They have to justify the rapidly rising cost of the residential private college "experience," which includes inducing a good number of students to borrow big for the credentials they could, in Georgia, actually get for free at the state school down the road.

To their credit, our administrators at Berry College might be clearer than most that it would be best if what the college actually accomplishes corresponds to its branding about what it accomplishes. The danger is that the substance of the curriculum might be transformed with the brand in mind. The even greater danger is that the quest for a distinctively excellent substance will be deemed futile. So many colleges have reached that conclusion that they sell themselves according to the amenities that grace their residential experience, and there's nothing more shameful and silly in American education today than the resulting amenities arms race.

And the desire for "substantial" distinctiveness (that drives St. John's in Annapolis/Santa Fe or Thomas Aquinas in California or Morehouse in Georgia)—which can be at the service of the genuine diversity that's the best point of American higher education—is mitigated by the desire to correspond to "best practices" as articulated by accrediting associations, foundations, and government bureaucracies. Best practices are, these days, pretty much about attending to method or form at the expense of content or substance. What we need are "measurable student outcomes" that are abstracted from content.

You can't say these days that every student needs to study this or that period of history or body of literature. That would undermine student choice and privilege mere information over flexible skills. Administrators find it tough to see, for example, that if the goals are critical thinking and analytical reasoning, how they might necessarily correspond to the particular disciplines of history or philosophy. Our allegedly disruptive thought that learning only occurs if it is a measurable competency—which has become banal management-speak dogma—actually, in a deeper sense, works against choice. It makes possible, in principle, the standardization of high education everywhere with the twenty-first century's globally competitive marketplace in mind. Education that's method abstracted from content knows no standard higher than productivity or power, and how to be productive is a global concern of workers everywhere.

Education for Sophists

The democratic, technocratic slogan is that we don't want to teach students "what to think" but "how to think." And there are easier ways, surely, of becoming a methodical critical thinker than messing with history made by or literature written by dead white males who had lots of personal "issues" that often prevented them from living productive and responsible lives. So at the allegedly cutting-edge college being founded by Ben Nelson's much-touted Minerva Project, students won't read "great books." Instead they will learn debating skills, practical writing, formal logic, and behavioral economics straight on.

Now it's true that guys like me hate Nelson for working so hard to replace the liberal arts college with the bookless and placeless (the students will change their location often so as not to get tied down or be less than cosmopolitan) training of a merely cognitive elite—specialists without spirit or heart, as someone said. But it's also true that Nelson understands that if the study of history is for "critical thinking," then educational efficiency means dispensing with tedious content and getting right to the thinking. History, after all, is merely information that can be Googled when you need it. And true philosophy is nothing but analytical philosophy, a method for thinking clearly or logically. The content of Plato is perfectly dispensable and certainly not worth obsessing about. That's why rigorously analytical programs think of the history of philosophy in the same way physics programs think of the history of physics, a somewhat instructive record of errors that occur when you haven't quite figured out how to think with the proper method for inquiry. That's why analytical graduate programs have sometimes followed physics graduate programs in that they no longer require the study of foreign languages. Everything you really need to know was written recently and is available in English. And, of course, an upside of writing following the logical rigor of mathematics is that there's little danger of something really fundamental getting lost in translation.

But Nelson's university—with its training in "debating skills" and "behavioral economics"—isn't really about the production of analytical philosophers or theoretical physicists. *The Big Bang Theory*'s Sheldon Cooper would be laughed out of the seminar room as the socially clueless nerd that he is. This university—which aims to replace Harvard as America's top educational "brand"—means to produce sophists. Now, Plato gave the sophist an undeservedly bad brand. Socrates said that sophists—unlike poets, politicians, and perhaps even parasitic philosophers such as Socrates himself—use what can be learned from natural science to solve problems people really have. Sophists are technicians or experts or consultants, and because their knowledge is scientific, it's valid everywhere. They can get and really do deserve the big bucks wherever they go. The reason Nelson will have his students change locations so often is so that they will understand themselves as rootless cosmopolitans—or freed from the prejudice that some local belief or concern trumps wealth and power in determining what needs to be done. So they will always give sensible advice when it comes to "calculating the probabilities" about how to sustain oneself or one's institution in a fundamentally hostile environment.

Professors, in this view, become nothing more than sophists themselves. They are to be evaluated according to their measurable productivity, and they too will work only if they have what it takes to flourish in the competitive marketplace. One downside of this way of thinking, of course, is the residential liberal arts college will disappear, as will any educational arrangement based on what we now call Socrates' "humanistic" objection, on behalf of both truth and virtue, to the sophists' technocratic focus.

Defending the Humanities?

So you would think that professors in "the humanities" would have enough class consciousness, the class consciousness shared by Socrates himself, to oppose with powerful arguments and rhetorical effectiveness this reduction of liberal education to sophistry. *The American Academy of Arts and Sciences* did issue a report defending the humanities. It's not a resolute defense, and it seemed somewhat desperate. The result was all kinds of articles that were more about recording than resisting the humanities' decline and fall in our techno-scientific time. The report reads like it was written by a committee, and it only rarely transcends the level of the management-speak of the sophist. Most of all, by calling the humanities "a matter of the heart," it actually reinforces the techno-cratic distinction between real knowledge (the head) and emotional responses (the heart). The report's overall effect is somewhat between special pleading and abject capitulation.

Lee Siegel, in a thoughtful essay in the *Wall Street Journal* "Who Ruined the Humanities," gave an optimistic spin on the humanities' inability to defend themselves. What we might be witnessing is the liberation of the humanities from the stultifying confines of today's institutions of higher education. And as a political scientist, I, like Aristotle himself, find myself caught between the categories of humanities and science—or what Aristotle would call poetry and philosophy. So I can't help but find myself asking what's worth defending about "the humanities" anyway. Here Siegel turns out to be a lot of help.

It's hard to know what "the humanities" are exactly, as opposed, I guess, to the sciences. The center of the humanities seems to be the study of literature. And allegedly the key sign of their decline is the fading away of the English major, despite the real evidence that most of that fading took place a generation ago. Just as grade inflation has apparently stabilized at a high level, the number of English (and philosophy) majors seems to have done the same at a low level.

When committees and commissions tell us about such trends, it is always in terms of a crisis, such as the crisis of civic literacy or scientific literacy or just literacy. We're told that the study of literature is indispensable for literacy, which it surely is above a certain level. But there's a lot more to this crisis. The lack of a formal humanistic education, as Siegel puts it, allegedly "leads to numerous pernicious personal conditions, such as the inability to think critically, to write clearly, to empathize with other people, to be curious about other people and places, to engage with great literature after graduation, to recognize truth, beauty, and goodness."

Now no one really thinks that people who weren't English majors or minors suffer from all those pathologies, nor does it make sense to think that English majors—because of their reading literature for credit—are free from them. Taking a couple of courses in literature as part of a "core curriculum" couldn't possibly make that much difference.

I do think that people who fill their leisure time by reading "real books"—literature, philosophy, and such—do have qualities of the soul that are in short supply in our middle-class techno-world. We're talking here about people who read for intellectual pleasure and not just for stress-relief recreation. One downside of our digital age is that they're probably more than ever the exception to the rule. In the film *Liberal Arts* (about Kenyon), we see a student for whom college is being obsessed with a single huge book. We also see that he's not fitting in with his fellow, better-adjusted students. In the HBO series *Girls*, we see a young woman who majored in "film studies" at a school in Ohio we know to be Oberlin, struggling (well, not struggling as much as she should) to earn a living as a writer in New York City. She has a decent prose style, but it turns out she has nothing to write about. One reason for this: she managed to get through college without reading any "real books" with real care.

Siegel reminds us that literature wasn't taught in our colleges until the end of the nineteenth century because reading novels and poetry "were parts of the leisure of ordinary life." That's what an educated person did, and didn't do, of course, for college credit. Thoughts and imaginations were shaped by literature as much as anything else. Sometimes they may have been silly thoughts and romantic imaginations—such as the chivalrous Southerners who were moved by Sir Walter Scott to choose an extremely bloody and optional war. And sometimes, as in the case of Abraham Lincoln, Shakespeare and the Bible almost all alone were enough to discover and "communicate" both the urgency and poetic and theological significance of the seemingly prosaic American proposition.

The study of literature for credit became common as the twentieth century rolled on. It was, in part, compensatory, to make up for the declining quality of educated leisure and for a waning of religious authority. The search for meaning in a bourgeois world, as part of higher education, became focused on the genres of novels, poetry, and plays.

There was, as Siegel also reminds us, a kind of "existentialist" moment that began after World War II and persisted through part of the 1960s. The focus on one's personal destiny in a world distorted by technology and ideology—a world that produced unprecedented mass slaughter—privileged literature over other forms of "communication." Insofar as philosophy was existential—and so obsessed with Camus, Heidegger, and Sartre—even it seemed more like literature than a technical or "theoretical" discipline. The goal was to save reflection on the truthfully irreducible situation of the particular person from the clutches of theory. The predicament of the person born to trouble—or at least a brush with absurdity—is what existentialist novels are about. And the insufficiency of philosophic prose to display that predicament explains why Sartre, Camus, and Walker Percy, for philosophic reasons, wrote novels. It is close, at least, to why Plato wrote dialogues and why St. Augustine wrote his *Confessions*.

As the great critic Lionel Trilling pointed out, it might have been near ridiculous to teach books that should make us radically discontent with our ordinary lives in the newly standardized format of American higher education in the 1950s. And it increasingly became doubly ridiculous to have those books taught by careerist professors without even the spirit and heart of specialized scholars. It might be triply ridiculous to expect administrators, bureaucrats, and other certifiers of competencies to be able to understand—much less articulate—a credible defense of "the humanities."

The existentialist point of "the humanities" is to experience the mysterious singularity of the particular being stuck for a moment between two abysses, born to love and die, to be moved by the sometimes inexpressible suffering of contingency and morality. It's also to experience the joy of "insight" with others, an experience that has nothing to do with "collaborative learning." As Siegel puts it, it's to experience the "transcendence" of our everyday world, and transcendence can generate issues of "reentry" into that everyday world, issues that can negatively affect productivity and ordinary effectiveness.

One such issue is that the noncareerist teacher of literature—including philosophy understood as literature—can't possibly explain why what he or she does might be good for critical thinking, effective communication, empathy, or "diversity." Siegel is right that most literature is not the place to look for writing that is clear in the business or technical sense. And empathy, of course, is a pitiful substitute for love. The preference for diversity over truth and the common good depends on the detached attitude of the tourist. It is something to be transcended, not affirmed as some educational bottom line.

Most experts today have figured out that the so-called suicide of the humanities began when they succumbed to the temptation of trendy theory. It was too hard to remain "inward," and so they turned outward, to moralizing on issues of "social justice," to finding the racism, classism, and sexism that discredits the claims to truth of the "canonical" books of the past. "Political correctness," of course, is meant to stifle "man's search for meaning." That's not because the person experiencing the hell of "pure possibility" of our high-tech world longs to be a racist. It's because the issues of race and class and all that have been already resolved. She's remains today's "leftover" being can't be told who he (or she) is and what he's supposed to do. Professors of literature decided to confine their moralizing to politics, the area of human life in which they could claim neither competence nor an authoritative tradition of responsibility. The turn outward in the name of relevance actually made the humanities seem more irrelevant.

Before their capture, "the humanities" weren't hostile to religion, although they did highlight how difficult belief is in our radically untraditional time. It was also in those existentialist days that the humanities seemed genuinely bohemian—even in the sense of Russell Kirk, bohemian Tory—or not merely bourgeois bohemian. They were about concerns that should animate one's whole life. But today, we sadly say, the humanities aren't typically a refuge from either the despotism of fashion or the despotism of theory, much less the despotism of careerism. That's one reason among many why they seem like a boring waste of valuable time for most students.

Given what most of our institutions of higher education are really like today, Siegel celebrates their abandonment of the humanities. Now literature is free to flourish somewhere else. It's true enough, I can add, that Socrates never taught for money. And he never could have gotten tenure. He didn't publish, and his student evaluations would have been uneven. It's far from clear why it would help a great writer to get any degree at all and certainly not one in "creative writing." Someone could argue, of course, that things were different when people routinely read real books outside of class. But there's no reason why they can't do so again.

Siegel's understanding of the humanities is perhaps too existentialist, too animated by contempt for the alleged diversions of ordinary life. The study of great books probably flourishes best when "contextualized" by the relational responsibilities of free persons. Liberal education through most of our history was somewhat "Stoic" or connected to the relational duties of ladies and gentlemen located in a particular place. And it was also, of course, usually somewhat religious or conditioned by what we can know and must do as beings made in the image of a loving God. The humanities, properly understood, are about who we are and what we're supposed to do as beings born to know, love, and die.

This is emphatically not an exclusively conservative conclusion. The politically liberal and proudly neo-Puritanical novelist Marilynne Robinson recalls the original antebellum, abolitionist, Christian mission of Oberlin; liberal education was available for everyone, including African Americans and women. Everyone studied, and everyone—including the professors—worked. The egalitarianism without condescension that motivates our noblest defenders of liberal education is often—even typically—of Christian and liberal inspiration. The point is, of course, that because we're essentially neither black nor white, male nor female, Jew nor gentile, liberal education—as opposed to, say, women's studies—is for us all.

There is probably something to Siegel's perception that the effort to defend the humanities everywhere in our educational system might be misguided. Maybe the focus should be on "countercultural" (which doesn't mean all about the 1960s) institutions that exist in a communal context and that have what it takes to resist standardization, trendy theory, and the understandable but still excessive focus on techno-productivity. Maybe they can in some indirect way elevate us all.

Or maybe we should just ask that there be a lot more celebration of the diversity that still characterizes higher education in America, even in particular institutions and sometimes within particular departments. The enemy of this diversity is standardization—what comes from shamefully intrusive accrediting agencies, government bureaucrats, the use of "branding" and various forms of management-speak to describe liberal education, the adoption of the skills-and-competencies model (which is okay for tech schools) to evaluate higher education, and the insistence that the standard of productivity should drive all educational funding. The enemy of diversity is the reduction of education to sophistry.

One advantage of standardization, of course, is that it holds slackers accountable. But we shouldn't work too hard to get rid of all those slackers (such as those "tenured radicals"). Otherwise, we'll too often mistake leisure for laziness. We might even mistake metaphysics, theology, poetry, and so forth for self-indulgent pursuits that don't prepare students for the rigors of the competitive twenty-first-century marketplace. More than ever, it seems to me, it is essential to hold members of our "cognitive elite" to a standard higher than productivity. All Americans' lives would be less pathological—and so, for one thing, more productive—if imaginations were, once again, filled with what can be loosely called the romance of the soul.

Studies show, E. D. Hirsch (the cultural literacy guy) has reported, that the key to flourishing in the world as someone with a strong personal identity in touch with the world as it actually is and ready to take responsibility for oneself and others is to have a huge vocabulary and an exact and imaginative understanding of what those words mean. The only way to achieve this competency reliably in primary and secondary school is through reading lots of "real books." And another study shows that an extremely reliable clue to how a child will fare in school and life is the number of bookshelves his parents have at home or, in other words, whether he or she has been raised in a seriously bookish environment where reading is privileged as a form of civilized leisure. It might well be the case that the best argument for the residential liberal arts is cultivating future parents who will raise their children in such a home.

Let me now say something about the teaching method we do or ought to find at those countercultural colleges, which is, partly, conversational. But it's not merely or simply conversational. The "Socratic method," for us, isn't much without "respect for texts." The point of the Socratic method, even today, is to help students gain the confidence to reasonably and erotically enjoy "real books."

The Socratic Method and Its Limits

Martin Heidegger called Socrates "the purest thinker" in the West, which, I gather, doesn't necessarily mean the best thinker. The sign of Socrates' purity is not writing down his thoughts, for fear they would become ossified, misunderstood, vulgarized. What you say always depends on the character of the person to whom you are speaking. Books speak to no one in particular, violating the common-sense principle that your teaching style ought to vary according to the learning style of your student.

One trouble with taking the purely Socratic approach too seriously is really believing that a great teacher is one who leads his students to the truth dialectically, with no books or other "outside authorities" needed. We have no firm evidence this approach really worked that well for the "historical Socrates"—as opposed to the idealized character Socrates, who shows up all the time in Plato's dialogues (or really wordy plays). It is highly unlikely it really works for the teachers these days who pride themselves in using that teaching method. We even see in Socratic dialogues that his really smart interlocutors don't have memories good enough not to be flat-out tricked by Socrates, who often reminds them about—by changing up—what he said before.

Now I don't try to trick my students that way, although I constantly remind them how easy it would be to do so. When I say, "remember we just said ...," they know it's because I'm saying something different than what I actually previously said—either because I screwed up before or to provocatively change my position for instructional or entertainment reasons. When I say, "I have to take a controversial stand," I follow with a stand that nobody would find controversial at all. "I do think women these days should be able to work." Or: "Slavery is just wrong." What passes for my pedagogical intention is to show that professors who preen about "being radical" or offensive are usually being quite conventional. It would be genuinely radical to say in class: "Religious liberty makes most people more unhappy than they should be." I do regularly put the latter, genuinely thought-provoking opinion in the mouth of Marx, when talking about "On the Jewish Question."

Another pedagogical point that I hope I make is that there are always limits to free speech. There are some things that even Socrates dared not say straight out, like believing in the gods is stupid, although Plato does sometime lead us to assume he must really think something like that. Once students make that assumption, it's time to remind them that Socrates also taught that those who are proud of their atheism—the sophists—also stupidly thought they knew more than they really did. Socrates doesn't make the mistake of feeding the sophists' vanity and needlessly corrupting the already arrogant youth by openly dissing the gods. He seems to use reason to make religion better.

Socrates shows us time and again that it's impossible to say everything you really want to say. A teacher has to think some about what his audience wants to hear. Socrates has to watch what he says to the strong and idealistic young men in the *Republic*. He says, for example, he knows he can't walk away without giving them some positive account of justice, although he actually believes such a confident account is above even his pay grade. It would be bad for them, given their reluctant but real openness to tyranny. It would be bad for Socrates, who might get the stuffing beaten out of him or have charges brought against him for impiety and corrupting the young. It would even be unfair to the young men for whom Socrates had "dialectically" taken the religious and poetic defenses of being just off the table. Without saying more, he would have rendered them defenseless before clever sophists who believe that money and power are the bottom line. It was his responsibility to convince them it makes sense to be good, to be just, because tyranny and wisdom aren't "on the same page."

No decent young person really wants to believe that money and power are the bottom line. And, you know, they aren't. Part of the Socratic method, more than ever, is to keep students from surrendering what they really know about who they are to those clever sophists. In this sense, classroom conversation is, in part, a polemic—even a shameless polemic—against the sophist's two weapons of scientism ("studies show") and relativism ("that's only your opinion").

So it's always important to remind students that justice always imposes responsible limits on free speech. The reigning view of justice is always somewhat tyrannical. As Socrates shows in the *Crito*, "the Laws"—the dominant view of who we are and what we're supposed to do—always demand more of people than is reasonable. In American democracy, as Tocqueville insistently reminds us, there's sometimes "the tyranny of the majority." A secular liberal would add here immediately, of course, that that tyranny explains why American political leaders can't be openly atheistic, and why President Obama had to feign being opposed to same-sex marriage until recently. A libertarian would add, of course, that's why no politician can tell the truth that our entitlements, on which an overwhelming majority of Americans depend, are unsustainable.

Socrates points out that the democratic prejudice is to exaggerate both the goodness and the real possibility of individual liberation. The "moral majority" is actually a popular prejudice against pure democracy; it's the spirited and pious prejudice that produced the trial of Socrates. Pure democrats claim to be all about an easy-going acceptance of diverse lifestyles, including, of course, the one enjoyed by Socrates. But radical democrats—meaning those who are extremists when it comes to "doing your own thing" being the bottom line—readily get angry and vicious at those who say that freedom must be limited by virtue, by coming to terms with the responsibilities necessity—beginning with the necessities of birth and death—imposes upon us.

The argument over same-sex marriage today should be a reasonable and friendly discussion of the relationship between freedom and virtue. But it's not, partly because even the Supreme Court says that all the words coming out of the mouths of those on one side of the discussion are motivated by animosity toward homosexuals as a class. That's a conversation stopper if ever there was one. Faculty members these days in mainstream institutions can only say what they please about same-sex marriage in class if they agree with the dominant view of sophisticated Americans—our "cognitive elite"—today. That's not to say that view is wrong but that it has become a dogma.

It's easy for me to be fair-and-balanced and acknowledge that most people on both sides of that issue, and plenty of others, are pretty dogmatic.

Faculty members teaching at evangelical and seriously Catholic colleges have to watch what they say as well, if they want to educate their students "from where they are," not to mention avoid being fired.

Professors, like Socrates, can't really educate without taking into account the reigning dogmas, including dogmas that exaggerate our personal freedom, as well as dogmas about who God is and what he requires of each of us. Free speech that moves minds and hearts is always fairly tricky. That's why, as I've already suggested, the freedom of speech is enhanced by respect for texts. And it's that respect that's most missing among our technocratic experts. It's not after all either a democratic quality or a technological quality. It rather depends on the conviction that there's a personal standard that trumps money and power. So the main thing wrong with education in America today is that texts have lost their authority to move us with their wisdom and beauty. In every area of life, we've forgotten that respect—respect rooted in our anxious longing for what we have not been able to supply for ourselves—is an indispensable prelude to wonder.

Respect for Texts

Someone might say—and libertarian skeptics often do—that classes in philosophy and literature are given quite an arbitrarily inflated value by being accorded with credit. Do away with the credit system and give degrees based on real demonstration of measurable competencies valuable in the twenty-first-century marketplace, and you'll find out what studying Plato's *Republic* is really worth. I admit that's a humbling thought, one that I'm sure my college's administrators would like me to have at least once in a while. And I've heard that our professors of finance and accounting and computer science (and even the political *scientists*) think I should be having such thoughts a lot more often than that.

Now, to be fair to libertarian techno-skeptics, they almost all believe (and many have discovered for themselves) that it's really worthwhile to read the *Republic* or Shakespeare. It's just that you can do that on your own time and for free. Well, I agree you should do that on your own time and for free. But it's pretty hard—if not quite impossible—to know why you should spend your precious time that way without a good teacher. It turns out that openness to books—and so openness to the truth—usually depends on trusting a personal authority to some extent. That person—your teacher—has to earn your trust. And in some ways that's harder than ever.

The democratic imperative to think for myself is typically a mixture of antiauthoritarian paranoia and a kind of unwarranted or excessive self-confidence in one's own "critical thinking skills." We techno-Americans tend to believe there's a method for everything, even or especially, as Descartes said, for thinking. But the question remains, "what should I think about?" Surely I'm stuck with thinking about who I am and what I'm supposed to do. And just as surely it's asking too much for me to answer the "who" and the "what" question all by myself. Even God himself didn't create himself out of nothing.

Now there's something admirable and something ridiculous in this "hermeneutic of suspicion." It has a noble Protestant origin, after all, in the determination to trust no one but myself—and not those Satanic deceivers who call themselves priests—in interpreting the word of God. But even choosing to read the Bible depends on taking someone's word that the Bible is God's word, and to submit, even to the word of God, after all, is undemocratic. Christianity might teach that we're all equal under God, but we won't really be liberated as "autonomous persons" until we free ourselves from being under God's personal thumb.

So at a point certain democrats dispense with the Bible and other people and try to find God in themselves. But the religion of me—all alone—turns out to be pretty empty and certainly not the foundation of much "critical thinking"—toughly judgmental thinking—about who I am and what I'm supposed to do. It's this personal emptiness, Tocqueville explains, that causes democratic religion to morph into pantheism—or the denial of real personal identity.

Obviously we'd know more about ourselves if we read the Bible as if it might be true—or not from the point of view of detached tourists who believe that what this or that "culture" once believed has nothing to do with us these days—or, more precisely, with me these days. And obviously Americans would know a lot more about what genuine critical thinking requires if they read Descartes. But to privilege his book on method over others requires submitting to the personal authority of those who have read and recommend it. We democrats really see the despotic danger of such submission. We've all read, for example, that Leo Strauss got his "neocon" students to read Plato to impose his own personal "noble lie" on America. Those democrats so paranoid about being seduced by philosophers, of course, don't know what students of Strauss do. The "noble lie" shows up in the *Republic* as part of the construction of "a city in speech" that was not intended to be a real project for political reform.

It's easy to respond that not to read the Bible or Descartes is to even be more thoroughly or thoughtlessly dominated by those books. The personal egalitarianism that drives most moral thinking today is full of biblical premises, and to think with those premises with no awareness of their foundation is, obviously, not really to think for yourself. We defenders of "human rights" assert that every human person is unique and irreplaceable. But we have no idea why. Certainly most of modern science is incapable of even beginning to explain why.

The same goes, of course, with Descartes's audacious choice of the modern technological project. Every transhumanist is a Cartesian, whether he knows it or not. If you become liberally educated, you can actually start to make connections between the Bible and Descartes. Then you will actually start to think clearly about how techno-liberation depends on the Bible's view of the person while being a rejection of the Bible's personal and relational God. A critical thinker full of theological and philosophical content might exclaim, "how reasonable is that?"

The big point here is the excessively resolute determination to doubt personal authority doesn't really lead to freeing oneself altogether from authority. What rushes in, in the absence of personal authority or relational personal identity, is impersonal authority. It's too hard—too dizzying and disorienting—to think all by yourself. Because you don't know who you are, you really don't know what to do. So what fills the void and makes action possible, Tocqueville observes, is usually either public opinion—or trendy opinion—or the impersonal expertise of science.

When we defer to public opinion, we, in fact, become relativists. We say there's no standard—when it comes to truth, beauty, justice, and so forth—higher than what sophisticated public intellectuals assert these days. When we defer to experts and what their "studies" or "data" show, we find ourselves in the thrall of scientism. We too easily believe neuroscience or evolutionary psychology or rational-choice theory as explanations for everything, as the definitive sources of knowledge of who we are and what we're supposed to do. It's not denying the truth and utility of science to be aware of scientism. It's the ideology that's the result of popularizing scientists speculating authoritatively beyond the limits of what they can really know through their methods.

Both deferring to public opinion and deferring to "popular science" are ways of denying what you really can see with your own eyes about who you are and what you're supposed to do. It's, as the philosopher Heidegger and the novelist Walker Percy observe, surrendering oneself to what "they"—to what no one in particular—say. It's freeing oneself from the "they" that's the point of existentialism. It's also the point of the efforts of both Socrates and Jesus.

Public opinion, let me emphasize, doesn't only mean what the majority thinks. It means the opinion of *your* public. As Rousseau incisively pointed out, sophisticated intellectuals in democratic times flee from "the vulgar" by being witty and fashionable—and so by not being critical of what the witty and fashionable believe at any particular time. We can see now, for example, that neuroscience as a comprehensive explanatory system—that incorporates, for example, neurotheology and neurohumanities—peaked out as scientism around about 2008. But the progress in the real science of neuroscience continues, even if it's given less attention by the witty and fashionable.

Here's a beginning to teaching respect for texts: there should be nothing in the classroom except a professor, students, and a great or at least really good book—a Supreme Court opinion or a classic political speech count as a really good book. No PowerPoint, no laptops, no smart phones, and so forth. And the professor should be calling constant attention to the text, reading aloud and dramatically, from time to time. At least the occasional class should be devoted to a single page or even a single paragraph, just to make clear how much there is for us to know.

Respect for texts, let me conclude, is, among other things, about overcoming the distinction between the humanities and the sciences. My biggest objection to the Academy's "Saving the Humanities," it turns out, might be that not only does it do an injustice to the humanities, it does the same to science, or especially to what the humanities and science as they're now understood share in common. There's nothing in the report about the joy of discovery and sharing the truth with others across time and space. There's nothing about "the community of knowers and intellectual lovers" that should include theoretical physicists, philosophers, novelists, poets, theologians—among others. Plato, we remember, excelled in all those specialized disciplines, because he thought that the discipline of specialization was at the expense of the comprehensive inquiry required to know who we are and what we're supposed to do. So the division of human inquiry into the humanities and the sciences is artificial and alienating. It's clearly at the expense of the humanities. Theology and philosophy, for example, are sciences—for science is nothing but genuine knowledge of the way things really are. And there may be no human mode of communication more empirical—not to mention more diagnostic— than a great novel. Dostoyevsky, for example, had a clearer insight than Darwin or Hegel or Marx about what the twentieth century would be like.

Berry College's Contribution to Our Educational Diversity

A respect for texts—and a respect for conversation and even a respect for method—is finally all about the foundation of the community of knowers and lovers that includes us all. The residential liberal arts college deserves a future only if it's set up to be a home for a small and intimate part of that community. Let me conclude by explaining why Berry College has some singular features that allow it to provide a "safe space" for that kind of welcoming home.

The "Berry College advantages" don't always (although they can) include an enlightened and sympathetic administration; they don't even necessarily include (although they have from time to time) colleagues to whom I can tell the truth and share the joy of discovery. Sometimes I have to be trickier with them than with the students, and let me tell you, I'm too often not tricky enough. The Berry advantages are, in fact, wonderfully accidental. They weren't chosen by anyone at all. That doesn't mean, of course, that they aren't worth choosing now.

The first is that Berry is a vaguely Christian school not connected with a denomination. There are a lot of seriously religious students (and a lot who are not religious) and a pretty typical, mostly secular, or at least liberal Protestant faculty. The result is a kind of freedom of speech and intellectual openness not found in either a strictly secular or narrowly denominational school. The Berry classroom, or mine, at least, is a safe space for both devoutly observant and complacently skeptical students. If I'm careful, it's even possible to have a real discussion about whether *Roe v. Wade* was rightly decided. When I gave a talk at Pomona in California, I asked students about the place of religion in higher education; they were almost uniformly amazed that anyone could think there was any. At Berry, that issue is a real bone of contention.

Our more bookish evangelical students often really become seekers and searchers, wonderers and wanderers, alive with the predicament of having a personal destiny open to a variety of possibilities. The evangelicals—say, Southern Baptists—are often equally dissatisfied with the superficiality of their churches and the relativism of the reigning secularism. And they sometimes have actually been raised to have respect for texts. They're open to the Bible teaching the truth, and so they're also open to the suggestion that the only reason to read any "great book" is that it teaches the truth. They want to hear about, say, Nietzsche, from Nietzsche's point of view. They're surprisingly reluctant to be satisfied with concluding, as evangelicals in general sometimes do, that "according to my 'worldview' Nietzsche is wrong." One reason, of course, is they're quick to get on board with his criticism of liberalism as a kind of inauthentic Christianity without Christ.

Another reason some Berry students are strikingly undemocratic in their respect for texts, of course, is that the South is more about personal respect, about even the authority of parents, and having good manners, than most of the rest of the country. So on my best days, I'm able to be alive to the mixture of Southern Stoicism, believing Christianity, and modern existentialism that makes liberal education possible in my particular place. I'm grateful that Berry affords me the space and the students to do what I think I'm supposed to do.

Chapter 4
Esotericism and Living in the Truth

The most important book published in political philosophy in years is Arthur M. Melzer's *Philosophy Between the Lines: The Lost History of Esoteric Writing*. It first of all establishes, beyond all reasonable doubt, that philosophers (and poets, and other writers) routinely deployed "a double doctrine." One was "exoteric" or "external" and "public." The other was "esoteric" or "internal" and "secret."

The intention of the French philosophers—or Enlightening, publicizing philosophers— was that the truth about these two contradictory doctrines becomes public knowledge. They turned esotericism into an exoteric or public doctrine. That was part of their attempt to bring about a world in which esoteric writing would no longer be necessary, where philosophers would no longer be persecuted for telling inconvenient truths.

In the ideal society to come, there would be no conflict between justice and human excellence. The residual esotericism that the enlightenment philosophers used was, in their minds, a temporary tool to purge the world of superstition and prejudice. This "political esotericism" of the authors of the Encyclopedia was in the service of an open society with perfect freedom of thought.

We could also describe their ideal world as a place without irony and double meanings, where esotericism would be remembered as that device which good men, such as Plato and Aristotle, used to protect themselves from political and religious oppression.

The Encyclopédie authors ousted esotericism as one way of making it a past-tense phenomenon. Soon, the kinds of things Plato and Aristotle said secretly could now be said plainly: for example, that religion is nothing but a political tool. Or that the risky virtues—beginning with courage—are for suckers, or that there's no other reason to obey the law than enlightened self-interest. We could add: love is an illusion, philosophy is basically the most intense and enduring form of hedonism, suffering is meaningless, and death is personal extinction.

The ancient philosophers thought that society couldn't handle anywhere near that much truth; social stability depended upon a veil of ignorance when it came to God, love, death, virtue, and civic attachment. The Enlightenment proved the ancients wrong. All those shocking truths are now the common sense of literary sophisticates, from Woody Allen to the author of the children's book and movie *The Fault in Our Stars*. And the popular adoption of these truths does seem compatible enough with the stable family lives of our "cognitive elite" today.

Our "new atheism" is nothing but an off-the-shelf version of the old or esoteric atheism. Enlightenment's result has been that religious and political cruelty continue to fade; we continue to purge ourselves of the residual illusions that hamper achievement of the reasonable goal of keeping the people around right now secure and free for as long as possible.

Melzer proves that the intellectual history of esotericism wasn't the perverse invention of Leo Strauss and his arrogantly deceptive Straussians. Any scholar who doesn't acknowledge the fact of esoteric writing is literally cut off from the deep wisdom of the past. But Strauss is a very significant figure in this history. He, even more than the eighteenth-century Enlightenment authors, made a big deal of the esoteric and exoteric distinction. He wrote to restore it as a fairly public doctrine, a doctrine that would orient public intellectuals and even beginning undergraduates. He, too, wanted the awareness of esotericism to be a mood or attitude that wouldn't just be for potential philosophers anymore.

Strauss, Melzer shows, was somewhat, but not mainly, drawn to esotericism as a political tool. It's true that Strauss did encourage his students to ally with American conservatism and defend American law and morality against various forms of corrosive, even if somewhat truthful, dogmatic skepticism and progressivism. So some Straussians insist that Americans must believe in the absolute truth of the principles of the Declaration of Independence, even if the privately Epicurean Mr. Jefferson was somewhat ironic about them.

But other, wilder Straussians, such as Laurence Lampert, say that it's good the Enlightenment and modern science continue to march toward a global triumph, and that the time for esotericism is over. Lampert criticizes Strauss for not having been loud and proud about his atheism and about "the sovereignty of becoming."

Judicious Catholic Straussians, such as Pierre Manent, consider whether the Enlightenment has led the West to revel self-destructively in post-political, post-religious, or post-familial fantasies, and whether it's now time to ask if there aren't even theoretical limitations to the philosophers' secret account of who each of us is, given that those private philosophical musings have become, in a distorted way, our public doctrine. Our Supreme Court, after all, has explained that the American idea of liberty evolves over time, which might mean that it purges itself of "political esotericism" and becomes all about personal autonomy or unfeigned Epicureanism.

We can say that many of our Straussians are ham-fisted enough in their esoteric efforts that even a sympathetic reader begins to wonder if they really mean what they say. With the best of them, their expressed devotion to God, country, and family is not feigned because they realize there is more to life than being a philosopher. That would mean, of course, that the best of the Straussians don't really think that Socrates taught the whole truth and nothing but the truth. Perhaps the esoteric Socrates perceived by some Straussians was less genuinely concerned with moral virtue and with those who understand themselves as parents and children, citizens, and creatures than many students of Strauss have been.

My own view is that Straussian writing doesn't work all that well when its main purpose is to defend the "healthy" political life that's the precondition for the future of philosophy in the world. One reason is that our view of personal identity, which includes our inalienable natural rights, depends upon a Christian insight that discredits a fairly exoteric Socratic teaching about the supposedly radical difference between the liberated life of the philosopher and the slavish life of everybody else, those benighted denizens of "the cave" or the city.

Consider that Socrates distinguished himself from the philosopher-kings by locating himself in the cave, and that his philosopher-kings are an exoteric, poetic construction two steps removed from reality (just as the character Socrates of the *Republic* is one step removed). Thinking of almost all people as "citizens" successfully socialized to be part of the whole called "the city in speech" and its regime was, for Socrates, an educational technique developed in response to Glaucon's tyrannical idealism. It was not Socrates' complete description of who particular persons are. Christianity introduced into the world a more public yet deeply authentic criticism of both the natural theology and the civil theology of the Greeks and Romans. Particular persons with singular destinies and irreducibly "inward" beings can't be reduced to a part of nature or a part of a country.

For the Romans, the Christians appeared to be atheists, because they openly and courageously denied the existence of the gods of the city. They aroused the anger of good Roman citizens, just as Socrates did of good Athenian citizens, and they chose death over dissimulation. St. Augustine highlighted the inauthenticity of the esotericism of the Roman philosopher Varro; Varro publicly affirmed, for the good of civic morality, the existence of gods he truly found to be ridiculous and degrading. So Varro, unlike St. Augustine, did not live in the truth. He wasn't open to the Christian good news that we're all born to live in the shared truth about our personal origins and destinies, a truth that commands our loving personal dedication more deeply than the law of the city ever could.

The good news is that because we're all transparent before the personal and loving God, we're called to do what we can to be transparent before each other. When Melzer deploys Augustine to display the place of esotericism in the history of thought, he does so to show that Augustine saw and understood the place of esoteric writing in the Greek and Roman philosophers, not that Augustine himself was insincere. That's not to say that Augustine always put what he thought in neon letters; he knew some would understand more than others. He didn't make a big deal, for example, of teaching that political life, particularly the city of Athens, was rooted in the sin of pride that was the source of unjustly excluding women from citizenship. He admits that he contented himself with making that point quickly and through a story. Parables have to be lovingly attended to by genuine seekers, but they fall short of being esoteric.

Although some Christian writers may have written esoterically (such as Thomas Aquinas on the limits of thinking in terms of "natural law"), the truth seems to be that Christianity itself claims to have surpassed the distinction between philosophy and law (or the tension between the philosopher and the city) that was the foundation of esotericism. And what should be called the return to esotericism by the Enlightenment philosophers was used as a weapon to disguise the attack on Christianity on behalf of liberated philosophy. But, as Melzer says, it wasn't exactly a return, because it presupposed the truth of key Christian insights about personal identity or the free individual. That's why the return to esotericism was temporary, or not a permanent reflection of the truth about who we are.

Modern philosophy, as Melzer shows, accepted or at least deployed the Christian's skepticism about politics. Religion and political life remain separated, and personal identity is understood to be free from political or natural determination. And so America's self-understanding has never been as a "regime" or a whole that corresponds to the non-philosophic soul. Melzer says that modern liberal or Enlightenment philosophy's intensification or elaboration of the key Christian insight actually obscures the truth that the key human distinction is between philosophy and poetry. More precisely, he says that this distinction was the foundation of multidimensional classical esotericism, although it hasn't been the foundation of either Christian enlightenment or modern, liberal, philosophic Enlightenment.

"All men are created equal" can't be vindicated these days by anyone who views it as an exoteric teaching or merely as the foundation of a public philosophy. The classical political thinkers, following the noble lie in the *Republic*, thought that the founding myth that all citizens are created equal had to be defended to keep political leaders from treating their fellow citizens as resources to be exploited. For them, equality was promulgated as a civic or public truth, not a natural or inward one. The classical political philosophers also thought, as Melzer explains, that slavery was indispensable for high civilization and therefore for the flourishing of philosophers. They tolerated that offense against what we regard as "social justice," and they were more than a bit ironic about the often tyrannical ambitions that fuel the human longing for perfect justice.

Aristotle is an exception, for he can be proved to have shown, although with great reserve, or even esoterically, that the convention of slavery does violence to what we really know about human nature. But that means that he was fine with the indefinite perpetuation of a despotic institution he knew was unjust. He accepted that slavery in some sense would always be with us.

The unironic defense of human equality depends, I think, on viewing every human being as a unique and irreplaceable person, a being with an irreducible personal identity. That questionable thought, which might be regarded as dogmatic, depends on bringing to the table more than the secret truths of the pre-Christian philosophers. It's that questionable thought, we might say, that made esotericism merely political or provisional. In a Christian or an enlightened world the need for it would wither away. Slavery, as even St. Augustine suggested, would disappear, as would the vain pretensions that were the foundation of the patriarchal exclusiveness of political life.

Just as the City of God doesn't distinguish between Jew and Gentile, Greek and barbarian, man and woman, or philosopher and citizen, there would be a reconfiguring of political life, the exoteric or public world, under the influence of the deep truth about who each of us is. In this way, political life could become a contract among free persons to preserve the peace and facilitate the inward relational life that's the flourishing City of God. And true theology would replace civil theology. The American Constitution dispenses with God as the foundation of political life, but it does so to protect the free exercise of religion.

In the case of Mr. Jefferson, his public devotion to all human creatures equally possessing inalienable natural rights and his corresponding eloquence against the cruel violence of slavery was compromised by his private Epicureanism, his heartfelt praise of the philosophic life that flourishes beyond hope and fear. In his public actions, Jefferson was altogether too serene about slavery's indefinite future. It's possible, even necessary, to be somewhat ironic about "natural rights." The rights-obsessed person, in Jefferson's philosophic view, is caught between Epicurean serenity and the dutiful life of the parent, friend, citizen, and creature. But is it possible to be ironic about the real existence of the significant human person and be devoted to the American "public philosophy"?

Leo Strauss's invaluable contribution, as Melzer meticulously explains, was to restore esotericism as a perennially relevant teaching method, and not just for potential philosophers. We so often forget how rare Strauss thought philosophers were. It's at least a question whether he regarded Diderot or Voltaire as philosophers—he certainly wouldn't apply this honorific to Thomas Paine, Jefferson, or all of our leading Straussians. From an educational view, as Melzer shows, the main problem with liberal society today is inauthenticity, a problem that intensifies as we work to reconfigure all rights around personal autonomy or "human rights." Jean-Jacques Rousseau complained that no one in the society around him was really a citizen or religious believer or a parent deep down; all bourgeois lives are consumed by "role playing."

That goes especially for our allegedly liberated intellectuals. They pronounce all kinds of terrible truths, but they don't really seem to be moved by them. They're not driven by wonder or awe or even real anxiety. They don't really understand that philosophy, or science, should entail learning how to die. They're already dead to, or diverted from, themselves. They care mostly about how they look in the eyes of others. Our scientists, it's true, sometimes more authentically lose themselves in the cosmos or their impersonal theories, but that still means that they are, when it comes to an inward consideration of their own natures, diverted.

Strauss wondered, and Melzer with him, why the truth about esoteric writing's past pervasiveness disappeared from our scholarly world. Maybe the best explanation is that the denial of the reality of esotericism is, at its most self-conscious level, a form of esotericism that supports the relativism that privileges what passes for wisdom nowadays.

The relativistic or "historicist" thought is that what is thought and said can be explained by the worldview or values or authoritative prejudices of a particular time and place. That means, for example, that Plato and Aristotle were basically apologists for the Athenian way of life and its conventions. A thinker can transcend only to a small degree his place in history. To interpret past philosophers in this manner requires one to collapse any distinction between their exoteric and their true doctrine, and then to judge the result defective in the light of the wisdom we believe we possess now. In a society where esotericism has become superfluous, it's better to not remember that it was ever deployed in the past.

Not only can one now write distinctly and clearly, without doing harm to oneself or anyone else, it's even possible to forget that anyone ever wrote differently. The denial of esotericism locks each of us securely onto the surface and in the present, allegedly for our own good and certainly with our own self-esteem in mind.

In Melzer's view, the denial of esotericism is a way of numbing people to the terrible truths they would rather avoid. Previously, philosophers kept people from really feeling the hard truth by supporting comforting illusions that cover it over. They enabled people to live authentically as citizens, creatures, parents, friends, and such. They acted on what they believed about God, love, family and country. Because they were passionately attached to serious opinions about the fundamental issues, a teacher of philosophy could work with what they thought they knew, to lead them toward the truth about those issues. The way to become a philosopher, the mature Socrates thought, was through questioning the assumptions that animate "earnest provincialism."

Melzer is open to the possibility that the numbness of inauthenticity promotes social stability as well as the salutary illusions used to do. But it turns out that it is worse for genuinely higher education, philosophic education, to encounter a society in which genuinely dangerous thoughts seem almost impossible. No writer in America today really fears the fate of Socrates.

As Walker Percy said, however, an American writer can have a kind of Solzhenitsyn envy, which might be understood as a version of Socrates envy. Solzhenitsyn's subversive defense of the truth against ideological lies caused him to be taken so seriously by his now-defunct country, the USSR, that he was thrown into the Gulag and eventually just kicked out. Contemporary American authors might envy the dissidents still truthfully writing between the lines in places like Iran, China, North Korea, Cuba, and elsewhere. For them, truthful words about freedom make a big difference, or even all the difference. A novelist or professor in today's America can say just about anything and people pretty much yawn. It's true that Straussians and Christians who teach in our mainstream colleges have to be prudently reserved until they get tenure. But big deal, then they can say what they think.

Melzer's only real objection to stability through authenticity is that it poses unprecedented obstacles to philosophic liberation. In my view, he follows Allan Bloom in exaggerating the flatness of soul of sophisticated middle-class Americans. It's just not true that they have become so lamely one-dimensional that they're no longer moved by love and death. Solzhenitsyn, in fact, was probably closer to the truth when he observed that just beneath the surface of America's pervasively upbeat pragmatism is the "howl of existentialism." Howling, of course, is what a desperate animal does when he or she lacks the words that corresponds to his or her longings. And only members of our species can be miserably lonely in the absence of personal love, anxious in the face of nothing, and haunted by the prospect of personal extinction. That's why, for example, so much of our pragmatism is now being deployed to fend off extinction. It's also why the pragmatist Richard Rorty's linguistic therapy of talking death out of existence, as well as the psychopharmacological therapy of drugging death to death, were doomed to fail from the beginning.

Ask a sophisticated American what idea, today, he or she would consider dangerous. Frequently the response is an idea that unnecessarily exposes a person to risk factors by promoting irresponsible or unhealthy personal behavior. Insofar as we become reflexively skeptical of the soul, and of the corresponding virtues and intellectual disciplines, we become obsessed with personal survival. People are more aware than ever of their personal contingency and haunted by the prospect of personal extinction. They're ever-aware of death, even as they refuse to accept its inevitability. There may be no more inauthentic life than one fueled by one-dimensional survivalism, with an aversion to danger that's both more natural and more dogmatic than the conventionalism that animated the political opponents of Socrates. It's this survivalism that causes us to put our faith in the technology that can save us, as well as the completely safe separation of sex or eros from birth and death.

The problem with a world where all communication is supposed to be clear and distinct, where there are no real secrets or elusive mysteries about the human soul, is that we lack the words, more precisely, we lack the modes of attentive reading and listening, that correspond to our real experiences. Although there are many motivations for and ways of writing esoterically, it is, on one level, simply introducing what poets and novelists characteristically do into the prose of specifically philosophical writing. It's better to show the truth than to tell it straight out.

The teaching method of Allan Bloom was, I think, a kind of exoteric exaggeration of the extent to which the individualism of Enlightenment rationalism has emptied relational life of its content. And so, Bloom explained, the true choices in our time are philosophy or nothing: living authentically with the truth about one's own mortality, or living inauthentically with it. The exaggeration that "capitalism" or "the Enlightenment" had transformed everything about us, which Marx employed to call us to political revolution, Bloom employed to call us to the hard truth about being a particular person who was born to know and die. And Melzer, by describing inauthenticity as our leading social problem, reminds us of the common debt that Bloom, Strauss, and Marx owed to the anti-bourgeois and proto-existentialist Rousseau. For many an existentialist, being authentic is being alone, but for the Straussians, there's also the philosophic compensation for the misery of mortality that comes with the joy of figuring out and sharing with others the truthful insight about who we really are. And insofar as that sharing occurs through writing, it has to be esoteric, because truthfully authentic lives will always remain few and far between.

That teaching method, I can't help but notice, has opened many young men and women to the possibility of philosophy, and it's not true that America today is short on highly educated and thoughtful Straussians convinced of the superiority of the philosophic life to all others. The idea of esotericism has turned out, in their cases, to have roused them from their bourgeois slumber. But I would say that they couldn't have been roused if their souls had really become flat, if they hadn't yearned to be a lot more than nothing. It wouldn't work, that is, if they didn't have longings that pointed beyond their biological beings as either social or solitary animals.

I do not, however, endorse this teaching method. That's because I'm Christian enough to believe that we're all called to live in the truth. And the great lie of the twentieth century wasn't "the law" but ideology. The great defenders of the truth, including but not only the truth of philosophy, were the anti-ideological dissident thinkers, particularly Solzhenitsyn and Václav Havel. Insofar as ideology is deformed philosophy, the dissident strives to defend the moral contents of ordinary life from forms of abstract rationalism that deny the real existence of the particular human person. Against the ideological absorption of persons into some natural or historical or technological process called "progress," every particular person is called to live responsibly in the truth about what each person really knows as beings born to know, love, and die. We're all called to live authentically as free and relational beings, as beings with more than a merely biological destiny.

As St. Augustine says, action and contemplation are for all of us. Even Socrates should have practiced the virtues of generosity and charity and parental responsibility, and all of us should have some time, because we're all given the inward inclination, to contemplate the truth about who each of us is and what we were born to do. This line of thinking is the way both to restore the dignity of liberal education and to recover the truthful foundation of the rights we all cherish. Consequently, I don't think we should practice esoteric writing, and I don't even think it ever faithfully or unambiguously served the truth. Truths that Melzer presents as once esoteric and now inauthentic commonplaces among sophisticates—i.e., that love is an illusion and suffering is meaningless turn out not to be true, deep down, after all.

I have done readers the disservice of barely touching on the contents of Melzer's wonderful book, which allows us to share abundantly in the author's joy of discovery. If I had a quibble, it would be that he doesn't give us, at least straight out, an example of esoteric wisdom that would be shocking to our atheistic era. Perhaps the fact of esotericism dazzles more than its actual content. Or perhaps we shouldn't expect Melzer to make a big deal out of being, as they say, genuinely transgressive. Those who buy the basic argument of his book, after all, now have every incentive to start reading it between the lines.

Chapter 5
True Liberalism Versus Democratic Excess

There are always limits to intellectual freedom. And there sure are in America today. I'm not talking about people being thrown into Gulags like Solzhenitsyn or put to death like Socrates for insistently speaking truths inconvenient for those in power. In a way, it's so easy to say anything in our country that it's even possible to complain that speaking freely doesn't cost anything—doesn't have any real value—these days. It's hard to be genuinely transgressive when there's almost no legal censorship, and so our artists and writers have to go to unprecedented lengths to genuinely shock us. But when Alexis de Tocqueville made the provocative claim that there's less freedom of thought in democratic America than there was in European aristocracies, he wasn't thinking about legal constraints at all. The punishment for stepping too far outside dominant or democratic opinion in America is ostracism, being banished from the "community" or the "conversation," and that was enough to keep American pens and even minds in check.

Today, the problem isn't so much the tyranny of public opinion. It's that ferocious intensity that separates our moral and political factions. Consider how heated our political rhetoric is now. Some say that the Democrats are all about facilitating baby killers, and others that the Republicans are racist homophobes who psych up mass murderers. It's true, of course, that political rhetoric always includes a tendency to demonize the other guys. What's more lacking than usual right now is the balance of generous inclinations that see political controversy as rooted in reasonable or at least understandable disagreement and so aim at political reform through persuasive conversation and prudent compromise. One reason for this imbalance is that our political process, as it now operates, leaves too little room for legislative deliberation (and too much for judicial intervention), for experiences that would show each side that the other isn't driven mainly by callous indifference or irrational animosity. Another reason is the niche-y nature of our various media outlets, which make it too easy for people to listen only to commentators who reinforce their prejudices and fuel their self-righteousness. So the truth seems to be that, more than ever, our country is divided into two separate but roughly equal (in size) bodies of public opinion.

Given this division, our colleges and universities should be much more attentive than they are to what Jonathan Haidt calls the lack of "viewpoint diversity" among our professors. A miniscule percentage of our professors in the social sciences and humanities vote Republican or consider themselves conservative, although roughly half of our citizens do. The argument for affirmative action that passes constitutional muster is that our faculties and student bodies should look like America, in order that there be a "critical mass" to defend the opinions that correspond to our diverse personal identities. Well, doesn't personal identity include political or ideological orientation? And in that respect our faculties don't look much like America at all. This is, as Donald Trump would say, a huge problem mainly because our liberals deny that conservative opinion has any intellectual legitimacy and deserves to be marginalized.

Our academic liberals aren't afraid to say that academic freedom ought to be limited by academic justice, that certain opinions can be excluded from "public reason" or enlightened discourse. There's a limit to the "viewpoint diversity" that is tolerated on our campuses, and that's one reason among several that our elite places aren't about to extend affirmative action to the marginalized group of conservative intellectuals. They pretty much deserve the microaggressions that come their way.

Enhancing this problem is the demand, flowing from both students and administrators, that the consumers of higher education be made to feel as comfortable as possible in a welcoming environment. Students and administrators at our most politically correct places are even demanding "trigger warnings" from their professors before being confronted with opinions that might make them feel uncomfortable or inferior. Feelings of inferiority, of course, can be triggered by anything that penetrates the bubble created by so many elite student affairs staffs, who act as self-esteem police for students. It goes without saying that the real concern is not professors preaching racism or sexism. Trigger warnings, apparently, should also be attached to teaching any "great book" that presents a different view of the place of women in the world than what we currently hold, or that strongly portrays what we now consider racism or anti-Semitism, such as *The Adventures of Huckleberry Finn* or *The Merchant of Venice*, even to dramatize the psychological and political damage caused by such injustice.

This illiberal spirit is fatal to the teaching of the "humanities"—meaning literature, history, philosophy, politics, religion or theology, and so forth. It's impossible to teach a great book without being open to the possibility that it teaches the whole truth about who we are. That means attending especially to the parts that most challenge today's fashionable opinions about justice, morality, God, and so forth. In reading Plato's *Republic*, for example, that means seriously attending to the possibility that really being devoted to justice means being for communism, not only of property, but of women and children—a communism based on the full equality of men and women in terms of fighting, philosophizing, and ruling. If students indignantly observe that communism is an offense against personal love and privacy, then they might conclude that political justice ought not to be the most passionate concern of free beings open to the truth about who they are. And they might learn what the book was actually trying to teach them.

Judging Democracy

But the main reason to read the *Republic* is to be open to inconvenient conclusions about the true strengths and weaknesses of democracy. Democracy is good because, in one respect, it's so open to freedom of thought and what we would call genuinely multicultural (or, more exactly, political) diversity. The dialogue's incredibly open-minded discussion about the merits of various human possibilities—aristocracy, timocracy (love of honor), oligarchy, democracy, and tyranny, as well as techno-domination, observant piety, poetic nobility, and open atheism—could only have occurred in a democracy. Imperial Athens did little to clamp down on controversial speech, the trial of Socrates being a major exception, and it was open to currents of thought and belief from many parts of the world.

Socrates' judgment in favor of democracy is clear in his notorious choice to be an Athenian stay-at-home. When he wanted a taste of multicultural diversity, he went to the Athenian harbor, not to other cities where his free thinking and intrusive moralizing would have gotten him into far more trouble. We can see that the young men with whom Socrates spoke for so long in the *Republic* could be led to think deeply and speak passionately about dangerous ideas and genuinely alternative ways of life, while never forgetting that even Athens was far from a perfectly "safe space" for such conversation. Increasingly unguarded talk about justice can take place with impunity only for so long. But embracing the noble risk is better than paying the price for choosing safety over truth. And, truth to tell, it's finally not democratic to choose the truth over comfortable opinion.

Pure democracy (not to be confused with impure or "real" Athenian democracy), according to Socrates, is the pure realm of freedom based upon the equality of human desires and aspirations. It lacks any principle of compulsion or even judgment. You're perfectly free to do your own thing, because nobody can tell you what your thing is. Wisdom and virtue—even the competence and virtues characteristic of ordinary relational or civic or business life—don't trump choice. So democracy is the realm of pure "diversity" or a sea of unobsessive randomness. The perennial human longing for this freedom can be seen in the fact that Marx's description of life under communism—doing what you please whenever you please without being defined by this or that activity—is identical to Socrates' description of democracy.

The pure democracy Socrates describes is, in fact, charming in its "diversity," in its absence of repression or sublimation and, officially, even anger. It's the only regime in which both philosophers and women can live as they please, without being chained to civic imperatives. But it also has ugly, truth-denying, and fatal weaknesses. Democracy is ugly in its relativism, in its easygoing refusal to rank human activities according to the standards of truth, excellence, and nobility. This refusal is a denial of what our eyes can see about the merit and the irreducible beauty of real human accomplishment. This refusal, from another view, is really an unempirical denial of the invincible necessities—love and death—that govern every human life.

The democrat claims to live an unobsessive or insouciant life—doing whatever he pleases whenever he pleases, as if he has all the time and all the freedom in the world. The only thing that angers him is any claim for necessity, which he immediately brands as oppressive authoritarianism. Human beings rank activities because they only have so much time; excellence or even competence requires specialization. Nobody can be good at everything. Not only that, human beings obsess and rank because they can't help falling in love; a pure democracy has to be thought of as a world without parents and children.

The atrophying of all the distinctions connected with the soul, however, leads to an obsession with the body, the necessity that can't be imagined out of existence. One result is that the elderly increasingly repulse the young by bringing death to mind. So older people, to avoid loneliness and marginalization, spend all their time trying to look and act young. A democracy is a terrible place to be old, because in the absence of respectful tradition and binding intergenerational ties, nobody knows what old people are for.

Even teachers fawn on students. Without the authority that accompanies truth, they have to fall back on the popularity that comes with being pleasing. That means that they can't call attention to any fact that undermines the students' complacent choices of their random personal identities. Teachers can't be so judgmental as to privilege some truthful or noble or pious or even necessitarian or survivalist principle by which it's possible to rank or judge the merits of various forms of human living, of various views of music, of God, of the good. "It's all good" is the democrat's lazy conclusion. And the record of human accomplishment has to be taught from the point of the tourist who revels in "diversity" without taking on the repressive baggage of thinking one "culture" is superior to another. Actually, that way of teaching privileges the superiority of democracy, the only place where it is possible to live as a detached consumer of the products of various cultures.

Pure Democracy as Hell

The most penetrating criticism of pure democracy—its most compelling teachable moment—is that, as far as we can tell, living there would be hell. That's the point of the philosophic film *Groundhog Day.* There the Bill Murray character mask his wounded soul by affecting the air of ironic detachment. He wants to appear to be living without order or necessity, like Socrates' democrat. But the truth is Bill (also his film name) is less easygoing than wounded, and so he's disconnected privileges from responsibilities and by feigning being impervious to love. His life, to say the least, is unimpressive to grown-ups.

Bill mysteriously enters into a more purely democratic utopia than even the one Socrates imagines. He's freed from time and death—the seemingly invincible limits to the dream of pure democracy—through living in the endless repetition of the same 24-hour day. It turns out that there's nothing worse than a world in which other people become nothing more than playthings at your disposal, and in which nothing you do has anything significance beyond immediate enjoyment. Hell, as Walker Percy said, is "pure possibility," being liberated from the necessities of birth, love, work, truth, and death. And the experience of hell turns out to be the remedy for Bill's self-indulgent, self-denying irony.

Bill becomes suicidal, but suicide is not an option for him. And so he has to invent order and necessity in his life to make it endurable. He begins to practice the virtue of charity for people who don't have the time to get to love or even be properly grateful to him. He devotes himself to cultivating his untapped talents, and he masters the piano, discovering the joy in music. He aims to gain the love of a particular woman by attending to the details of her longings. She becomes more strange and wonderful to him as she continues to elude his complete comprehension and control, just as he appears, each day, more strange and wonderful to her as he becomes more virtuous, more accomplished, and finally more loving. His reward for his noble efforts, the film concludes in a corny way, is his return to time and death.

It's often said that the dream of pure democracy—which is the same unobsessive randomness as Marx's dream of communism—corresponds to the deepest human longing for liberation, and it's a shame it can't become real. The truth is that it's a dream based on a denial of the love and work that make life worth living, and thank God it can't become real. The world John Lennon imagines, without God and anything worth fighting for, would be one that we would want to fight our way out of.

The Unsustainability of Pure Democracy

Still, the most urgent problem with pure democracy is that it's unsustainable, and so it tends to be easy prey for a highly passionate and ambitious tyrant. A pure democracy lacks the courage and devotion that inspires citizens to risk their lives and fortunes for its defense. It lacks the spirited intensity that's the source of noble contempt for mindless materialism, just as it lacks the disciplined deferral of gratification required to be a productive materialist. In terms of tyranny, democrats can be readily seduced to their personal freedom not only to particular tyrants but to impersonal forces such as technology and public opinion formed by no one in particular. It turns out that people have to have a spirited point of view—the spirit of resistance—to defend themselves from the forces always threatening to envelop them.

So Socrates turns out to be, among other things, a friendly critic of democracy in the name of democracy's real future. He gives his interlocutors the impression that there's no going back to pure aristocracy or pure oligarchy, but he causes them to think of ways aristocratic and oligarchic and timocratic elements are indispensable for any functioning political order. The cure for what ails democracy is sometimes less democracy.

In thinking about America as they encounter Socrates' account of pure democracy, students become open to the possibility that many social pathologies are democratic excesses. They will also observe, of course, that our country is far from purely democratic. We have a strong oligarchic component to our regime or way of life. We are obsessed with money, in part, but only in part, because we have to be. And we have a sense of honor, if one in some decline. Honor is the countercultural motivation for those "special forces" on whom we depend for our protection.

And a true aristocracy, Socrates explains, is ruled by the best, those unsurpassed in wisdom and virtue. We still have a genuine concern, of course, for merit and meritocracy, which we see in its purest form in business, sports, and science. We even see that concern in our choice to hold elections rather than a purely democratic lottery in selecting our representatives and executives. Ordinary people get to vote, but they usually choose the best candidate (from a personal view) and not ordinary stiffs such as themselves. America's future depends on those non-democratic elements—with their money, virtue, and competence—having a place in our country and its self-understanding. There's nothing more ridiculous than the contemporary democratic utopias that flow from both Marx and the transhumanists that suggest that we'll all soon live in unprecedented abundance and nonjudgmental freedom for an indefinitely long time with very little work, in a world with no real devotion to justice and God and no real personal love. The libertarian critics may agree with the Marxists that the point of life is freedom for unfettered enjoyment, but add that the exercise of that freedom will always depend on attending to necessity by being productive. Oligarchic means—including the relevant moral and intellectual virtue—are indispensable for enjoying what we can of democratic ends.

Learning from Pure Democracy

What students might learn from the *Republic* is that admirable and sustainable political orders and societies are mixtures of diverse elements, and, from the points of view of truth, justice, excellence, endurance, and love, conditions are genuinely getting better and worse. The study of the *Republic* is meant to disrupt the prevailing liberal or libertarian narrative in which the history of our country has been pretty much evolution toward greater and greater justice understood as maximum conceivable personal autonomy with no corresponding cost to love, living well with death, courage, truth, competence, and ordinary relational life. The future of democracy depends on having a kind of "selective nostalgia" for what's best about non-democratic life, without being, as Yuval Levin says, "blinded by nostalgia" by imagining any point in the past as better than it really was. There's a lot to be said for democratic freedom and egalitarian justice, if only we're able to use them well.

Another way of putting it: The point of Plato's *Republic* is to get students more than a little bit uncomfortable about who we've become and to think about our shortcomings in comparison to other places and times. I'm not sure how many trigger warnings would have to be attached to a class about reading that great book carefully. A lot, that's for sure.

We also learn from Socrates that the job of the philosopher is to teach against the dominant prejudices of those to whom he is talking. He criticizes the sophists—or the enlightened technocrats of his time—for thinking they can reduce moral education to a technique. And he criticizes the democrats—such as his accuser, the poet Meletus, for thinking—in the name of equality—that all citizens are equally competent when it comes to education, a mistake no sophist would make.

Alexis de Tocqueville, following that Socratic example, said that had he lived in the medieval world he would have been preaching the liberating hunt of prosperity against the indolent and often repressive focus on spiritual life or the soul. But in a democracy, the task is to defend the soul and great human individuality against both single-minded materialism and promiscuously leveling egalitarianism. In our case, the effort is to disrupt the vain prejudices of the sophisticated class—professors, journalists, and experts of all kinds—that pass for wisdom. It's not that the dominant class doesn't know anything, but it knows less than it thinks it does, while the allegedly less enlightened class knows much more about who we are and the art of living well than the arrogant elitists assume.

I often tell students: Your time in a residential college—the closest thing you'll have to an aristocratic experience in our oligarchic democracy—is to learn what you won't learn on the street in a democracy. Use your leisure of the residential college to be all about philosophy, literature, theology, art, music, and even theoretical physics to cultivate your soul for lifelong educated leisure. You'll have to focus on money soon enough. If you can really read, write, and think, money just won't be that big an issue. You'll flourish better in our technological mixture of oligarchy and democracy if you're somewhat ironic about its inflated claims. You'll flourish better if you know enough that money and technology needs to be subject to worthy human purposes, and that "lifelong learning" is most of all about connecting your privileges to your responsibilities.

Many politically correct professors and bureaucrats do seek to defend the "humanities" and liberal education from the oligarchs who want our country dominated by an alleged meritocracy based on productivity. They really believe that moral equality trumps productivity, that there are more noble standards of merit than generating power. But they discredit their position by not acknowledging that their claims for justice through "diversity" are contestable. And in place of the claims for truth embedded in the great texts of our tradition, they have substituted the angry propaganda of identity politics. If identity trumps truth, however, there's plenty of reason for a woman to bypass women's studies in the name of the true liberation she can achieve by becoming a highly competent member of the meritocracy based on productivity. The money she earns gives her the power to define her own identity as a free individual—and not as a member of a particular race, class, gender, or sexual orientation.

In a world that has trivialized political and cultural distinctions through the leveling weapon of "diversity," all that remains are the rigors of the marketplace, which makes its judgments according to a quantitative standard that's unquestionably real. If we are to join Socrates in arguing that there's more to life than wealth and power and personal preferences, we have to reinvigorate liberal education by freeing it from the shackles of democratic excesses.

Libertarian legal scholar Glenn Reynolds (basically an oligarch when it comes to education), an astute educational reformer, begins with the proposition that the various politically correct hijinks of professors and especially our increasingly bloated class of administrators has made higher education much more costly and much more obviously ridiculous. So the excellent libertarian economist, George Leef, actually welcomes the most recent student uprisings on behalf of diversity as facilitating educational reforms already underway reconfiguring all of higher education in terms of techno-competence. The more aristocratic judgment of the genuinely innovative literary critic Alexander Zubatov, however, is more pointed.

> [W]hen we in the West stopped genuflecting at the altar of our greatest cultural achievements and started acting sheepish about them, while canonizing, in their place, all kinds of second-rate productions because they ostensibly better represented the viewpoints and experiences of non-Western countries and sundry protected categories, we turned

ourselves into an international laughingstock and lost the confidence of much of the educated public outside the anointed ranks of the literati.

Making the humanities too much about conforming to some democratic view of justice made them irrelevant as a countercultural force that can mitigate the effects of moral and intellectual relativism and challenge the economist's idea that the only solid principle of merit is productivity.

The very idea of *higher* education, of course, is undemocratic, and so its future depends on Americans drawing upon countercultural resources that are, in some way or another, aristocratic inheritances. Tocqueville observed that the most precious inheritance any democracy has is its religion. Tocqueville was astonished, maybe most of all, by how religious the Americans were. He was far from thinking that American religion expressed the whole truth about who each of us is. He simply observed that religion is strong—by curbing our self-obsessive materialism—where democracy, by itself, is weak. And he tells us, from an explicitly Socratic view, that we should regard religion, by directing us to the contemplation of the high and immaterial destiny of each particular human soul, as our most precious inheritance from aristocratic ages, one indispensable for producing great theoretical, artistic, and practical accomplishments that stand the test of time.

Many American colleges and universities are distinguished by their religious missions. There are, of course, limits to intellectual freedom at these schools, too, but the limitations are different from those found at our allegedly cutting-edge elite institutions. The question of God, for example, is still alive in many of those religious schools with a kind of passionate intensity that's absent elsewhere. And there's often the conviction that the best books—and not only the Bible—open us to the truth, and so it's easier today to read the *Republic* with the truth in mind at the Southern Baptist Union University in Tennessee or the Mormon Brigham Young University than it is at Swarthmore or Oberlin.

Our country is even graced by colleges that are private and neither confessional nor politically correct. They, like Berry College in rural Georgia, where I teach, may have the most academic freedom of all. At

Berry, most, though far from all, of the students are religiously observant, as are some, but probably not most of the faculty. Here, it's possible
to have a freewheeling discussion with both sides well defended on
same-sex marriage and the future of marriage in general, abortion, and,
more generally, on whether angry fundamentalism or slacker secularism
is the greater threat to intellectual liberty in our time. The same is true
on whether Nietzsche was right that "God is dead," and whether our current untenable, self-indulgent morality is comprised of Christian values
detached from foundation in Christian belief.

As long as I teach responsibly—or by privileging the opinions of the
author in question over my own—I find that there's no possibility that
academic freedom will be trumped by academic justice, and that students
are almost too ready to challenge sophisticated opinion and pop scientism with enduring truths, and just as ready to challenge "fundamentalist" opinion with what we can really know through science. When Walker
Percy tells them, in effect, "Evolution happened, get over it," they get on
board. But students are also mostly ready to get on board with Percy's
doubts that "the theory of evolution" can explain everything about who
we are as beings "lost in the cosmos." Surely one purpose of a genuinely
humanistic institution is to assess attentively the theory of evolution, dis-
tinguishing between genuine science and ideological scientism.

It would be easy to go on, but let me leave you with some takeaways.
Democratic education is liberal education insofar as it promotes an openness to the diversity of viewpoints. But it is illiberal insofar as it choses
diversity over truth, virtue and beauty, and insofar as it denies the various
forms of necessity that shape every human life. The point of an educational conversation is to move from the partial truths embodied in various
opinions toward the shared joy of figuring out the whole truth and nothing but the truth. That movement, as we see in the *Republic*, is necessarily rife with various forms of microaggression, but it's the only route to
the true liberalism of coming to terms to who each of us is as a free being
born to know, love, and die.

Chapter 6
Higher Education and the Morality of Capitalism in Our Time

Education is always somewhat determined by the practical requirements of the way of life of a particular people. Our forms of education are largely for a middle-class society full of free people who work. And so it's inevitable and beneficial that education in our country is largely guided by the morality of what's called liberal and democratic capitalism. But surely countries can be praised for also aiming higher or sustaining forms of education that look beyond the reigning practical imperatives in the direction of the relatively timeless truths about who each of us is and what we're supposed to do. My purpose here is to begin by looking at the state of our middle-class morality today, defined as it is both by the twenty-first century's globally competitive marketplace and a kind of libertarian securitarianism, and then to view critically the fading place of higher education in our world.

Let me begin with the take-away exaggeration that the morality of capitalism has won. All of American life is being transformed by the imperatives of the twenty-first century's global marketplace. Our two parties are converging in a kind of libertarian direction. The Koch brothers, we read, are "moderating" the Republican Party by purging it of its concern with social issues that are really reactionary prejudices. Silicon Valley is "moderating" the progressivism of the Democratic Party by purging it of policies that stifle growth and innovation by stripping members of our meritocracy based on productivity of their honestly earned property and money. The results of the withering away of the impediments to globalization are astonishing. More people than ever have access to the world, past and present, through what they can call up on their various screens. The average lifespan continues to get longer, and the realm of personal freedom or autonomy, as our Supreme Court explains, continues to grow. More than ever, America is defined by a meritocracy based on productivity. Race, class, gender, sexual orientation, even the imperatives of biology (such as birth and death), and so forth mean less than ever in constraining the opportunities for free and industrious individuals.

Forces opposed to the reign of that meritocracy, such as unions, are in retreat. Unions depended on American industries' relative lack of competition from the rest of the world. Given the intensification of that competition, unions have become excessively counterproductive and unable to deliver the goods to their members. Other safety nets that ordinary people have come to depend on to cushion the influence of the rigors of the market on our lives are also atrophying. These include pensions, all kinds of tenure, government entitlements, employer and employee loyalty in general, relatively independent local communities, family and churches. More and more, the American worker is becoming an independent contractor selling his or her flexible skills and competencies to whomever can use them at the moment. We have here, all factors considered, a multifaceted new birth of freedom, an expanded menu of individual choice, and a reduction in some ways of personal security and relational flourishing (the latter especially for ordinary Americans).

But we're spending more money on government entitlements than ever, you say! Sure. And everyone with eyes to see knows that the present entitlement situation is unsustainable. Medicare and so forth are going to have to be trimmed and reconfigured to have much of a future, and most young people don't, with good reason, expect to see a dime of Social Security. There are, of course, many reasons for the unsustainability of our at least conceptually minimalist welfare state. It must be emphasized that the main one is not some culture of dependency; it's the change in our demographic situation since the early Sixties that can be attributed to our creeping individualism. Due to the progress of medical technology and individuals' more rigorous attention to risk factors, people are living longer than ever, much longer under the protection of Social Security and Medicare. And they are having fewer babies. We're thinking of ourselves less as relational animals hardwired to generate biological replacements and more as free individuals who work and do not need to be replaced (or less as creatures told to be fruitful and multiply and more as beings who give each of us infinite personal worth). We have too many old and unproductive people and too few young and productive ones to keep the Ponzi scheme that's been our entitlement regime in motion. So one reason among many why "capitalism has won" is that we now know, contrary to the prediction of Tocqueville, our individualism actually seems to ensure our "road to serfdom" never gets to serfdom.

One paradox about our unprecedented situation is that Americans are becoming more and less middle class. When Alexis de Tocqueville (in *Democracy in America*) said that ours is a middle-class democracy, he meant that almost all Americans (outside the slave states) thought of themselves as and were free beings who work. To be middle class is to be free like an aristocrat to work like a slave. Well, not exactly like a slave. The American works for himself and his family and believes that everyone has the right and duty to do the same. What the aristocrat calls leisure, he calls laziness. A free middle-class country will inevitably have vast disparities of wealth, but a kind of rough equality of hope; a hope supported by the perception of some connection between talent, effort, and success and by the fact that wealth circulates rapidly and fortunes are made and lost so readily and rapidly.

America, Tocqueville noticed, was also characterized by a rough similarity of habits and opinions, and Tocqueville offended us most when he observed that there's little real diversity of thought in America. Nobody (outside the literary South) talks up the advantages of an aristocratic leisure class for culture; everyone has a technological (as opposed to a "purely theoretical") understanding of what science is and everyone appreciates the utility of the family and religion. Most people apply the spirit of industry even to literature, vacations, and "free time" generally. Most people speak way too complacently about the way self-interest can explain and justify social duties.

The worry is getting more common that inequality is increasing and mobility decreasing. Probably more than ever, the gap in wealth mirrors a gap in productivity between, as the deeply astute libertarian futurist Tyler Cowen (in *Average Is Over*) has shown, a cognitive elite of maybe 15% that owes its wealth to being skilled and industrious in either working with "genius machines" or in marketing the products of or managing the work of those who do, and the rest of the population that's, in fact, becoming less productive and so less prosperous. Cowen proclaims that "average is over," meaning that the middle class, in the sense of the middle management who produce and earn something in between the highly productive and the marginally productive, is withering away.

The division of labor is increasingly pronounced between those who do "mental labor" and those who relatively mindlessly work off scripts devised by top management and marketing, often located in some centralized and even undisclosed location. The perfection of the division of labor plus technological development (robotization and the screen, for examples) are making many jobs in "the middle" obsolete and people who work below that middle less productive.

Consider that perhaps the most stunningly efficient workplace in America right now is the Amazon warehouse; it was somewhat less efficient, not so long ago, when it employed nearly 200 employees. Productivity and reliability soared as the astute use of robots cut the actual number of persons to under 20. Even the nicer, more homey chain restaurants such as Panera Bread are replacing cashiers with kiosks, and the geniuses in their home office in St. Louis anticipate that the more impersonal service will be quicker and more nearly error-free.

"Average is over" means, for Cowen, that many or most of those Americans who could formerly think of themselves as middle-class will become "marginally productive" at best. And maverick conservatives, such as Joel Kotkin, in a similar spirit, write about the "proletarianization" of the middle class. Others still have noticed that some of the features of the "idiocracy" displayed in the funny dystopian movie of that name are already with us.

Social critics such as Charles Murray (in *Coming Apart*) describe the American "cognitive elite" as smarter and more sensible than ever, with excellent work habits, surprisingly stable family lives, and a due attention to what the studies show about health and safety. Our sophisticates may talk the 1960s talk about "Do your own thing," but few people actually *live* that bohemian way or free from the prudent calculation about probabilities that makes one's being and the being of one's own more secure. The high level of un-bohemian or un-romantic economic and familial responsibility is impressive; time and energy are lavished on both work and kids. Sure, our productive meritocrats typically only have a kid or two. But, for women especially, the scarcity of time is still more of a problem than it was for many more child-laden middle-class families of the past. Young, successful women now typically earn as much or more as their husbands, and equal investment of both spouses in the lives of the kids remains more an ideal than a reality. We learn from Murray that our elite, our meritocracy based mostly on cognitive productivity, is just smarter than the elites of the past. But it remains decisively middle class, and certainly less of a leisure class than the more WASPy elites with some of the manners of aristocrats of our even recent past. It is also middle class in the sense of having little of the aristocratic conviction that privileges that flow from wealth generate responsibilities to care for those less gifted or fortunate than oneself.

It might even be the common case that the ties that have bound rich and poor together, from sharing a common Creator to common citizenship, are weaker than ever. Tocqueville feared that America might end up with a kind of industrial aristocracy that was more intellectually and emotionally detached from common people than the aristocrats of old, and that detachment would be based on the progress of division of labor. This unfashionable, for conservatives and libertarians, fear seems more warranted than ever. It must be emphasized that this detachment is based upon real differences: Rich people are now smarter and thinner, while relatively poor people are fatter and dumber than ever. One class is full of people who have what it takes to flourish as productive participants in the twenty-first century's global marketplace, the other doesn't. And this meritocracy is actually becoming hereditary, more than any time in our history; "the best" are mating with the best primarily because they don't have much contact with anyone outside their gated communities in the super-rich zip codes and their exclusive public or private schools.

Murray describes the deterioration of the work ethic among the bottom 50%. Others focus more on increasingly pathological families, the collapse of neighborhoods, the disappearance of the common life that was the parish or other form of religious congregation, and the failures of schools to produce graduates with the basic literacy that is required of almost everyone who works for himself. There is, I think, a tendency for libertarian conservatives such as Murray to overrate the culture of dependency generated by the welfare state as the cause of the deterioration of middle-class habits and values. Someone might immediately add the sharp drop in the number of unionized industrial jobs. Those jobs were often full of repetitive drudgery but ennobled by the fact that their wages and benefits (not to mention their security) made it possible for a man to earn enough to raise a middle-class family. Too many think, not without reason, that the jobs available to them won't make it possible to have that kind of relational dignity. So they punt on working, and so punt on being responsible husbands and dads. The real problem, of course, is that they lack the skills and competencies required to be productive enough in an economy such as ours, and the jobs available to them pay less, because of the rigors of the market, than they used to pay.

Some pillars of middle-class justice are in question. One, of course, is the "trickle down" theory that probably originates in John Locke. Under a free economy protected by a liberal government, the productive capabilities of the industrious and rational among us will be unleashed, and they will get what they deserve: huge amounts of money. But everyone else, as a general result of the rapidly increasing amounts of wealth and power, will be better off too. Libertarians still defend that proposition today, with the new emphasis on the democratic effects of the diffusion of technology, such as the screen and health care. They also say that many studies exaggerate the extent to which economic inequality is growing and the stagnation or worse of economic progress for many Americans. Those studies miss the "after tax" redistribution of income that occurs through government programs. That criticism is correct, but it's not particularly reassuring. For one thing, it only distracts us from the real problems, which have to do with declining productivity and so declining real wages of so many Americans. And there's the related problem that real productivity can increase while most workers are worth less.

Americans are more middle class insofar as they lack a shared elevated standard, such as the ones that have come from religion and tradition which trumps the middle-class definition of us all as free beings who work. But they are less middle class descriptively. There is quite the "leisure gap" that separates our cognitive elite from the bottom half of our population. The former work harder than ever; they are, in fact, workaholics with (when you add caring for kids) very little leisure time.

Not only that, they stressfully perceive themselves as working harder or having less "free time" than they really do. Meanwhile, many ordinary people (mostly men), increasingly detached from meaningful work and responsible family life, have more free time than ever, too much of which they fill with activities that don't deserve to be called leisure or even recreation. For them, the screen is mostly a diversion filled with sports, games, and sadly, porn.

The hollowing out of the middle class—and the atrophying of the experience of common citizenship— described here are at the foundation of the insurgent Trump and Sanders campaigns. My best guess is that neither will have an enduring effect on the evolution I've described here. The result, after all, will be President Hillary Clinton, the favorite candidate of Wall Street and Silicon Valley.

It's probably more true than ever, in any case, that we lack the cultivated leisure class that values "the best that has been thought and said" (as well as painted and sung) for its own sake and has endless amounts of time to attend to the nuances of excellence. And someone might say, although none of our prominent political leaders, that our biggest social issue is cultivating those with the leisure, earned or given, made possible by high technology to aid as many Americans as possible in rising far above merely middle-class life. As most experts understand it, however, our biggest social problem is how to get more and more Americans the skills, competencies, and habits required to flourish, or at least make it, in the twenty-first century's competitive marketplace. The problem, maybe somewhat overstated, is that too many don't even have what's required to be proletarian cogs in a machine, to be reliably, if marginally, productive. And so all the educational experts say that we have to work harder to transform all of education around the requirements of the competitive marketplace; even our colleges have to become much more intentional in making graduates competent.

Being Libertarian and Securitarian

The conclusion that the road to serfdom never gets to serfdom can be contradicted by our increasing obsession with personal security, beginning with health and safety, which is producing progressively more intrusive government regulations. That self-obsession, however, is primarily characteristic of members of our cognitive elite. It shouldn't be confused, of course, with the revolutionary envy of the many, and the regulations it generates don't aim at economic redistribution. It's really the opposite of a class-based form of animation. Sophisticated Americans feel their personal contingency more than ever, and they spend more time than ever fending off personal extinction. They are often "libertarian" on all matters of personal morality, and even the free market, but they are puritanically moralistic and highly regulatory on the health-and-safety front. The same campuses that allow students to do what they please when it comes to sex (as long as it's safe and consensual, of course) are banning smoking everywhere.

So the claim that this is a libertarian moment, of course, depends on what libertarian means. The unjustly neglected political philosopher Bertrand de Jouvenal (in *On Power*) distinguished between being "libertarian" and being "securitarian." Many of today's young people want to be both. They want to practice safe libertarianism in the unfettered enjoyment of the pleasure of sex. Contraception—now an entitlement guaranteed by an intrusive government mandate—is about detaching sex from the hard realities of birth and death. Better than safe sex, from that view, is the virtual sex available on the screen, which, if the film *Her* is correct, will soon be personalized through a relationship between a biological man and an Operating System that sounds like Scarlett Johanssen. Imagining the body, of course, is safer than actually touching it, as no living body can be made compliant enough to one's own personal preferences to be completely comfortable.

The techno-goal is to subordinate erotic longing to rational control, to keep it from being risky business or being the source of dangerous liaisons. So sex, from this view, in the name of "relational autonomy" is being freed up for individual enjoyment from repressive cultural or relational restraints. From another, it is driven more by securitarian concerns than ever. Libertarians, especially among the young, aren't so good at seeing the connection between the liberationist "hook-up" culture not only tolerated but affirmed by our colleges and the somewhat justified securitarian concerns about "the culture of rape" that allegedly flourishes on our campuses. That connection is, nonetheless, really there. Our campuses are both more libertarian and more securitarian than ever. Students and consumer-sensitive administrators demand a campus that's one big "safe space" where students feel perfectly comfortable doing what they please, without fear of violence or even being criticized, as they define who they are as autonomous beings.

Now there are some libertarians that are about mocking every effort by government to protect individuals from the risks embedded in the "spontaneous order" that is social life. Those libertarians, some of whom are found in the Tea Party, are about deploying libertarian means (or freedom from government) for the more natural relationships that make life worth living. They believe we're social and relational beings—and not free individuals—by nature; they're, in that respect, more Burkean, Hayekian or Christian than Lockean or Randian.

One example of the deployment of libertarian means for non-libertarian ends is the effort to struggle against government and corporate bureaucratic efforts to standardize American education through methodical expertise. Most opponents of the Gates/Obama Common Core, accreditation, and certification want to preserve the genuinely higher or not merely technical or "politically correct" parts of American education. They include, of course, our wide variety of (mostly religious) private primary and secondary schools, home schooling, and, of course, the freedom of our religious colleges and institutions to define their own missions and ways of achieving them. Government and agencies enabled by government, from this view, are in the name of "diversity" understood as a corporate/government project, aiming to detach people from the personally binding authority of social institutions such as the church. The pursuit of "diversity" intentionally undermines the genuine moral and religious diversity that has flourished uninhibited in our free country. That's why, say the libertarians for non-libertarian ends, we have to clamp down on all programs (such as federally subsidized loans) that allow the federal government to determine the agenda of higher education, and that's why, for the good of our churches, we have to get government and the employers (such as the institutional churches) they can mandate out of the insurance business.

But from the point of view of many libertarian economists, "libertarian means for non-libertarian ends" is an incoherent view about the truth about who each of us is. Cowen, for example, celebrates a world in which free and prosperous individuals can enjoy the productions of living cultures without themselves being saddled by the repressive baggage of said cultures. It is true that Cowen has said it would be better if ordinary American workers, especially men, became Mormons, to benefit as reliably productive workers from the intrusive personal discipline that church imposes on its members. He's not saying, of course, that government should do anything to facilitate the flourishing of that church, but perhaps he wouldn't be against private employers having some such initiative. But Cowen also chastised the Christian, libertarian economist Congressman David Brat for referring to the distinguished economist Deirdre (formerly Donald) McCloskey as him/her. For Cowen, a people who think and live like free individuals accept the transgendered without reservation or irony. Let's say the Mormons are pretty weak on that front.

So it might be easy to conclude that it's Cowen who's caught in the contradiction! He sees that most people need the discipline of personal, relational authority to live well, but he sees no truthful foundation for thinking of oneself as other than a free individual. Another way of expressing the contradiction is that Cowen really thinks that the members of our productive meritocracy don't need to be Mormons; they discipline themselves by thinking and acting rigorously according to what they really know about themselves as productive and consuming beings. He's for Mormonism only for the undisciplined, unintelligent, and unenlightened many. There's no reason at all, from this view, that Mitt Romney should be a Mormon.

Another contradiction worth noticing is that so many "whole-hog" libertarians seem much more securitarian than, say, those brainy Mormons who want to use libertarian means on behalf of the non-libertarian ends of their highly relational and rather patriarchal church. Consider, for example, that even the libertarian technophilia of Cowen, Brink Lindsey (in *Human Capitalism*), Donald Boudreaux and many others emphasize that unfettered technological progress benefits everyone, and those democratic benefits aren't properly appreciated when liberals or old-fashioned progressives whine about bourgeoning economic inequality. Medical technology, for example, has greatly extended the average lifespan, at least for those prudent enough to live according to what we now know about the various risk factors that imperil one's very being. And that way of thinking, of course, points in the direction of the emerging techno-project of using our creative freedom to transform not only nature but human nature in the service of indefinitely long or even quasi-immortal lives of particular individuals. Many libertarians, such as the brilliant Peter Thiel, easily morph into being kind of evangelical transhumanists, who find hope in the prospect of the Singularity, of the time soon to come when the free or conscious individual can be located in a much more secure machine than the ephemeral, biological body. The progress of technology serves freedom or the ever-expanding menu of choice, and that includes the security of being pro-choice on death.

Higher Education Today

Let's turn the focus to what this emerging victory of libertarian-securitarian brand of capitalism means for higher education. It's always been the case that higher education has been about preparing people for what the branders now call "lifelong learning." From the traditional perspective we're given by Aristotle's *Nicomachean Ethics*, work is for leisure, and leisure is for contemplation, for thinking about who you are and what you're supposed to do. So a lifelong learner takes pleasure in cultivating his soul or educating his mind by reading the best books that are written for that purpose, including philosophy, theology, novels, poetry, plays, and so forth. And that pleasure can be about moving from reading to listening and looking, to music, art, film, and so forth. From this view, making money is easy, but knowing what to do with it is hard, because the latter depends on the cultivation that allows a person to take pleasure in what is intrinsically worthy for rational and virtuous beings such as ourselves.

Contemplation here doesn't mean theoretical physics or metaphysics, which are, as it were, purely mental activities and so not for men and women of action. It means more like reflecting on the practice of the virtues that make life worth living. The Southerners who are self-consciously Stoic (like George Washington or the fictional Atticus Finch) were Aristotelian in their focus on the virtues of generosity and magnanimity as being characteristics of any rational person. So liberal education is about being able to rule yourself and others, as those whom President Obama praised as "the proud men of Morehouse" do when they fearlessly return to their local communities with the intention of assuming positions of prominence. Lifelong learning is intertwined with a life of taking responsibility for what you can't help but know about yourself and others in the place where you live. That means, of course, that worthwhile work is *for* love and virtue, and not the other way around.

Today, however, lifelong learning seems to mean mainly having the flexibility to pick up new skills and competencies in response to techno-development and the changing needs of employers. So one reason among many that employer-based health care doesn't make any sense to anyone is that it artificially limits the worker's option to move on, and, more important, the employer's option to push him or her out the door. And it also, of course, keeps the employer from feeling guilty when he downsizes those who have become marginally productive. In an increasingly disruptive and innovative global marketplace, those without that flexibility that comes from being comfortable working with machines and thinking abstractly (or unparticularly or impersonally) just haven't been prepared for today's world of work. In the meritocracy increasingly based on cognitive productivity, being unable to abstract yourself from yourself and your attachments to take on new roles and contexts guarantees that you'll be left behind. There's much good, of course, in being an independent contractor or out there on your own, but it's at the price of being displaced. The "how" of generating power, more than ever, works against the "why" provided by the secure relational context in which most people find personal significance. The new understanding of lifelong learning presupposes being stuck with being displaced.

This capitalist morality—this morality of productive displacement— can, Tocqueville reminds us, also be called middle-class morality. All human beings, from one view, are middle class, stuck between the other animals and God. We're beasts with angels in us, and it's the angel who teaches the beast how to satisfy his desires. But not only that, it's the angel that causes our desires to bloat and become more complicated and so harder to satisfy. So it's that being stuck in the middle who becomes increasingly defined by technology and remains restlessly dissatisfied, even in the midst of unprecedented prosperity.

Middle-class Americans are very judgmental about work. Aristocracies were poor by comparison because nobody cared or could seem to care much about money; aristocrats had to at least pretend to be above it, and the servants or slaves had no hope for it. Aristocracies were poor and unjust in comparison to us, Americans know, because nobody really worked and the people who had the wealth and power didn't really earn them. Nobody has a right not to work. What aristocrats called leisure, middle-class Americans call laziness. We can pity the poor only if they are "working poor." That means middle-class education has to be for everyone, and it is education for freedom.

But that education for freedom isn't higher education, and it isn't the kind of intellectual and spiritual liberation we associate with liberal education. So Tocqueville claimed to find almost no higher education in America, and little genuine concern for the leisurely cultivation of the soul. Aristocratic education, which includes metaphysics, theology, literature, and theoretical physics, is the proud and seemingly sterile cultivation of the mind or soul. Democratic education, which is pretty much exclusively practical or technological, is oriented around the security and pleasures of bodies. The democratic claim might seem vulgarly materialistic, but it's also based on the truthful insight that nobody is too good to work. The truth is that all human beings have interests or rights, and real freedom; real self-knowledge comes from acknowledging that egalitarian fact. Liberal education, from this view, is based on the illusion that some of us are more, and some of us are less, than all of us really are.

Still, as Tocqueville observes, middle-class education produces merely middle-class "brains." It prevents us from being all that we might be. Democracy is capable of turning even art and literature into industries, and of transforming language in such an insistently technical direction that the words that correspond to what's true about metaphysics and theology simply disappear. Tocqueville's biggest objection to middle-class America might be that there's no class of the people with the leisure to take the education of the soul seriously, no class with the high opinion that the purpose of the human being is to know the truth for its own sake. His objection, from another view, is that Americans don't have a high enough opinion of themselves as beings with singular destinies that take us far beyond the confines of their interested concerns of the material world.

This democratic skepticism reduces all real education to acquiring the techno-vocational competencies required to obtain money and power. That skepticism, Tocqueville claims, aims to obliterate all real intellectual diversity in our country. There is an unprecedented diversity of interests, and that's the diversity that the celebrated *Federalist 10* deployed to protect minorities in our country from being tyrannized over by an overbearing majority. But that diversity is grounded in a deeper uniformity that understands everyone pretty much as beings with interests and rights and nothing more. As we see more than ever today, diversity in one sense is at war with diversity in the moral, intellectual, and religious sense. Tocqueville saw remnants of alternative ways of life in America, but he predicted their extinction in the face of middle-class universality.

Tocqueville's Exaggeration as Today's Emerging Truth

Tocqueville's claim that there was almost no higher education in America was clearly an exaggeration. It's also one that clearly seems out-of-date. We have a huge and diverse array of colleges and universities, and they all think of themselves as providing higher education (see *The Chronicle of Higher Education*). But by higher education Tocqueville really did mean theoretical science and the leisurely, meticulous reading of the "great books" in their original languages, with the same sort of attention to high-minded enjoyment of art and music. How much of that is going on in our colleges and universities? Well, some, and maybe even more than Tocqueville seemed to suggest, but less and less with every passing day. The takeaway point to be made to students is that if it's about textbooks, PowerPoint, collaborative teamwork, civic engagement (as beneficial as that can be), service learning, and all that, it's not higher education.

Fewer and fewer of our colleges market themselves as offering liberal education. And others that stick with the "liberal arts" brand (because it's classy) are emptying themselves of liberal arts substance. "General education" or the core curriculum at most colleges is becoming smaller and more optional. The main way traditional courses in the humanities are justified is in their ability to aid in the acquiring of skills and competencies required to flourish in the competitive marketplace. It goes without saying that taking courses in history, literature, and philosophy aren't obviously the only or even the most efficient ways of acquiring those skills. Liberal education as an end in itself has become an optional luxury these days, and one that doesn't add the value required to justify the high cost of college. But critical thinking and analytical reasoning do, because of their obvious benefits in a high-tech world dominated by a cognitive elite that prides itself not on its wisdom, but on its productivity. Our elite, despite its unprecedented wealth, remains middle-class in its conviction that free beings are all about work.

In the crucial respects, higher education is becoming more vocational or careerist, and the most penetrating and effective criticisms of our colleges and universities tend to be from a libertarian or middle-class point of view. College, the critics say, has become ridiculously expensive and irrelevant. It has become a "bubble" in two senses. Like in the case of the housing bubble, costs are expanding rapidly while quality is getting shoddier. The big scandal, of course, is that the government facilitates easy-credit borrowing that allows the consumer to borrow big without considering long-term consequences.

College is also a "bubble" insofar as it insulates students from the increasingly tough imperatives of the marketplace. It is an artificial environment not unlike that inhabited by the "bubble boy" on the legendary *Seinfeld* episode, one that can't be justified as fit for people who can and must eventually survive in the real world. One result of college costing so much is that students are treated like consumers—or not even future producers. And so campus life is all about privileges without corresponding responsibilities.

The combination of bubbles means, of course, that students are paying a lot for degrees that won't pay off. Lots of students leave colleges with both big debt and no prospects of becoming prosperous enough to easily make the monthly payments. Our colleges are charging students ridiculous rates not to prepare them effectively to be free beings who work. It's just a matter of time until, just like the housing bubble did, these bubbles burst.

It's amazing how much the critics of our higher education agree and how pervasive their influence is. Consider this: the election between Obama and Romney could be understood to have been between two kinds of American corporate capitalist oligarchs. Obama had the support of Silicon Valley, while Romney had the support of more old-school corporate giants such as the Koch brothers and the DeVos family that runs Amway. Two forms of big money and big data had a showdown, and one of course proved itself more savvy or more in touch. But both sides of this struggle agree that what's wrong with American education is the bubbles, and the bubbles have to be burst in a techno-vocational, more efficient and productive direction. Also agreeing are various foundations, the consultants and experts that surround the Harvard Business School, accrediting associations, and academic and government bureaucrats, such as those following the powerfully intrusive lead of Bill Gates, who came up with the incredibly mediocre or relentlessly middle-class national Common Core. The cutting-edge thinkers in this mode are mostly libertarian economists and various state public policy institutes, which are often facilitated by Republican governors, but, when it comes to the future of higher education, they don't think any differently than their Silicon Valley counterparts such as Gates.

These critics believe they're outing higher education in America as the shameful project of decadent aristocrats called professors. Their lives are full of privileges without the corresponding responsibilities. The truth is that the privileges have become indefensible. Tocqueville, in his classic account of the causes of the French Revolution—*The Old Regime and the Revolution*—explains that the eighteenth-century French aristocrats retained privileges that only made sense when aristocrats wielded actual political power, and these privileged men came to use their leisure to engage in an irresponsible "literary politics" or to talk up revolutionary theories without any real thought concerning their likely real practical consequences. They set the stage for the radical disruption that was the revolution. Our professors, their critics say, are "tenured radicals" who preach their theories without having to be concerned with the consequences of the self-indulgent teaching on their students' real futures. The result will be revolution, but not the kind they desire. Today's disruptive educational transformation will consign them and their "humanities" to the place in the trash can of educational history they richly deserve.

Disruptive Innovation vs. Higher Education

When the critics, beginning with Clayton Christensen, write of disrupting higher education, they mean to apply to higher education a process that transforms various techno-industrial sectors in the competitive marketplace of the twenty-first century's capitalism. When a product—say, a tablet—is developed, it is initially quite expensive, and its developers focus on making their machine better, assuming that the consumer is as concerned with quality as with price. Then a competitor ingeniously devises a "knock off" that performs the essential operations at a "good-enough" level and prices the designer version of the product out of the market. It's the tendency of capitalism to drive prices down by responding to the consumers' views of what their real needs are. Colleges, just like any other industry, will survive insofar as they disrupt themselves to drive costs down, disposing ruthlessly or at least with eyes wide open of the irrelevant bells and whistles that bubbled tuitions up for reasons irrelevant to the real demands of the market. It's the good-enough colleges that have a real future, the colleges that give students exactly what they really need and want at the lowest possible price.

Some conservatives say that the main cost-control issue in American higher education today is tenured faculty who don't teach enough. It would be better if their lazy self-indulgence could be better controlled by more accountable administrators. Tenure, from this view, is a kind of union, and "faculty governance" is collective bargaining. It would be better if administrators could be empowered by the "right-to-fire" situation found in our more entrepreneurial states. What the union-taming governor wants, he doesn't understand, the administrators have already been achieving. In the industrial world, the war against unions is suddenly becoming more aggressive and more effective because unions can't deliver the goods anyway given the dynamic realities of the twenty-first century's globally competitive marketplace. The same is true of the war against tenure. Tenure is withering away, and astute administrators know better than to launch a frontal assault that would result in really bad public relations and many unnecessary casualties.

The truth is that the number of tenured faculty is rapidly diminishing as a percentage—the tenured and those on a "tenure track" now are a still fairly unoppressed and, I admit, often fairly clueless minority—of the "instructional workforce." There are doubtless good reasons why, at some places, tenured and tenure-track faculty should teach more. It would be better if more students had their "personal touch," just as it would be better if they graded their students' papers themselves at research institutions. But, given how cheap adjuncts are, it's a big mistake to believe that tenured professors taking on an additional class or two would be a significant savings. It's often even the case that administrators would rather they not teach more.

At some places at least, the situation seems to be that the administrations are buying off tenured faculty with low teaching loads and various research perks. That incentivizes them to be compliant with the transfer of instruction to adjuncts and other temporary faculty. It also allows them to accept the emptying out of the content of "general education" as requirements focused on the content and methods of the academic disciplines—such as history, literature and philosophy—are replaced by those based on abstract and empty (or content-free) competencies.

Tenured and tenure-track faculty often come from highly specialized research programs where, even in history and literature, the tendency is to know more and more about less and less. There are also allegedly cutting-edge approaches, such as neuroscience, "digital humanities," rational-choice theory, and so forth, that take the researcher away from being attentive to the content that's been the core of undergraduate instruction. And then there's the pretension of "undergraduate research" (which originated in and makes a lot more sense in the hard sciences) that it's best for students to bypass the bookish acquisition of content about the perennial fundamental human issues and questions and get right down to making some cutting-edge marginal contribution.

All in all, it's often not so hard to convince specialists to surrender concern for merely general education. Or at least to convince them that the imperatives of the marketplace and the increasingly intrusive accreditation process demand that the value of their disciplinary contributions be reconfigured in terms of competencies. That way, they're led to believe, they'll be able to hang on to their curricular "turf." The study of history (or philosophy or whatever) can be justified, after all, as deploying the skills of critical thinking, effective communication, and so forth. One problem, of course, is that those skills can be acquired more easily other ways, ways that aren't saddled with all that historical or philosophical content.

And when the disciplines of liberal education are displaced by competencies, institutions tend to surrender the content-based distinctiveness that formed most of their educational mission. The biggest outrage in higher education right now, for example, is not this or that report of students or administrators whining about microaggressions or being insufficiently trigger-warned. It's that Notre Dame might be about to surrender its requirement of courses in philosophy and theology for all students for competency-based goals. What distinguishes or ought to distinguish Notre Dame is the seriousness by which it treats philosophy and theology as disciplines indispensable for all highly literate Catholic men and women, or not primarily by its provision of a Catholic lifestyle.

As institutions surrender their liberal arts substance (while sometimes retaining their classy liberal arts brand), they become pretty much identical in terms of their educational goals. Lists of competencies always seem to me vague and rather random, but they still seem to turn out about the same everywhere. Their measurability usually depends on multiple-choice questions and the sham exactitude of points distributed on rubrics. And in general the data gets its veneer of objectivity through the intention to aim at sometimes stunningly low and only seemingly solid goals. It's easy to mock the earnest redundancy of the competency phrases themselves. "Critical thinking"—well, if it wasn't critical, it wouldn't be thinking. "Effective communication"—well, if it wasn't effective, it wouldn't be communication.

In any case, the thought being surrendered is that the dignity of thinking and communicating must have something to do with what is being thought or communicated. It's just not true that the same methods of thought and communication can be applied in all circumstances. Thinking about what or who is a man or woman is way different from figuring out how to rotate your tires or even maximize your productivity.

Communicating information is different from "winning friends and in-fluencing people" (or persuasion and manipulation) and from commu-nicating the truth through irony or humor or esoteric indirection—through the parables of the Bible or the dialogues of Plato. The forms of communication that distinguish the great or even good books that pro-vide most of the content of liberal education elude measurable outcomes, and it's not immediately obvious that they have much value in the mar-ketplace. Actually, the kind of insight they provide can be invaluable in marketing, as anyone who's watched an episode of *Mad Men* or read one of those eerie, philosophical, uncannily effective pitches of Don Draper knows. But the administrators would reply, "Well, sure that Don's a ge-nius, but he's so damn unreliable. We don't want professors like that!"

As the low but seemingly solid goal of competency becomes about the same everywhere, the delivery of education can become less personal or quirky and standardized according to quantitatively validated best practices. Courses can become more scripted, and then delivery can be increasingly open to the use of the screen. So the "intellectual labor" of college administrators—the number of which is "bloating" and the perks of which (at the highest level) are coming to resemble those of corporate CEOs—is directed in much the same way as it is in other sectors of the economy. What's going on, for example, in the Amazon warehouse or in large chains such as Panera Bread, is occurring on our campuses. The idea of "competency" being enforced by the accrediting agencies—ba-sically run by administrators and following a "class-based" administra-tive agenda—serves the goal of disciplining instruction through measurable outcomes and then displacing actual instructors, as much as possible, by education delivered on the screen.

As colleges become more identical in their competency-based cur-riculum, the question that obsesses a college president is how to make his or her institution distinctively attractive in the intensely competitive mar-ketplace for the increasingly scarce resource of the student. There's the in-creased sensitivity to the student as consumer. One result is the amenities arms race. Typically, these innovations are the product of administrative initiatives in which "shared governance" does not come into play.

The excellent libertarian scholar Glenn Reynolds is so disgusted by such developments that his modest proposal is for campuses to be honest and market themselves as luxury cruises. That means spend, and spend more, on the amenities and cut, and cut more, the cost of actual education by reducing the ranks of career faculty and replacing them with various forms of online instruction and MOOCs (Massive Open Online Courses). No college or university, so far, is going quite that far. But many are pretty far down that road. And even the small colleges that talk up the presence of real faculty have begun to describe these as worthy agents and advocates for students—in a way, just another amenity offered to the discerning consumer.

Add to the amenities arms race all the increasingly intrusive and usually stupidly counterproductive compliance requirements of the federal government and accreditation agencies and politically correct administrative initiatives having nothing to do with education, and it's easy to see where most of the so-called bubble in college tuition really comes from. It's not faculty compensation or the cost of instruction in general that are going up much more quickly than the rate of inflation.

Well, you might say, putting the focus on competencies must at least have the advantage of banishing at least some politically correct blathering from the classroom. Exactly the opposite is true. It institutionalizes political correctness. Some competencies are always attitudinal, about sensitivity to diversity and all that. Students learn that sensitivity is displayed through not only having correct opinions, but the right kind of enthusiasm about them. In the discipline of philosophy, for example, justice is viewed as a question, one to which there is genuine diversity of thoughtful answers. In the era of the competency, the question of justice has been answered, and all that is left is to be engaged in the right way in promulgating the final solution. So the world of the competency mixes techno-enthusiasm with dogmatic social liberalism on the justice front.

Some conservatives still understand the war against political correctness as for capitalism and against socialism. There was a time that "tenured radicals" thought it was their job to take students out of their consumerist comfort zones by displaying the inegalitarian degradation that's the result of the capitalist commodification of everything. There are, to be sure, some faculty still around who think it's their job to talk up socialism because capitalist propaganda dominates the media that would otherwise be the only influence on students' lives. But, for the most part, the center of political correctness has moved from the faculty to consumer-sensitive administrations, and it serves not socialism but libertarian securitarianism. The point of trigger warnings, whining about microaggressions and all that is to spare students the discomfort of hearing discouraging words about their personal quest for maximum conceivable autonomy. They actually demand to hear more than "not that there's anything wrong with that" in response to all their choices that don't violate the securitarian trinity of health, safety, and consent; they demand to have the dignity of their exercises in self-definition affirmed and celebrated. That kind of sensitivity to diversity is perfectly compatible with Silicon Valley capitalism. As Rusty Reno has pointed out, the truth is that Silicon Valley celebrates both competence and diversity, the latter as a replacement for morality. That reduction of morality to sensitivity is not compatible with liberal education, which has to proceed as a highly judgmental activity.

Well, a remaining limit to freedom is doing what's required to be productive, and today's political correctness facilitates that single limit by devaluing bohemian, "solidarity," place-based, and faith-based standards that used to clearly rank higher than autonomy and productivity. And the imperative of productivity doesn't smack students in the face until after they graduate. As paying customers on campus, they're consumers, not producers. Even if it is claimed that they have mastered this or that competency, the truth is being competent or becoming competent on campus are lifestyle options.

From Competency to Literacy?

Those few conservative reformers who genuinely want our career liberal arts professors in the classrooms filled with as many students as possible have a noble goal. If their reform is seriously personal—or, as we say these days, reform conservatism—then they should oppose every effort of our administrators to displace respected professors with proletarianized adjuncts. The reformers should also work to reduce, as far as possible, the place of competency and the screen in figuring out the kind of general education—the kind of content-driven literacy—that is part of genuinely higher education. Respected professors, it turns out, as we conservatives should understand, are part of the indispensable content of higher education. The genuinely personal and relational point of view, let me add, is what the anti-communist thinkers Solzhenitsyn and Havel called the genuinely dissident point of view. It's the point of view that resists the reductionist excesses of both capitalism and communism—both consumerism and ideological terror—on behalf of "living in the truth" about who each of us is.

For now, we dissident faculty are about resisting standardization and surveillance of all kinds, whether it be from the government or the foundation or the accrediting agency. Because it's impossible to dispense with "branding" altogether in our digital world, we want to replace the idea of competency with that of literacy. And we do so with the real job market in mind. It turns out the main complaint of employers today is not that graduates lack this or that fairly minimalist techno-competency that could, after all, readily be learned on the job. It's that they don't have the level of literacy, the good habits, the sense of personal responsibility, and the fine manners that we used to be able to count on most college grads—or even most high school grads—having.

So let's begin with a question that bothers educators more than it should, "Is liberal education about learning content or acquiring a method of thinking?" For me, it's undeniable that content is prior to method. You can't think well without knowing what to think with.

The argument for content is typically framed around the need for literacy. Surely every American citizen needs to possess civic literacy. That means having knowledge of the key moments and documents of our long and bookish political tradition of liberty, as well as knowledge of how our form of government actually functions. From this view, civic literacy is prior to the often-touted method of "civic engagement." To take part in our political process responsibly, citizens need to be informed or not just about shooting the bull over alleged outrages.

In any country, civic literacy is intertwined with historical literacy. In the case of America, that seems to mean both knowing the history of our country and the place of our country as part of Western civilization—a civilization based on a very definite kind of poetry, philosophy, and theology, as well as the one in which the modern conceptions of freedom and technological progress arose. It is a civilization animated by different views of who the free person or individual is—and so by disputes over the proper relationships among personal or individual freedom, economic freedom, civic freedom, familial freedom, and the freedom of equal creatures under the personal and relational God (which includes both freedom of conscience and the freedom of the church as an organized body of thought and action).

It would be easy to add here, of course, economic literacy, given how dependent our country now is and has always been in some measure on the global competitive marketplace. And, of course, technological literacy. Nobody really thinks economic productivity and technological progress are good for their own sakes. The "how" of money and power are for the "why" of properly human purposes. Still, there's no way to hope to subordinate the "how" to the "why" without understanding how the how works. The last thing liberal education should do, especially these days, is facilitate the vanity that comes with having unreasonable contempt for what making money and deploying technological creativity can do for us all.

Even libertarians, who often seem to be unreservedly technophiliac cheerleaders for the unimpeded primacy of market forces, don't really think money and power are the bottom line. They don't even think money and power are merely good for satisfying "subjective preferences" and nothing more. For libertarians, typically, the bottom line is the free or sovereign individual, the being undefined by class, caste, or oppressive relational imperatives. That understanding of freedom, of course, requires a real philosophical literacy, and its defense requires real knowledge of its philosophical and theological alternatives. That understanding of freedom is also far from whimsical; it requires taking responsibility for oneself and one's own and refusing to be thoughtlessly dependent on others.

But there's even more. The purpose of modern technological efforts is to deploy smart and even genius machines to enhance human productivity to the point where most of us live in abundance with considerable leisure. Libertarians, for good reason, point to the screen as a kind of liberty that has been made available to us all. Through the screens on our smart devices, we all have access—for free—to most of the great cultural achievements of Western civilization. We also have access, of course, to all manner of mindless games and pornography. There's no way anyone could be satisfied by saying that the whole progress of Western civilization has been toward producing a kind of idiocracy where most people spend their days immersed in online games and porn—perhaps enhanced by legalized marijuana.

There will, of course, be no effective laws limiting access to most of what can conceivably be made available on the screen, just as there'll be no laws limiting Google's hugely intrusive efforts to know and manipulate our preferences. So the only alternative is an effort to educate people to use their leisure and their technology well, to have what it takes to fend off mindless addiction and Silicon Valley scripting. So literacy has to be expanded to include musical, artistic, and literary literacy. It's great that what used to be available only to lazy and unjust aristocrats is now available to us all. But it would be much greater, of course, if our democratic understanding of education aimed beyond techno-vocational literacy to an elevation of personal choices concerning what to do with the unprecedented power at one's disposal.

That means, if you think about it, that the content of education should mainly be found in books. It really makes all the difference—when it comes to both economic success and the choice of worthy leisure—if a particular child is raised in a home animated by love of reading. We should prize no skill more than being able to attentively read a "real book," a book that's more than a source of self-indulgent entertainment or technical self-help. That skill is all about effective access to content. It's for building a huge and precise vocabulary that opens the particular person to the daylight of meaning—to living in the truth—that comes with connecting words to the way things really are.

That skill, after all, is the source of the freedom that comes from being able to use techno-happy talk ironically, to see, in the field of education, that "collaborative learning," "competency," and even "critical thinking" are lazily abstract ways of diverting oneself from the challenge of figuring out who an educated person really is. Being able to read with the joyful shared pleasure of discovery is, after all, what literacy really is. It also may be the only way of being able to deploy the screen with the ironic moderation that puts it in its proper or reasonably quite limited place in our lives.

Chapter 7
History, Transhumanism, and the Emptying Out of Higher Education

North America's higher education systems tend to justify their rising and often scandalous costs by boasting the great practical and personal benefits they bestow on their graduates. At the risk of acquiring some university presidents and admissions officers as enemies, I'd say our colleges and universities produce great benefit to society—at the expense of particular students. Let me begin by observing that this is a modern issue. Beginning with the Enlightenment, we as Westerners—especially North Americans—have focused higher education on the study and advancement of technology. As Alexis de Tocqueville observed nearly 200 years ago, we criticize the contemplative, ancient science of Socrates, Plato, and Aristotle for being sterile, for producing nothing worthwhile or genuinely useful. Leisurely contemplation is a waste of valuable time. It isn't "making a difference." It isn't "getting us anywhere."

It is distinctively modern to identify, as most of our research institutions tend to do, scientific inquiry with technology. Theory is still around, of course, but we only take it seriously to the extent that it yields technological benefits. American taxpayers, for instance, are generally happy to subsidize the National Science Foundation because science can contribute to national security and to the health and safety of individual lives. Because technology promises such widespread benefits, we prize STEM graduates over those who frittered their time away in philosophy or art history or women's studies or even purely theoretical physics (in the mode of the weird science of the unverifiable string theorizing of *The Big Bang Theory*'s Sheldon Cooper).

When popularizing scientists such as Neil deGrasse Tyson disparage the study of philosophy, we object for a moment to their vulgarity (people generally concede that Socrates and his kind make for classy cocktail party references), but then nod in agreement. Tyson sensibly, if smugly, says that being preoccupied with "asking deep questions" mainly produces a "pointless delay in your progress" in tackling "this whole big world of unknowns out there." It is self-indulgent to obsess over lofty, ultimately silly questions when we know for certain that only technological progress can save us from the menacing asteroids, pandemics, natural disasters, and climate change (whoever or whatever might be its cause) that threaten our extinction.

The way to get North Americans interested in the space program isn't to wonder about what is going on somewhere out there, but, as the film *Interstellar* displays, fuel paranoia about the precarious state of our species because, at this point, we're able to call only one (increasingly unreliable) planet our home. From an orthodox Christian or Augustinian perspective, there is much to admire in Pope Francis's recent encyclical on the relationship between social ecology and natural ecology, but, here and there, it gets pretty hysterical about getting our natural future under our control. What's wrong with *Laudato Si'*, as James Schall points out, is that it's all about sustaining creation and not at all about personal redemption. "Repent, repent, the end is near" is a perennial piece of Christian personal wisdom. But it loses its truthful force when applied to the species or life itself. No matter what we do, after all, we will continue not to know the day or the hour.

When it comes to the science of sizing up the risk factors that imperil personal survival and success, from cholesterol to carcinogens to excessive screen time, Westerners are more vigilant than ever. Thanks to scientific progress, we are aware of more and more of those factors, and thanks to various forms of technological progress we can do more to combat them. Many men, women, and children alike enjoy greater security and health as a result ("nudged" along by the government technocrats). At the same time, however, collective anxiety rises because we experience these benefits as increasingly more contingent; we're all too aware of how much more we might do to bring the various threats under our rational control. This anxiety fuels the techno-imperative to stop thinking and start hurrying. There's no time left, we hear, to wonder about the causes of or the significance of climate change, we have to deploy all our resources now.

A few decades ago, the popular refrain was "only the good die young." That's because they put heroism or adventure or love over mere survival. Now we say that only the stupid, reckless, and self-indulgent die young. People with brains use them to do what they can to stay around. Well, they might be risk-takers in the business world, but there's a big difference between constantly flirting with bankruptcy in the mode of Donald Trump and an authentically dangerous liaison or what the *American Sniper* did pretty much every moment he was at work.

We cannot help but notice that the deepest of our Silicon Valley entrepreneurs (surely the most cognitive part of our cognitive elite), such as Peter Thiel, are also transhumanists, promoting the unfettered progress of technology as the ultimate form of personal hope. They take care of themselves now in anticipation of the coming of the Singularity, that moment in the not-too-distant future when personal consciousness can be downloaded into a machine infinitely more secure than one's ephemeral, biological body. Thiel's *Zero to One*, a witty and engaging account of the redemptive power of the startup founders to impose technological "intelligent design" upon all of nature, speaks like the only kind of prophet our sophisticates can believe in.

This hope of invincible personal security in the near future fuels beyond measure the hurry-up paranoia that subordinates the present to the future. From a technological view, nothing could be more tragic than dying the day before the Singularity, especially if one's demise can be attributed to ignorance or carelessness when it comes to a risk factor revealed by the progress of science. That's why Thiel suggests we turn our attention away from physics and toward nutrition. He observes that "we know more about the physics of faraway stars than we know about human nutrition," and it is the latter science's success in forcing nature to yield its secrets that might well be the key to keeping us around until we can dispose of our bodies for something infinitely more durable. "Nutrition matters for everyone," and so Thiel wonders why "you can't major in it at Harvard."

Now, from one point of view, our understanding of technological progress, thanks to Thiel and other transhumanists, has become more personal. There are two new features, after all, of the utopian eugenics of our time: the orientation around the particular person and the possibility of real, singular success. The eugenics displayed in Plato's *Republic* aimed to produce more perfect citizens, or fodder for the city (as we're reminded in the philosophic Superman film *Man of Steel*). And more recent eugenics efforts—those that emerged in the late nineteenth century and reached their extreme form with the Nazis—were about improving the race or the species; particular people were, again, regarded as mere parts of impersonal wholes allegedly greater than themselves. These more recent efforts of the various totalitarians subordinated personal being to the process of History, to being "history fodder" for the coming End of History.

The End of the End of History?

The criticisms we have for the illusions of History are overwhelming. There is almost nothing more misguided than giving your life for History, as opposed to sacrificing your life for people or even a country you actually know or love. History, we now all know, was at the foundation of terror-driven ideologies that aimed to keep each of us from living in the truth about who we are and what we're supposed to do. In our age of "human rights" we think we know that the freedom and security of particular persons is the "bottom line." We don't think we have to give that bottom line any deeper foundation; it's those bleeping' foundations—God, nature, nation, class, or whatever—that were all illusory causes of cruelly gratuitous suffering and killing. All persons are free and equal; each is mysteriously given the capability to construct his or her personal identity; each lives for himself or herself, and living relationally with others out of love or fear of being alone is a lifestyle option that carries with it no particular duties.

From this perspective, Thiel and the other Silicon Valley transhumanists are our cutting-edge thinkers deploying technology for its proper purpose of indefinitely securing the being of each person. Such thinking is not about History in the obvious sense. The illusion of History is that when we achieve the perfect political order, one in which every free person is equally recognized in his freedom, then we will all be happy or at least satisfied. At History's end, as Allan Bloom complained, we become incapable of imagining a world better than the one we have. But the truth is that even if History, in one sense, has ended, and we no longer have fundamental political dissatisfactions or political hopes, we are still not happy. We can still imagine a world better than we contingent and ephemeral persons are stuck in for now. We won't be happy until we're literally liberated from nature for unconstrained personal freedom, but that goal cannot be achieved historically or politically. That's why Thiel lets us know that these days our heroes are, in the mode of Machiavelli, not founders of political orders or great civilizations, but founders of start-ups. They lead the way toward a life in which we can be pro-choice on everything, including love and death.

To honor Tom Darby's pathbreaking work on the End of History, I will speculate more than I otherwise might on the partial irrelevance these days of the Strauss-Kojève debate on whether eternity or History is the bottom line when it comes to self-knowledge and fundamental reality. If each of us could become, in a way, eternal, then Strauss's objection to philosophy morphing into wisdom would become, at least, questionable, as would Kojève's speculation that at History's end members of our species become like the unfree species again. The future is, from the transhumanist view, not radically necessitarian but radically libertarian.

To be sure, we also still have the Marxist criticism of the Hegelian version of History's end. As long as the final solution is merely political or civic, then our satisfaction is merely abstract and at the expense of a reality that is becoming more miserably competitive or Hobbesian. So the libertarian futurist Tyler Cowen candidly acknowledges that "average is over," and society, driven by the imperatives of the twenty-first-century global competitive marketplace, is increasingly divided into the cognitive elite that is—and deserves to be—more wealthy than ever because of its unprecedented productivity in collaboration with genius machines, and a class that is increasingly stuck with working off scripts devised by others, if its members (such as all those superfluous men) can find work at all. Collapsing, or at least in crisis, are all those relational institutions that used to link us together in a middle-class way of life—the churches, schools, families, local communities, and even common citizenship. People are being liberated from the repressive prejudices of politics and culture to be nothing more than workers, producers, and consumers. And, of course, even higher education has to be purged of the relational concerns inherited from the past that waste time and treasure by getting our minds off who we really are.

Libertarian Liberation

Our libertarians and our transhumanists respond that this isn't a complete picture of the liberation characteristic of our time. People are living longer than ever, and that progress may have only just begun. And nothing is more important than being healthy, and especially not dead. Besides, we all have equal access to the screen that democratizes access to entertainment, information, and all the cultures past and present. It allows us all to become consumers of all the world has to offer. In any case, we have no right to criticize those who choose porn over Plato.

The key point here is that life is becoming more virtual or detached from the body. We—meaning, at least, the Supreme Court speaking as the authoritative interpreter of the spirit of our times—have detached marriage from the biological imperatives of procreation, and we liberated love from the desires of animals. As the film *Her* shows, the love of ingeniously responsive Operating Systems might be purer and more satisfying that having to deal with intransigent women with bodies. All post-political, post-religious, and post-familial claims for autonomy are rebellions against embedded institutions suitable for beings limited and directed by their embodiment.

The claims for autonomy are for the irreducible uniqueness and infinite significance of one's own personhood. "I am not a part" is the libertarians' battle cry. So, as the Court says, we have no right to think of women as reproductive machines for the state or of marriage as a republican institution that aims at the creation and formation of future citizens. "I am not a parent, and I am not a citizen." Our cutting-edge libertarians, who call themselves "libertarian originalists," aim to configure the law around the idea of autonomy or radical individualism, opening our borders to all the individuals of the world and outing citizenship as nothing more than a form of rent-seeking. The Hegelian view is that the end of history comes with perfection of free and equal citizenship, but citizenship means less and less in the twenty-first-century global competitive marketplace.

Libertarian Securitarianism

Still, there are many ways in which the radically liberated person experiences himself or herself as insecure. The dominant ideology of our time, in fact, is not the heroic or adventuresome libertarianism associated with Ayn Rand's talking symbols or John Wayne's lonesome cowboys. It's more like what Bertrand de Jouvenal called "libertarian securitarianism." Consider what students demand on our campuses: They claim the autonomous privilege of living exactly as they please, without being assaulted or bullied or criticized or even unaffirmed. College is a safe space, and the only rules, in fact, are safety and consent. And the result of "treating students like adults," without the characteristic relational responsibilities of adults (or spouses, parents, children, and so forth) is the acceleration of obsession with security. Not without reason, of course. The more "libertarian" (or, to be fair to real libertarians, loutish or libertine) students are only restrained by rules that basically prohibit criminal behavior (sexual assault and rape), and not at all by what we now think we know to be repressive manners and morals. So the more security-obsessed students think they need, more than ever, the protection of the law at all times to secure both their safety and their autonomy.

The satisfactions of recognized autonomy are too insecure or contingent to be the end of anything. To be satisfied with recognized autonomy also depends, of course, on a kind of stable self-knowledge that no one really believes in anymore; we hear, for example, that sexual behavior should be regarded nonjudgmentally as a harmless source of enjoyment, having nothing to do with who each of us really is. But we also hear that somehow my fluid sexual identity—detached in autonomous beings from biological imperatives and somehow both chosen and given—constitutes the whole of who I am. It's pretty easy to conclude that I'm so fluid that all I really know is that I'm not nothing, and I'm stuck with doing what I can to give myself some kind of identity—engineering my being into existence—every day of my life.

The most pervasive cause of libertarian securitarianism flows from our detachment from the relational components of personal identity, from what we mistake as merely "being parts." One obvious irony is that we live in a time when our sophisticates lack what is required to speak of what the Christians (such as the philosopher-pope emeritus) call "the free and relational person," the being made in the image of the Trinitarian God, the source of the personal *logos* that governs all of being. It is the discovery that the personal *logos* is really History—or the unfolding of human freedom—that's at the foundation of every Hegelian account of the end of History. But now we don't believe in either the Christian or the Historical form of the personal and relational *logos*. We believe that to be personal is not to be relational, and so to be personal is to be radically isolated or detached.

Personal vs. Relational

We see the division between the personal and the relational in our reigning theories. To be personal is to be autonomous or self-defining, and the celebration of autonomous liberation from traditional repression is the narrative of the humanities. The relational being—or, more exactly, the social mammal—is the narrative of the Darwinian natural sciences from evolutionary psychology to neuroscience. As the most philosophic of the Darwinians, Larry Arnhart and Jonathan Haidt, explain, for all animals the good is the desirable, and we are hardwired to desire what is best for our species. So for "eusocial" animals, virtue is doing one's duty to one's family and community, and vice is to prefer oneself to others. This distinction between virtue and vice is specific to our species because we're the eusocial species that (unlike the ants) has evolved brains so big that the conflict (characteristic of self-consciousness) between serving oneself and serving society (and ultimately the species) came into being. From the autonomous point of view, the real conflict is between being a free being and being a sucker. The Darwinian response is that, so understood, the conflict is between the Lockean's endlessly futile pursuit of happiness and happiness itself, between calculated self-interest and unreflective empathy or, as Thomas Jefferson said, between the head and the heart, between the free and rational "I" and the animal instinctually equipped by nature for social life.

Our theorists tell us we are, following Locke and his successors, free or autonomous by nature, free by nature to overcome what nature has given us, and that we free persons are distinguished from the rest of nature by our ability to negate nature in the service of selfish desire. Our theorists also tell us, following the lead of various forms of neo-Darwinism, that we are no different in the most important respects from the other social animals. Our sophisticates, in particular, are proudly paranoid about their autonomy, while also believing, quite incoherently, that Mr. Darwin explains it all. It is an improvement in the direction of the truth to recognize that Locke and Darwin are both partly right, and we see more by playing the partial truth of one off against the partial truth of the other. If Locke is perceived as too right, we have too many anxious and lonely people and a birth dearth that threatens the future of the West, and eventually our species. If Darwin is perceived as too right, we deny the very existence of the free person, with the equally disastrous moral and political consequences.

Following this line of thought, with Arnhart and especially Haidt, we become moderately conservative, thinking that traditionalism, family values, observant religious belief, and patriotism are indispensable antidotes to the creeping and sometimes creepy libertarianism of our time. We might even become "neoconservatives" in the pre-Iraq sense, or Irving Kristol sense, thinking that liberal politics and a free economy depend on conservative sociology. From this perspective, however, religion is seen as useful as a social bonding mechanism, but it is a given that its claims about the free and relational creature can't be regarded as actually true. And so an appreciation for and the need to cultivate religion and patriotism become part of higher education, but not an open-minded investigation of the truthful metaphysical and theological claims of religion or even political philosophy insofar as they have no foundation in either Locke or Darwin.

The Christian claim, contrary to Darwin, is that *logos* is personal, that knowing, including self-consciousness, is only possible in beings who are neither minds nor bodies or even a mixture of the two. Knowing is a personal quality—a characteristic of a being with personal longings. Our deepest longing is to be fully transparent before another knowing and loving person, and at even the highest levels of thought personal reality remains. Socrates' view that philosophy is learning how to die isn't true if it means that philosophy requires getting over yourself or coming to terms with your personal insignificance. In that respect, the Christian (or the Hegelian) agrees with the Lockean. But the Christian adds that to be personal is to be relational, knowing is knowing with others or the joyful sharing of the truth. Knowing is both irreducibly erotic and irreducibly interpersonal, which is not to say that the truth depends on personal affirmation or recognition. So to be relational is not to be a sucker surrendering self-determination by wallowing in animal instincts that we might mistake for love. The creature in love with the personal and relational God never "loses himself" or surrenders his identity as a particular person with a name and a singular destiny.

Because our theory detaches being personal from being relational it supports the conclusion that should allow us to transform ourselves away from our Darwinian natural condition on behalf of a secure personal reality if we can. Anything we might lose along the way is well worth the price. In fact, we know we can change ourselves in ways we can believe in: The theory of evolution might have been completely true until our species showed up, but we have been all about transforming nature with our free or personal status in mind. We, not the dolphins, are discontent with what nature has given us, and we have what it takes to do something about it. It is easy to ask the neo-Darwinians who want to collapse the distinctions that separate us from the dolphins to account for the complete absence of dolphin priests, presidents, princes, poets, philosophers, physicists, and so forth, as well as for the lack of evidence that dolphins wonder about the origin and destiny of personal being or the place of each of us in the cosmos. Also conspicuous by its absence is dolphin technology—or the capacity to make being itself progressively more personal. The fact is the very future of the dolphin is in our hands. For now, we think they're cute and smart enough to keep around, but things aren't so good for the stupid and tasty tuna. But then, any time we want, we can worship the sacred tuna and condemn the dolphin species to oblivion.

We see the priority of "being technological" to being either passively open to the truth of being or being relational in our obsession about oblivion or "extinctionism." We really think that the future of our species, or the very future of life itself, is in our hands, and so we have to deploy Green technology to counter what we have done to trash the place with technology in general. We aren't about living well with what Mr. Darwin says is the fate of all species, or what the physicists tell us about the fate of all planets, or what the philosophers tell us is the fate of all persons. We are the species that can do something about what has been, up until now, the truth about personal and species extinction; the impersonal "laws of Nature and Nature's God" don't apply to us.

Thiel and the other transhumanists point out that caring about the species or the planet are sentimental diversions. There is no going "back to nature" for us. The future is the continued progress of the separation of personal being from nature. It is driven by the most truthful insight of our time: What we really want to do is keep personal being—my being—from being extinguished. We always "rage, rage against the dying of the light," and the technology of our time promises at least indefinite longevity through regenerative medicine and other forms of biotechnology, and eventually quasi-immortality through the detachment of personal, timeless consciousness from the inevitable extinction of all biological being. Up until now, as Thiel explains, persons have either had to be fatalistic about death (which is hard and never works perfectly) or divert themselves (through, among other things, relational life) from its truth. But now we can actually do something about it. The success we've already had in pushing death back in most particular cases over the last century is just an eventually insignificant prelude to what's to come.

So Thiel rails against "political correctness"—or reigning theories that reflect "the end of history"—because they are based on the false assumption of, say, John Rawls that human beings can be satisfied with a kind of egalitarian justice which recognizes each of them in his or her autonomy. "Political correctness," from this view, is a lullaby that stifles true or technological innovation. Thiel accepts the stock existential criticism of Marxism or Hegelianism; history cannot culminate in satisfaction or happiness or, especially, the unobsessive enjoyment Marx describes as long as we remain self-conscious and mortal. We can't, of course, become unselfconscious, and so we must cease being mortal.

From Thiel's view, then, the humanities in our colleges have been deformed by a stifling political correctness that turns our attention away from what is really possible these days. Reigning intellectual authorities such as Rawls have a kind of vague optimism rooted in banal thoughts about "fairness and distribution," but they are "indefinite optimists." They don't give us the "specific vision of the future" most needed, a vision rooted in an "intelligent design" aimed at overcoming our natural limitations. So even our optimists, with their vague confidence in the progress of justice, cause us to be "set in our ways."

The pessimistic philosophy of the ancient world, Thiel goes on, was even worse, mistakenly accepting "strict limits on human potential" and turning higher learning into "cop[ing] with our tragic fate." Modern philosophers, such as Herbert Spencer and Karl Marx, were truthfully hopeful in "expect[ing] material advances to fundamentally change human life for the better." Marx, Thiel reminds us, celebrated "the technological triumphs of capitalism" as the key to overcoming the scarcity we've been given by nature and entering the realm of absolute freedom. But Marx and Spencer were pretty clueless when it comes to really understanding the full potential of technology, particularly in our time.

Transhumanism and the End of History Rightly Understood

That doesn't mean Thiel, and transhumanist Silicon Valley in general, dissent from what can be called the nonpolitical components of political correctness. "Social liberalism," Thiel proclaims, has won. That means we should think of people as free to determine their sexual identities, and not to be defined as biological beings divided into males and females and directed by the imperatives of having and raising babies or oriented around familial and civic love. Each of us, in truth, is a free person, measured by our productivity or ability to push back nature in the service of freedom. From an educational view, the result is a kind of stifling of controversy by a refusal to take seriously the guidance of traditional or religious or civic morality. The result is not "the end of History" but the dogma that we have gone beyond the category of History. It is not some quasi-Hegelian progressivism but libertarianism. It is the abolition of the categories of nation-state and citizen, the opening of borders, and the pursuit of maximum conceivable mobility.

So the light at the end of the tunnel, as libertarian futurist Cowen tells us, is the time to come when we'll be freed from nature by "genius machines"—and as genius machines—to play endless games. Then, as Marx predicted, all human activities will become hobbies, and we can be "foodies" like Cowen or highly discerning—if quite detached—consumers of the great art produced by the living cultures of the past. There will be no more need for birth because there will be no death. The world will be something like the heaven described by the Christians. But for the Christians even in heaven we retain our bodies and our capacity for relational—if not sexual—love, and the point of heaven is to be in love in the eternal present with the personal and relational (or Trinitarian) God. Maybe love is a merely biological quality that will wither away when the need for the family and children does. That is not to say the transhumanist world of pure or unconstrained consciousness will necessarily be composed of beings locked up in trans-erotic solitude. Maybe we will be fully transparent to each other, experiencing what the Trinitarian God allegedly does, being one being while somehow retaining personal identity. It will be upside pantheism without the downside of personal dissolution. In any case, who can really know?

The point of transhumanism is to achieve what Marx promised at history's end not through political revolution, but through technological transformation. Scarcity will be definitively overcome when we no longer have a scarcity of time, and we're free from the anxiety that accompanies the experience of personal contingency. For now, our job isn't to foment rebellion that will overcome the alienating division of labor. It's to continue to perfect the division of labor in the service of indefinitely accelerating the personal productivity of those adept at intellectual labor, at working, as Cowen explains, with genius machines, herding those nerds who do that work, marketing the innovative and disruptive products of that work, and being (as the economists are) cheerleaders for the future to come. The bottom line is talking up the freedom that fuels productivity, and that means privileging the experiences of those displaced persons who can think abstractly, that is, flexibly insert their skills into a wide variety of roles by using their minds to resist being tied down by the oppressive prejudices that govern the authoritative conventions of relational life. That means our future of being itself depends on reconfiguring all of higher education—education for our cognitive elite —in the service of technology broadly and rightly understood. That is, in fact, what we have been doing. Everything that resists the sovereignty of technology is being emptied out.

Higher Education as Technology

It is quite understandable, and in many ways beneficial, that we have reconfigured so much of higher education around the progress of technology and the science that serves it. Consider, for example, all the enthusiasm around "undergraduate research." My objection has always been: Undergraduates shouldn't be doing original research; they don't know anything yet. That objection, however, makes little sense from the techno-progressive view. We are always living on the cutting edge of knowledge, and our job is to make a small contribution to its indefinite advance. The "history" or past of science is a series of outmoded errors; there is no need to think about the origin of what is known now to move ahead. The focus is on "disruptive innovation."

The experimental approach that rightly dominates inquiry in chemistry and physics has expanded into techno-lite fields like communications, marketing, economics, and most of the social sciences. It has also moved into history and literature, with the "digital humanities" movement. Even the text is no longer understood primarily as a source of enduring personal wisdom, but something to be accounted for and manipulated by understanding its genealogy. The point of the digital humanities movement is to deconstruct "the myth of genius" by understanding even great literature and poetry as collaborative technological productions. Something similar could be said about emerging fields such as neurotheology, which understand even our seeming openness to God as something to be explained and manipulated according to the experimental method of the natural sciences.

From one point of view, the technological model of progress is very personal, insofar as it is oriented around the security and autonomy of particular persons, but that personal progress is achieved by surrendering the personal dimension in understanding and research. We see that in our colleges "general education" is shrinking and becoming more optional, in part to allow promising students to get right down to specialized research. The principle of specialization, of course, is becoming a cog in a machine, making a small contribution to a whole process beyond one's own comprehension and control. So often the choice of "research questions" doesn't flow from one's own informed curiosity about nature and human nature, but from what scientific and technological progress seems to require at the moment. The important thing is to make some contribution.

We also see an increasing emphasis, even at the early stages of undergraduate education, on collaboration. Articles in experimental science and technology often have more authors than they do pages. The premise is that the objectivity of science overwhelms personal differences in perspective, and so no contribution is to be understood as having been made by anyone in particular. In the digital humanities they even explain that the plays of Shakespeare were not really written by that particular bard, but were the collaborative effort of theater workers in his time and place. The skill of collaboration is "teamwork," becoming a part of a whole greater than oneself. An advantage of collaboration might be that nobody has to take personal responsibility.

The Progress of Technology vs. Personal Progress

I am not taking a stand here against the progress of science or technology or what is required to achieve it, but every benefit has its cost. The progress of technology is, in some measure, achieved at the cost of personal virtue and self-understanding. Tocqueville, in his formidable *Democracy in America*, warns us that we may become so enamored with controlling and improving everything around us that we actually lose our most "sublime faculties," those that give us a taste for the infinite, a love of greatness, and ways to understand ourselves as more than material beings. It is thinking of ourselves as more than material or technological beings that gives us the confidence that we can make genuinely enduring contributions—those that won't be overwhelmed or rendered obsolete by technology.

I could go on to cite astute thinker after thinker who says something like this: obsession with material progress, with technological control, comes at the expense of the soul. By "soul" I mean nothing more than what animates beings with the particular destiny of being born to know, love, and die. The soul endures, though, even in the most arid of environments, and without some account of our "soulful" experiences, our lives easily become a miserable mixture of techno-obsessions and lonely personal emptiness.

William Deresiewicz, in his provocative and popular *Excellent Sheep: The Miseducation of the American Elite and the Way to a Meaningful Life*, echoes Solzhenitsyn, to a point, saying that the unwillingness of our elite universities to assist students in finding purpose and "constructing" their souls is perhaps the big reason for the anxious emptiness that lurks beneath the calculated careerism of our best and brightest. Harvard's outstanding evolutionary psychologist, Steven Pinker, has reasonably responded that his university (like almost all the others) hires professors for their promise and accomplishments in advancing the frontier of some form of specialized knowledge. Nobody asks them what they can contribute to the students' search for personal and spiritual meaning. And Pinker is right to say that Deresiewicz speaks nobly about college as time for students to contemplate, without explaining what contemplation is or why it is actually a form of knowledge. According to Pinker, the point of college is to advance the critical thinking and scientific knowledge of rational people. They can, if they find the need, work on their souls on their own time.

Neither Pinker nor Deresiewicz, truth to tell, can speak with confidence about higher education as the education of the soul. Each in his own way lacks what is required to teach young men and women about who they are and what they are supposed to do as rational and moral persons. They have no confidence, for example, that Aristotle might be right about the proud and truthful virtues of generosity, magnanimity and justice. And certainly neither is open to considering Thomas Aquinas's insistence on the virtue of humility as a truthful balance to the magnanimous person's complacent lack of both wonder and anxiety. Deresiewicz's most insightful moment might have been when he pointed to brilliant professors at relatively obscure religious colleges as being singularly able to confidently teach about what animates beings born to know, love, and die. Pinker, by contrast, quickly dismisses their distinctive contributions as the inculcation of discredited superstition. The takeaway, though, is that Deresiewicz cannot flesh out why real higher education—the real pursuit of *scientia* or knowledge of the way things real are—is more than technology or science technocratically understood.

The danger of our time, as Martin Heidegger said, lies in the reduction of everything, including our fellow human beings, to resources to be manipulated and exploited. The danger, in other words, is that we understand everything in terms of technology. Our specialized, collaborative, "undergraduate research" modes of education really do have the strong tendency to think of particular students as resources to be deployed in the service of technological progress. We sometimes even think that the whole point of higher education is to prepare students to take their place in our meritocracy based on productivity, but each of them, in truth, is much more than a productivity machine. That means that in some measure our educational goal is to leave each of them worse—hollowed out, less than they really are—in order to make society, or particular persons in our society, more comfortable and secure.

Yet we really do believe, when we take time to reflect, that each particular person is a unique and irreplaceable whole. We believe in what the philosopher Hannah Arendt called the irreducible fact of "natality," that each human life is a new beginning. For "whole being" with an irreducible personal and relational identity, education must always begin at the beginning, taking on the fundamental questions about moral and intellectual virtue—and about faith and reason, utility and nobility—beyond which it is impossible to progress. For example, those who have read Aristotle, St. Augustine, and Moses Maimonides know that anyone who puts his personal hopes in the Singularity is worse than a fool. Among the more pernicious effects of our overbearing pride in technological progress is that we think we know more or better than Aristotle in every respect.

While acknowledging that most education these days will be technological and utilitarian, let me lobby strongly for more "general education"—education designed for the irreducible yet relational whole that is a particular human person. After all, the technological approach to the conquest of nature presupposes the singular value of the particular person. That value isn't self-evident; it was the discovery of the early Church Fathers reflecting on the relationship between revelation and Greek philosophy. That discovery included the insight that to be personal is necessarily to be relational, that even "consciousness" is necessarily "knowing with." *Logos*, or openness to the truth about all things, as far as we can tell, is only present in relational persons, in beings made in the image of the Trinitarian God.

That means that we can't be so busy that we identify higher education with becoming a useful part of some project. It is in the West, after all, that we have come to understand particular human beings as having irreducible personal identities. Even in our "spiritual" moments, we don't lose ourselves in some whole. Even our experience of the Creator is that of the person who made each of us created persons in particular. So much of "general education" should be teaching the so-called "great books" as conversational or relational, and as if they speak to each person with the truth we're "hardwired" to share in common in mind.

The most urgent question remains: Whom am I as a particular being with a particular identity, one beneficially shaped by irreducible natural limits and hardly the center of all being? What am I supposed to do as a free, loving and relational person in search of truth? Including, of course, the truth that it is impossible to live well if death is regarded as an unbearable limit to be overcome through my own efforts. The "non-technological" thinkers and teachers have always put those questions first. And no technology can invalidate the philosophical, theological, poetic and "existential" answers they have given us for consideration. Without such thoughtful consideration, we wallow in inauthentic diversions that barely mask the existential howl that renders us dazed, confused, and altogether impotent in subordinating technological progress to our personal and relational ends. The truth is, as Solzhenitsyn says, that technological progress shouldn't be regarded "as a stream of unlimited blessings," but "as a gift from on high, sent down for an extremely intricate trial of our free will."

We should cut back, at least, on developing the competency of collaboration and encourage the discipline that comes with really taking yourself seriously, really wondering about who you are and what you're called to do. There is, as both Tocqueville and Walker Percy say, nothing more strange and wonderful than what animates the human soul. Physics, even string theory, is relatively boring by comparison. After all, we are, by our natures, the only alien beings in the cosmos, and it is relatively easy for us to know everything about it but ourselves—the knowers. And there is nothing we need more than self-knowledge to live well. The truth is that we are not conscious machines destined for immortality through our own techno-creative efforts. Neither a pure mind nor a pure machine nor some mixture of mind and machine knows anything about what it means to be in love or to be responsible for others. The more we think truthfully about ourselves as whole, free and relational beings, the more we can put technology—as we have put History—in its proper place.

Chapter 8
Campus Safety:
Reflections on Current Outrages

Thanks to *Rolling Stone* and Lena Dunham, a big and sensational media issue today is rape on campus. Both the magazine and the author/actress appear to have published false accounts of rape that were written to fit a preconceived liberal or feminist agenda. Vulnerable women are raped by "a Republican" (Dunham) or gangs of fraternity boys who think it's their white, patriarchal privilege to treat women like chattel. The editors of *Rolling Stone* were so pleased with the latter narrative that they didn't check the most obvious facts, although it would seem that anyone should be suspicious of a story that fits their prejudices so seamlessly.

In their malpractice, the sophisticated liberal/feminist media have ended up instead publicizing the counter-narrative of their foes: The politically correct mainstream media, campus affairs staffs, and Department of Education are waging a war against men. Based on sketchy or false data, the Department of Education and its allies in the media have caricatured our campuses as a kind of state of nature where there is no effective check on the lawless aggression of men. Extraordinary means must be deployed that bypass ordinary standards of due process in order to cast sexual predators off campus. The goal is rarely to lock them up—that could only be achieved by the police and courts—but to purge them from the academic community. Our campuses need a different kind of a policing that aims to make them utterly safe spaces, freeing students, especially women, gays, and other marginalized groups, from any perception of risk. Discomfort is to be banished from interpersonal experience, whether in the dorm room or the classroom, by regulating every interaction with detailed rules concerning what constitutes "affirmative consent," supplemented by "trigger warnings."

The real outrage, so the counter-narrative goes, is not that women are subject to sexual assault and rape on campuses (which are far safer than society at large), but that men's rights are far less protected there than they are beyond the walls of the institutions of higher education. The same goes for the rights of those who dissent from the reigning political correctness, including political and religious conservatives.

What may be surprising to those far removed from campus life is that one can find elements of truth in both narratives of outrage, the one grounded in political correctness and the other in individual rights. Ours is both a libertarian and securitarian time. Americans, especially the young, seem to want to be liberated from every vestige of religious moralism found in our public policy. But they also seem to be more obsessed with protection from danger than ever before. There's an intensifying paranoid, puritanical, and prohibitionist impulse when it comes to health and safety risks, fueled by the experience of intensified personal contingency that comes with the atrophying of the various safety nets that institutional authority once provided.

You may object that libertarian securitarianism is more than a bit of an oxymoron, but that's the point. We live in a time of conflicting impulses. Our characteristic self-indulgence is the thought that we can have a sustainable society that maxes out both liberty and security.

At first glance, our residential campuses are bubbles, artificial environments that insulate students from the life of the competitive marketplace. The more exact truth is that our campuses offer students the privileges of liberty without the corresponding responsibilities. They can do what they please, whenever they please, as long as they respect the minimalist principles of safety and consent. When it comes to sex, they're not only allowed but encouraged to express themselves freely, as long as they do so in safe and consensual ways. Such a bubble culture flourishes because the natural, relational roles that structure life, being a husband or wife, mother or father, son or daughter, and that force us to recognize the limits of individualism in defining who we are, aren't features of "liberated" campus life.

The campus instead can be close to a consumer-sensitive libertarian and securitarian paradise, where students are offered a comfortable, "no worries" environment in health-club dorms with gourmet food, recreational facilities, student-affairs staffs that function like concierges, and classes that are virtually impossible to flunk. Students are remarkably free to frolic with each other in the service of pure enjoyment. Sure, that's an exaggeration and not true at all about some campuses. But like any good exaggeration, it points to an inconvenient truth, this one about privileges without responsibilities.

But not only is this paradise a really expensive product of social engineering, it's a luxury cruise that's not to everyone's liking. The dorms are often pretty much "no rules." That's because students are allegedly being treated as autonomous adults. More exactly, they are, as consumers being catered to with little asked in return. The resulting freedom might actually be more of a burden than a delight for many women and some men. The strong among them, for example, "hook up," while the weak are condemned to "sexile," finding themselves homeless in paradise. And the whole world of coed dorms, we know, from Plato's *Republic*, originated as a male fantasy that dismissed the more feminine desire for privacy and intimacy, or respect for relational boundaries and natural sex differences.

Another important feature of the unnatural state-of-nature that's campus life is, especially at liberal arts colleges, a dearth of men. It's sometimes argued that political correctness and the excessive consumer sensitivity of our colleges have made them rather infantile places, places unworthy of men. From a broader view, however, it's also easy to see that men are not faring as well in society these days, and sometimes, in the age of empowered single moms, they can even seem rather superfluous. Our educational system from grade school to graduate school seems to fail many boys. And our corporate workplaces, which increasingly favor compliant employees who can work quickly and sensitively off scripts prepared by others, are pretty much, as C. S. Lewis said, for "men without chests."

Well, that whiny observation isn't really fair to women, who are surely, in aggregate, as spirited as men. But who can deny that women generally are better at faking it than men, meaning they're more relationally adept and have better control over their smiles and the tone of their speech? At Chick-fil-A, for example, employees are told to say "my pleasure" in response to every customer request, no matter how rude or unreasonable. Those words almost always ring hollow from the mouths of men, who, we know, would rather say, as used to be permitted, "no problem" with a bit of edge, meaning you, the inconsiderate and un-grateful customer, have needlessly caused me a problem.

Women servers probably share those male preferences, but they, as Tocqueville says, are better attuned to knowing what it costs both to please and not please. To take all this from the dining room to the class-room, women are often better "collaborative learners" than men. They're better, often, at using the "team" to their advantage, even though men typically pride themselves in thinking they're team players.

Still, the increasing scarcity of men on the residential, and especially residential liberal arts, campus is a headache for administrators, who know that if the disparity grows too large it will discourage applications from young women who want a normal social life. The "enrollment man-agement" news at my college has recently been quite good, with the ex-ception that the gender disparity crept beyond the 60-40 mark that's thought to be a comfort zone. Part of our "war for more men" has been to add a number of new sports, which, it's hoped, will make the campus more "manly" in the inoffensive, basically athletic sense. This approach worked the year football was introduced, with the coach having to recruit a roster of more than 100 guys. With a student body of a little over 2,000 undergraduates, that got us, for the moment, to 50-50. But, I think, only for the moment, as the early returns this year already show signs of re-verting to being light on men.

I have no idea why men not interested in sports but very interested in women do not flock to most of our residential liberal arts colleges. I thought the most effective recruitment brochure we ever had featured a single man holding forth a great book surrounded by eight enthralled (or seemingly enthralled?) women. The fact is that the median man at my college is not as relationally mature or quite as well prepared and just maybe not quite as smart as the median woman. That might be be-cause there's a slight de facto preference in recruiting for the scarcer gender, and it certainly is because that's the way things are with men and women of college age throughout our population. Someone sent me a complaint found on *Rate My Professor* that I tended to give women A's, while for men my grading system seems a game of chance. My only semiserious response: that's because I really grade on merit.

So men show up at the typical liberal arts college to see comparatively few of their kind and an abundance of women; many or most are smarter, more mature, and more attractive than the men actually are. That these women are stuck with being interested in them can't help but cause an undeserved self-esteem surge, one which just might not enhance their best personal qualities. The sexual marketplace on campus therefore isn't anything like "real life" or what nature intends. And the state-of-nature or privileges-without-responsibilities characteristic of campus life detaches sexual relationships from their biological and civilizational imperatives as described by Darwin. This detachment, I will boldly say, is more repulsive to the more mature women than it is to the men, who are often, not always, of course, big kids.

Relational life in college is therefore more likely to be disappointing to women than men. They often don't find anyone in college worth marrying or even with whom to have a "committed relationship," and they're frequently surprised by how much their relationships improve after college. I'm not saying that this leads to a huge amount of sexual assault, but it does lead to a lot of reluctant and disappointing sex that takes place outside the confines of the trust established through love and mutual respect. Some women adapt to this situation better than others, and some even flourish. But many experience it as a threat to their self-esteem and personal identity. Some men do, too.

Now, the official doctrine is that there are techniques that can make sex equally safe for both men and women, overcoming a double standard given to us by nature. Safe sex means liberated sex, or sex detached from the constraining biological imperatives of birth and death (and disease). Everyone has a right to "hook up" safely and consensually, or without the fear that pervades sex in the state of nature.

This may be a right, but it's one that men can usually exercise a lot more easily than women. For most women, to be reasonably fearless, as opposed to the false sense of well-being that can come with being liquored up, requires either earned personal trust or confidence in the possibility of very effective law enforcement. The securitarian impulse overwhelms the libertarian claim to absolute personal autonomy.

That's why the libertarian campus, where students are treated (except when it comes to health and safety) as perfectly autonomous adults, produces a "politically correct" reaction. Peter Wood has observed that most assertive students on campus these days are either libertarian or politically correct. The libertarian students, we can guess, are those satisfied with what they perceive as the secure freedom of campus life. They're perhaps not thorough-going theoretical libertarians, all about succeeding as unencumbered entrepreneurs. The genuinely innovative and disruptive founders of tech startups and such usually flee from constraining dogmatisms of campus life well before graduation. But the libertarian students do want to be freed from all forms of moralism to do as they please. They think the politically correct stuff they hear in class is an offense against freedom and common sense, but they don't take it seriously, just as they don't take seriously the politically correct rules generated by intrusive administrators.

Lots of campus libertarians, or more precisely, so as not to offend libertarian intellectuals, libertarian-securitarian slackers, tend to be jerks who flirt with hedonistic nihilism. When they read Ayn Rand, they do it in the perennial spirit of immature young men, rationalizing their untutored perception that they're better than the relational institutions that have raised them. They're like the young men who enjoyed hearing Socrates go after the respected elders of Athens for not really knowing much at all. That enjoyment, as Socrates' accusers rightly alleged, is hardly the wondrous pursuit of wisdom that animates future philosophers. It's usually not even "critical thinking."

The politically correct students, meanwhile, also want to do as they please, but they think they need much more intrusive protection from potential rapists and bullies. They really do feel insecure in displaying their personal identities, and they're very touchy when it comes to the perception of aggression in what should be their safe spaces and comfort zones. They feel put upon by patriarchy, privilege, and power everywhere, and so they demand not to be judged in word or deed by anyone who's critical of who they are and what they do.

It's easy to mock the politically correct faculty and administrators who prey upon such fears, but it's both mean and unrealistic to deny that the fears are somewhat warranted. We learn, for example, that the self-indulgence of campus life is especially hard on earnest and naïve first-generation college students, and it might really be true that our campuses are more distorted by "classism" than "sexism." Campus life, in the absence of a shared moral orientation, really is a war of all against all for the scarce resource of status, and that war diverts everyone from the real purpose, the good that should be shared in common and the source of a high form of friendship, of higher education. The last observation includes faculty and administrators, too.

The college or university is also too often a place where the rare natural predators (sociopaths and psychopaths) can run amok undeterred by, at best, unreliably enforced rules. The enforcement process, detached as it often is from the practiced investigative eyes of the police and lawyers, leads too often to the illegal extremes of cover-ups at the expense of the accuser and lack of due process for the accused.

The somewhat justified paranoia that animates both the accusers and the accused on our campuses today might be traced to an environment that's too much about autonomy and not enough about cultivating trust based on shared responsibilities and loves. A community cannot be formed in the absence of rules and virtuous expectations beyond safety and consent. The residential liberal arts college was structured to be a genuinely aristocratic experience that develops the kind of friendships that come with cultivating the moral and intellectual virtues described by Aristotle, in many cases modified but not obliterated by biblical faith. Without some community agreement on the goods that should be shared in common by mature adults, the adult environment allegedly secured by reducing shared virtue to autonomy produces the opposite of the adult behavior presupposed at the foundation of genuinely liberal learning.

Our libertarianism and our political correctness share the same roots in a rather extreme philosophy of autonomy. And it's not the toughly rational and judgmental form given to us by Kant, but the soft or more self-indulgent form shared by John Rawls and Robert Nozick and many of our public intellectuals. We have to think outside the "autonomy box" to be open to the possibility that our campus life is demeaning, rooted in a theory that portrays free and relational persons as much less than they really are. That theory is not a proper foundation for higher education and especially not for the "experience" of the residential college.

It's not true, of course, that all students on campus are either libertarian or politically correct. There are those science, technology, engineering, and math majors lost in their theories and experiments, often lacking the social confidence to be libertarian, and completely clueless when it comes to the angry concerns of the politically correct. And there are the religiously observant, who conscientiously object to the moral claims, or moral emptiness, of the social and political worlds that surround them. There are also plenty of students who remain decent and relatively unassuming men and women primarily interested in acquiring the skills and competencies required to enter the world of work to support their families. Last but hardly least, there are still pockets of students animated by real books and music and all that. Our most sustainable residential campuses, it seems to me, are those that intentionally work to provide safe spaces or facilitate friendly environments for these nonlibertarian and nonpolitically correct goals of genuinely higher education. My Berry, in fact, is one of those genuinely countercultural colleges.

The point of the residential college campus is to allow students to spend some time apart from, to rise above, the rather ignoble libertarian securitarianism that deforms our time. For now, too many campuses seem in perverse ways to be even more libertarian and more securitarian than the rest of our country, even its most sophisticated precincts. Those residential colleges without a point, it seems to me, aren't worth the big cost (funded too often by student loans) required to sustain them. So they probably don't, and shouldn't, have much of a future.

Chapter 9
God, Political Science, and Werner Dannhauser

Anyone who takes higher education seriously attends to the words of legendary teachers. They're likely to be undisciplined, witty, and unfashionable about great books; ironic about the careerism of their colleagues, students, and administrative bosses; self-indulgent; and insistently erotic, without being creepy.

Let me appreciate just a few of the thoughts of the legendary Werner Dannhauser (1929–2014). Even as I add my own spin to them, I'm doubting that I'm saying anything that great teachers of politics, such as: Dannhauser, Allan Bloom, James Schall, Michael Harrington, Harvey Mansfield, Mary Nichols, Michael Sandel, Jean Elshtain, and Carey McWilliams, didn't know and say better than I ever could.

Dannhauser did nothing but concern himself with the more compelling concerns of our strange and wonderful species: God, politics, love, and death. In so doing, he put himself, willingly and without any regret that his students could detect, outside the domain claimed by political science today.

Political science, insofar as it thinks of itself as a science, is about power and control. As Dannhauser acknowledges, that focus does give our "positivistic" political scientists something in common with many modern political philosophers. The early liberals Thomas Hobbes and John Locke, he reminds us, wrote with the intention of maximizing human power and control in the service of personal security and freedom. Their tradition is sustained by today's political scientists who think of themselves as methodically serving the cause of human rights.

The limits of that understanding of political science stem from the technological orientation in general. It's not that a Machiavellian mastery of the sources of power and the mechanisms of control isn't useful; we can see that mastery deployed, for example, in the brilliant success of our Framers in sustaining our liberty through constitutional means over the centuries. It's just that, compared to God, love, and death, it's relatively boring. No kind of technological success can obliterate the "existential" questions that shape the personal destiny of every particular human life.

Dannhauser gives us an empirical observation that "the current generation of students is more interested in God than in sex, possibly because they have more than they need of the second, and almost nothing of the first." So Dannhauser, "violating all political science curricula," assigned the proto-existential Christian Blaise Pascal to students bored by Hobbes and Aristotle. "Suddenly," he says, students paid attention. He had, to use the trendy phrase, "engaged them where they were."

He adds a second empirical observation: "God goes undiscussed in the study of politics these days, despite the fact that the hunger to meditate on Him is perhaps the single profoundest hunger in the human soul." How could the hungriest part of our hungry hearts be irrelevant to any account of political behavior?

Well, it's not true that political scientists neglect religion as a cause of political behavior. They'll even overdo thinking of religious belief as a cause. As in, what's wrong with those conservatives out in Kansas, letting their nutty fundamentalism stop them from considering their true economic interests? Religion, they sometimes agree with Locke or Marx, is a kind of popular delusion that needs to be exposed and purged from political life. At most it's a fact to be reckoned with in any calculus of power and control. The Democrats learned that lesson when they forgot to talk about God during the first day of their 2012 convention; Republicans are no less cynical when they God it up to mobilize their base.

What Pascal tells us is that the longing for God is a real and irreducible part of who we are. It might be, as Jean-Paul Sartre and other atheistic existentialists say, an absurd longing, or it might be an indispensable clue, as Pascal claims, to not only who we are but what we are supposed to do. Either way, it's as integral as our desires for self-preservation and comfort, the desires Hobbes and Locke reckon with, and just as natural as our desire (identified by evolutionary psychologists) for instinctual identification with other members of our species for reproduction and social bonding. Our better evolutionary psychologists, of course, explain religion as an indispensable or at least very useful mechanism for that bonding. Churches, they observe, are good for families, and flourishing families are what we need if our species and our country and our prosperity are going to have a secure future.

Today's Lockean/libertarian individualists sometimes object that we free individuals don't really see ourselves, deep down, as parts of any whole greater than ourselves, be they families, churches, countries, or solar systems. Once we acknowledge, however, the Pascalian evidence that we are both irreducibly free and relational, we can see that our longings point us beyond ourselves. They even point us beyond our families and species toward a personal God who sees each of us "just as I am."

Seen from this highly modern or postmodern vantage point, Dannhauser provocatively suggests, even Aristotle can seem a trifle boring. Interestingly enough, Aristotle, too, had tried to come up with a political science that owes little or nothing to our hunger for God. The classical political thinkers, who didn't make the mistake of reducing political analysis to power and control, did address the proud longings of the best of human beings to live genuine lives of virtue in light of the truth. Yet even they tended to reduce most human beings to citizens or parts of some political whole. They understood the rarely-achieved liberation from political life for the sake of the life of the mind, to be a pursuit of wisdom that held no place for a relational God. Aristotle seems not to have taken seriously enough the longings that Pascal would come along and describe.

Another legendary American teacher, the socialist Michael Harrington, understood socialism to be a kind of wager we should make, that the right kind of egalitarian political community could assuage the loneliness that modern persons experience in a mass society. If he were around today, I can't help but think, he would concede that socialism failed to do that even as it failed to obliterate our deepest longings. We can say that both socialism and modern technology—and nobody can deny the wonderful and beneficial successes of the latter—have failed to make God "past tense." The space in ourselves for being moved by God or his absence is still there, maybe larger than ever.

Let me conclude with a couple of resources Dannhauser didn't have for integrating Pascal into the teaching of political science. Alexis de Tocqueville's *Democracy in America* is often taught as perhaps the most astute and comprehensive book ever written on democracy and on America. Recent scholarship establishes that Tocqueville's singular powers of observation and explanation depend, in significant measure, on his reading of Pascal. Tocqueville's uncanny feel for the persistence of American restlessness in the midst of prosperity owes much to what he found in Pascal—a description of the various busy distractions deployed by people who can't bear to face up to what they think they know about God's absence.

Tocqueville says the most truthful experience each of us has is of being caught for a moment between two abysses, and it's that experience, first described by Pascal, that is in the great displays of individuality, and also the worst displays, that come with human liberty. It is thought and action in response to that experience that explain why each of us is stranger, more mysterious, and more wonderful than either the stars or Carl Sagan's *Cosmos*.

For an updating of Tocqueville's analysis, we can turn to the best of our friendly critics in recent decades, such as the anti-communist dissidents Aleksandr Solzhenitsyn and Václav Havel. Solzhenitsyn, from his Vermont perch, said that he heard beneath the Americans' happy-talk of techno-pragmatism the howl of existentialism. The uncannily deep comedian Louis C.K. said that one reason he refused to let his daughters have smart phones or spend much time in front of screens is that they too easily divert us from the loneliness that's inescapably part of us. We live in a time, to paraphrase both Pascal and the Beach Boys, when each of us is not expected to enjoy the experience of simply being alone in one's room. Because we don't really talk about God or his absence, we're stuck with either howling or being techno-diverted. Really discussing our longing for God is necessary.

Let me emphasize that I'm not talking up teaching religious dogma here. I'm pretty sure Tocqueville did not believe in the truth of Catholic dogmas concerning the Trinity, personal salvation, or the sacraments. The key point is that he thought himself unfortunate not to be a believer; the absence of God made him anxious. Werner Dannhauser, for his part, seems to have been a fairly agnostic Jew. But by the same token he, along with Pascal, didn't really think that "the God of the philosophers" could replace our longing for the God of Abraham, Isaac, and Jacob.

Admittedly I seem to have gone way beyond political science toward the conclusion that a revitalization of the social sciences and humanities depends on inquiry becoming more "existential" again. So be it. What is required, to use the tired cliché, is that we break down the disciplinary barriers to focus on the whole human person. I'm not saying that the hunger for God is the whole story, but ignoring its reality is a big reason that the social sciences and humanities are failing to attract the best and brightest these days.

As Dannhauser understood, such a recovery of the scholarly enterprise would place no theocratic or collectivist limitations on personal liberty. No, what I'm talking about is recurring, very much as Dannhauser did, to the perennial reflection on what our liberty from the coercive constraints of political life is for.

Part 3
America's Heretical Currents

Chapter 10
Moderately Socially Conservative Darwinians

Sophisticated Americans these days think of themselves, or at least talk about themselves, as autonomous beings, free from old-fashioned social restraints, and free even from the limitations of nature. Men and women both feel free to define who they are for themselves, without being saddled by the imperatives of their biology, their bodies. Our sophisticated form of sex is now, of course, safe sex—or free enjoyment detached from the biological events of birth and death. Meanwhile, even as new medical technologies keep extending our life spans, we are more than ever death-haunted and worried about the contingency of our personal existences. This leads to the newest and most genuinely personal form of hope: that with the prudent avoidance of risk factors, the ways nature and other people are out to kill us, we might be around for the Singularity—the liberation of our self-consciousness from all the limitations of biological embodiment.

Among the consequences of our libertarian drift is the demographic crisis. We have more and more old people and fewer and fewer kids, a fact that threatens the viability of our social safety net. The caring connections that bind together the generations in any healthy society are eroding for not-unrelated reasons. Not only do young people see having children as constraining their autonomy, they increasingly see the unproductive elderly as a costly burden as well. And studies show that Americans are increasingly anxious, experiencing life as too contingent and isolated to be happy or in love, or just content in the present with the goodness of life and other people.

Our aspirations for autonomy can be traced back to René Descartes, who saw each person as an individual self, an "I" existing independently of the impersonal and mechanical natural world. To Cartesian science, nature is nothing more than a source of raw materials for us to become the masters as well as the possessors in order to secure and sustain our particular existences. In a roundabout sense, Descartes' best student was arguably America's founding philosopher, the classically liberal John Locke. Under the U.S. Constitution, written in the spirit of Locke, each of us is liberated from social and biological categories of gender, race, religion or sexual orientation to be free persons or individuals. Without denying for a moment the great success of the free political institutions founded in this spirit, we can wonder whether it is good for us to believe, and to live as though, we are simply autonomous beings.

Science offers one way to get beyond the personal isolationism of American Cartesianism. The view that the personal or autonomous self is free from impersonal or mechanical nature is contradicted by the increasingly pervasive view that biological science, and evolutionary theory in particular, can explain the whole truth about who we are. Some Darwinians who are attuned to philosophical currents, such as political scientist Larry Arnhart and psychologist Jonathan Haidt, point out what they see as the deep flaws in Cartesian science and the autonomy-maximizing morality it supports. In his insightful book *The Happiness Hypothesis*, Haidt explains that the ancient philosophers' passionately unempirical worship of reason as a tool to control their animal lusts morphed into the modern worship of the "I" detached from animal passions. For the ancients, reason had to be in charge; for the moderns, the self has to be in charge. But the truth is, as even Plato had to admit in his own way, that reason always serves some passion or another. And all our passions, the Darwinians teach, can finally be traced to the requirements of our evolutionary development as embodied or material beings. So the most basic human moral question, for these evolutionary scientists, is not how we can ensure that the passions are controlled by a rational will but rather which passions direct us toward our true purposes and our true happiness as social animals.

Who Wants to Live Forever?

The Darwinian thinkers' thoroughgoing naturalism leads them to be characteristically confident that as reason progresses, it does so alongside our moral sense. Psychologist Steven Pinker argues in *The Better Angels of Our Nature* that the progress of reason leads to moral progress, so there is more morality and less sociopathological cruelty in the world now than ever before. That is also why naturalist and founder of sociobiology E. O. Wilson is so confident that the human domination of the earth is due much less to some liberated techno-impulse than to our superiority as social animals. Because science itself must be in the service of our species' social flourishing, it doesn't occur to Wilson that scientific enlightenment could undermine social cohesion or humane progress. Larry Arnhart, meanwhile, who is more attuned to concerns about the morally degrading effects of evolutionary science expressed by philosophers like Friedrich Nietzsche and Leo Strauss, dismisses or mocks the idea that there are scientific truths that we are better off not knowing. Wilson and Arnhart agree that the reality of human nature as revealed by Darwinian science must be good for us to know. Arnhart calls for Darwinian liberal education, and Wilson explains that the true narrative about who we are as a species, one that dispels the more narrow tribalism of religious illusions, might well help bring about a twenty-first-century paradise in which human beings find themselves fully at home with, and completely responsible for, humans flourishing as natural beings made for our planet. Scientific truth is not only about making us masters and possessors of nature, but also about setting us free to be fully who we are, and so to be as happy as our evolved nature intends us to be.

Because Descartes' unlimited techno-domination is not the main or truest current in modern science, today's Darwinians believe that the transhumanist hopes and *Brave New World* fears about making ourselves more or less than what we are by nature are overblown. It is not true that we are aliens thrown into a hostile natural environment, as the Cartesians say. But it is also not true, as philosophers like Leo Strauss claim, that nature is the home of the human mind. Nature is the home of the human animal. We cannot, in truth, transcend the limits and directions given to us by our embodied, social lives, and we would be nothing but miserably disoriented if we could. The Cartesians and Lockeans are all about the aimless, empty, and unreal pursuit of happiness; the Darwinians are all about the happiness we find in our real, embodied social lives. They concur with Aristotle, the scientist who discovered that we are most likely to be happy if we live according to the purposes or functions that we have by nature.

Arnhart and to a lesser extent Haidt know that the objection they have to Descartes applies to Christians like Augustine and existentialists like Heidegger. Christians and existentialists think too personally or unnaturally; they deny that the person can be defined by his or her biological limitations, and that personal identity and personal destiny can be reduced to animal nature. The Darwinians contend that there is not, as the Christians, the existentialists, and the U.S. Supreme Court claim, some mystery to each of our beings, and that we do not define for ourselves who we are either through faith in God or personal decisions. And we are certainly not absurd leftovers who constantly have to fend off suicide once we realize that there's no point at all to our particular existences. The Darwinians explain that our religious experiences or our existentialist anxieties are based on fantastic self-deception, socio-pathological natural disorders, unnatural social isolation, or material deprivation. Such experiences are not caused by any real transcendence of the world of nature, because nature is the only reality there is.

Darwinians downplay the connections between love and death, and they find something abnormal in making too much out of one's own death. Arnhart, for instance, admits that we are moved somewhat by the terror of death, but he does not count immortality or even indefinite longevity among our natural desires. We desire instead a complete life, one long enough to fulfill all our natural, social functions. We do desire to live on through our genes and so through our children. So what seems to be our desire to transcend our biological limitations can be explained in terms of fulfilling our biological function. Even our desire for immortal glory is really about social service to our group or tribe, our country, or to some other social whole of which we are a part. Because the impulses of our social natures will characteristically trump personal obsession, Arnhart is confident that we will use biotechnological progress not mainly for some futile effort to keep ourselves around far longer than nature intended but rather for the health and wellbeing of our children.

Arnhart and Haidt, despite their philosophical sophistication, defer to the more rigorously scientific Wilson in attributing fundamental significance to evolutionary science's recovery of the idea of human nature in our time. For centuries, the dominant modes of thought, likely beginning with Descartes, have suggested that human nature is an oxymoron. To be human is to be undetermined by nature, to be free, to not be explained by the methods of natural science that capture the truth about mechanical nature. Even Locke, who trumpeted natural law, explains that what distinguishes each of us is self-identity or personal ownership. In the service of who we are, we recreate ourselves and our environment, inventing our way to an artificial or cultivated reality not given to us by nature. From a personal or self-won view, nature provides only some almost-worthless materials. This self-invention or movement away from nature toward some indefinite perfectibility, whether accidental or conscious or some combination thereof, is what philosophers from Rousseau through Marx and Nietzsche to Heidegger would call History.

Hive Mammals

The study of history or culture has become known as the humanities, a kind of knowing different from that of the natural sciences. But the consilience, a term popularized by Wilson's 1998 book of that name, promised by Darwinian science overcomes that split in human knowing. Darwinians think of our cultural evolution as an extension of our natural evolution, and they see both as having an equally social and biological foundation.

Wilson sees members of our species as much more like bees and ants, the insects that he studied during his distinguished career as an entomologist, than even our fellow primates. These insects achieve their unrivaled social cooperation, which includes a complex division of labor and shared responsibility for taking care of the young, through robotically perfect obedience to social instinct; these instinctual traits define what Wilson and other entomologists have termed "eusociality." We human beings much more consciously employ our intellects in the service of social instinct to reach our own heights of cooperation. The social intelligence of human beings, the self-aware animals with complex speech, leads to a tension between the selfish desires created by individual-level selection and the social impulses created by group-level selection, a tension that hardly exists for the instinctively self-sacrificial eusocial insects.

The success of our species in dominating the earth comes from our ability to resolve this tension in the social or group direction. It is true that the selfish individual usually prevails over the altruistic one. But groups dominated by altruists or animals strongly guided by social instinct typically defeat groups full of selfish individuals. Despite the cost on the individual level, Wilson observes, "all normal people are capable of true altruism," of selflessly feeling for and acting on behalf of others. Along with other biologists like David Sloan Wilson, E. O. Wilson has been working to rehabilitate the idea that traits like altruism are sometimes favored by evolution because it strengthens the competitiveness of groups, rather than individuals. Actually, this idea of group selection is still controversial among many of today's Darwinians, like Steven Pinker and Richard Dawkins, who argue that altruism evolved through kin selection that favored animals who help only their genetic relatives (a theory that E. O. Wilson himself helped to advance in the 1960s). Still, Wilson and Wilson now argue that the evolution of our species privileges group survival over personal survival.

But whether our social instincts evolved through group selection or not, each of us is, as E. O. Wilson contends, "a compulsive group-seeker, hence an intensely tribal animal." It is as members of tribes and groups that we struggle for status or significance or honor. It is through identification with groups that we develop the social virtues of loyalty, trust, and heroism. Such identification or empathy, Wilson explains, is coercive in the sense of being instinctual or almost automatic. For Darwinians like Wilson, it is in service to a group or tribe that we find the only real significance nature can accord us.

Haidt, who claims that evolutionary psychology is nothing more than the fleshing out of Wilson's audacious insights about the relationship between natural selection and human behavior, follows Wilson in saying that each of us is shaped by both individual selection and group selection. It is true that we are selfish and struggling by nature. But, as he argues in *The Happiness Hypothesis*, we are also "hive creatures who long to lose ourselves in something larger." The only thing that gives us a sense of purpose worth dying for, that saves us from what would otherwise be our lonely and self-destructive personal obsessions, is the group, or our relationships with members of the group. We cannot live well without knowing there is something that makes self-sacrifice justified. We are unable to achieve what the bees and ants have, complete instinctual self-surrender. But our happiness is still fundamentally about having the right relationships. We are, as Haidt puts it, both sociocentric and individualistic, but we find home, place, significance, and happiness in the sociocentric mode, being "full of emotions finely tuned for loving, befriending, helping, sharing, and otherwise intertwining our lives with others." So we find happiness not in autonomously pursuing it as a right but by satisfying our natural social desires to belong.

That's why Haidt regards Émile Durkheim as the most evolutionarily sound of the social theorists through his idea that human happiness, human longevity and human health can all be predicted from the quality of one's social relationships. Even those who seem naturally introverted (but not sociopathological) become happier when forced to be more outgoing. Consider that Tocqueville makes a similar observation, finding that Americans are happier, or less restlessly miserable in the midst of their prosperity, when they are forced by the presence of free and local institutions to act as citizens. Calculation, Tocqueville explains, is displaced by instinct. And American men, he adds, are happier because their social circumstances and calculation about the most effective division of labor compels them to marry. Whatever they might say in their proud, delusional perception of their Cartesian freedom, they cannot help but learn to love and even live for their wives and children.

But despite the profound importance of social relationships for human happiness, we are, by evolution, tragically divided as animals both so intelligently self-conscious and deeply social. The unity we seek with others will always elude us, and it is good for our species' domination of the planet that it does. There is something to the existentialist whine that hell is other people. Social life will always be a source of painful disappointment, as we are never quite capable of finding what we seek in our relationships with others.

We can, however, also go too far in the direction of autonomy, and today we risk doing so. Haidt finds himself agreeing with religious conservatives in fearing that our culture of autonomy risks creating "a flat land of unlimited freedom where selves roam around with no higher purpose than expressing and developing themselves." He hastens to add that religious conservatives are wrong about a lot, but he also agrees with them that the specific danger of our time is too much of this autonomy-driven flattening, creating a world full of too much that is "ugly and unsatisfying." The main enemy of happiness in America today, Haidt contends, is not oppressive and closed-minded traditions, but the corrosive ideology of extreme personal freedom, a Lockean or Cartesian misunderstanding of who each of us is. It "encourages people to leave homes, jobs, cities, and marriages in search of personal and professional fulfillment." When we spend our time pursuing our own happiness and use other people as instruments toward that end, we make ourselves miserable by detaching our relationships with others from our social instincts.

Natural Justice and the Liberals

With an audacity rare among psychologists, Haidt agrees with social conservatives that we have lost something fundamental: "a richly textured common ethos with widely shared virtues and values," a society concerned with honor, loyalty, propriety, sanctity and so forth. What we have experienced, he says, is "the death of character." We have mistakenly privileged personal freedom over the social and cultural resources required to form and sustain the genuinely personal identity in the face of the eusocial (or ultrasocial, to use Haidt's preferred word) aspects of our species. That does not mean, he clarifies, that we should go back to, say, the 1930s. Our more moderate task is to recover the common ethos required for character formation without the cruel and narrow social exclusion that flowed from bygone hostile groups based on trivial differences. Social instinct, Haidt suggests, need not weaken as it becomes more expansive through scientific enlightenment; our empathy now opposes itself to injustices such as racism and sexism. Even if we cannot rival the moral richness of ancient Athens, we can tolerate some moral flattening, but not too much, as we strive to reduce our own "anomie" or moral isolation while far exceeding Athens in justice.

But what is justice for Haidt, and on what basis does he condemn the injustice of the ancient Athenian regime? Political philosophers have generally tried to ground justice in the demands of reason, but Haidt argues that reason is not fit to rule. In moral matters, he explains, reason seeks justification for what one wants to do anyway rather than the truth about what is right and wrong. This puts him on the side of Glaucon, Socrates' interlocutor in the *Republic*, who said that people only care about having the reputation for justice, rather than actually being just. In other words, they care how it affects their relationships with others, particularly others within their own tribe. A reliably just society is one ruled by those with genuine authority, who form characters and hierarchical relationships around shared conceptions of loyalty, sanctity, and the like. But if justice is simply what curbs egoism and preserves the integrity of the group, then shouldn't Darwinians accept the ostensibly just city of the *Republic*, the closest we could come to being hive animals, as the ideal by which all other societies be judged?

The Darwinian answer is that projects that take justice too seriously and that try to socialize away the tension between the individual and the group actually aim to extinguish the complexities embedded in the human being, the eusocial animal who succeeds through social intelligence. To be effective, social cooperation cannot simply be the product of calculation or self-interest rightly understood (as the Lockeans would have it), but it also cannot be imposed in a way that would abolish individual choice or responsibility (as in the *Republic*). For all his sympathy with social conservatism and its understanding of the importance of relationships for morality, politically speaking Haidt is more of a libertarian. He's the increasingly rare kind of libertarian that idealizes not the liberated individual who chooses to design himself from an ever-expanding menu of choice but rather the intelligently eusocial animal who takes responsibility for his own relationships.

Haidt notes that socialists and big-government liberals have too much faith in reason and not enough in social instinct. They think of themselves as imposing order on a chaotic mass of individuals, believing that the Cartesian description of the world as full of liberated and isolated "I's" pursuing selfish interests is, regrettably, accurate. But social cooperation is more warped or crowded out than assisted by an intrusive government. Authority and sanctity and character formation flourish better when government is limited by a robust common morality rooted in social groups. Institutional religion, for example, cultivates the social virtues better than coercive government ever could, although it can also easily be distorted to serve violent tribalism. But even when religion is not so distorted, Haidt claims that it is ridiculous to expect it to generate unconditional empathy, or unconditional love, as the Christians claim it should. The empathy that religion encourages, Haidt says, is generally limited to members of the religious group and is generally motivated by concerns over one's reputation within the group.

What liberals have to offer is their generous and humane defense of victims oppressed by and excluded from one group or another. But their caring and their anger blind them to the damage they are doing to the hive overall. The changes they fight for often weaken groups, traditions, institutions, and moral capital. Consider, for example, that welfare programs in the 1960s reduced the value of marriage, increased out-of-wedlock births, and weakened African American families. To Haidt, justice combines liberals caring with the recognition that it could hardly be just to undermine the indispensable conditions for happiness of eusocial animals. On his moderately socially conservative view, both libertarians (who sacralize liberty) and social conservatives (who sacralize certain institutions and traditions) reliably espouse partly correct views of who we are. The balance achieved through the clash of partisans is better than one set of factions prevailing at the expense of the other. Better still would be partisans who really listened to each other, who saw the limits of reason in the eusocial animal even in their own cases.

Evolutionary Science and Sexual Morality

With a few prominent exceptions, such as the political scientists Larry Arnhart, Francis Fukuyama, and the late James Q. Wilson, most of the scholars studying human nature from a Darwinian perspective profess to be as liberal as the next academic. And while the idea that biology and evolution have a role in human behavior has long been sharply opposed by many on the left, many more moderate liberals share the views of Steven Pinker that evolutionary psychology is part of the antidote to the conservatism of fundamentalist religion. But the explorations of particular public controversies by sociobiologists suggest that the relationship is not that simple.

In his latest book, *The Social Conquest of Earth*, E. O. Wilson criticizes what he sees as the dogmatic, unscientific ignorance of Pope Paul VI's 1968 encyclical *Humanae Vitae*, which explains the Catholic Church's ban on artificial contraception. In Wilson's interpretation, Paul holds that God intended sexual intercourse to be only for the purpose of conceiving children.

The pope seems very Darwinian when he states that the purpose of members of our species is to pair-bond, reproduce, and raise their young. On this view, sex is deformed when detached from those natural, social functions. But Wilson helpfully explains that Paul missed another purpose for sexual intercourse discovered lately by scientists; human females differ from those of the other primate species in not obviously displaying "estrus," or being in heat. That means that a woman bonded with a man invites continuous and frequent intercourse. The evolutionary or adaptive function here, Wilson tells us, is that women use sexual pleasure to make sure the father is always around to help raise the children. Because the large brains that give us our high intelligence take so long to develop, human children need intensive help for much longer than the young of other species. It would hardly have been adaptive for social animals like us, Wilson says, to leave the natural mother of children stuck with raising the kids alone.

Wilson even adds that when it comes to raising children, there is just no good alternative to two "sexually and emotionally bonded mates." The mother, even "in tightly knit hunter-gatherer societies," simply cannot count on the broader community or tribe. So, to Wilson, the superiority of the two-parent heterosexual family with children is both natural and enduring. Other kinds of families are less natural or adaptive which is not to say that they aren't better than nothing. Wilson's conclusion should not be taken to imply we should diminish our empathy and support for the struggle of single moms, or our admiration for gay couples with the generosity to choose to provide a home for children who do not have one.

It is striking how many areas on which Wilson and the pope agree, including that marriage is for having and raising children; the capacity of women to be sexually available must be understood in the context of the stable, enduring marriages that are required for children to be raised well; women suffer when they make sex too readily available to men who are unwilling to accept the responsibilities of sexual and emotional mating. None of this, of course, is to say that Wilson's Darwinian approach to sexual ethics would lead him to join the Catholic Church in opposing the use of contraception, or the woman's use of sexual pleasure, outside of marriage. On his account for example, the single mom might use both to bond with a mate who could help raise her children.

Another example Wilson offers of evolutionary science employed to correct ignorant dogmatism involves homosexuality. Once again, the mistaken judgment of religious conservatives, Wilson says, is that sexual behavior not aiming at reproduction is wrong. One might think at first that evolutionary biologists would at least agree that homosexuality is maladaptive, but new findings suggest a subtle contribution of homosexuals to group fitness. Wilson highlights studies showing that homosexual-tending genes have been favored by natural selection to a limited but real extent, and so all societies have had some people with natural homosexual inclinations. The reason for this, he explains, is that homosexuals have contributed specific talents and qualities of personality not generally found in heterosexuals. So, Wilson argues, attempts to repress homosexuality and oppress homosexuals actually hurt society by suppressing beneficial diversity. Homophobia should give way to a scientifically informed valuing of what homosexuals contribute to the flourishing of the group or tribe.

It seems fortunate for all involved that Wilson's biological determinism happens to lead to such a congenially liberal conclusion. His discoveries purport to show that a more humane appreciation for homosexuals does not depend on a Cartesian science based on the liberation of the autonomous individual. Nor does it depend on mysterious beings defining who they are for themselves, as the Supreme Court claims, unguided by nature. It is easy to wonder whether, if evolutionary science purported to reach the opposite conclusion (that homosexuality was maladaptive and doesn't serve the group or the species), Wilson would encourage us to abandon our appreciation for it.

Relational and Personal

Evolutionary scientists claim to overcome the dualism stemming from the false belief that we are more than biological beings, that is, the various forms of distinction between animal nature and personal or individual freedom. Yet their talk about the tension between individual selection and group selection has a sort of de facto dualism. The socially intelligent human animal does not automatically behave in accordance with instinct like the bees and ants, and he does not experience himself simply as either a whole (and surely an organism should be a whole) or as a part (as the eusocial ants and bees are parts of the hive).

Despite their best efforts, the Darwinians' descriptions of human beings reveal that we are too wayward to exist simply for some impersonal process. Wilson, for example, tells us the rest of nature would cheer if the members of our species were to disappear, and so we must assume conscious responsibility for not trashing beyond repair the planetary environment on which we depend for our very being. He also grants that we just might not have enough empathy and enough science to meet that responsibility. The techno-domination that is supposed to bring about Wilson's vision of a scientifically informed paradise on earth could just as easily produce an unprecedented hell. Doesn't the promise of paradise, as the more political Arnhart and Haidt remind us, depend on forgetting that the tragic conflict between our selfish and social instincts will continue to be the fundamental characteristic of the human animal?

Another penetrating criticism of Darwinian social thinking comes from Christians like Robert P. Kraynak. In "Justice without Foundations," Kraynak argues that those implicitly dualistic evolutionary theorists, though modern men and women and humane scientists, still cannot help but affirm the Christian view (semi-secularized by Lockeans) that human beings are more than members of a tribe and possess an irreducible personal dignity. Although evolutionary psychologists try to reach the same political conclusions as people devoted to the human rights of individuals mysteriously liberated from nature, evolutionary science offers no real evidence that could ground our sense of personal significance apart from the requirements of the group and ultimately the species.

The moderation of Darwinian conservatism comes from its implicit recognition that evolutionary psychology falls short of explaining everything about who we are. The Cartesians are onto something regarding our irreducible personal freedom and our dissatisfaction with our personal limitations, existential loneliness, misery without God, anxiety in the face of personal demise. In this sense, the reduction of religion to a form of social bonding and adherence to group morality does not capture everything about religion. Surely Heidegger is right to say that, in the absence of a personal God, one's own death and the dread it inspires are not social or relational experiences.

Pushing in the other direction, of course, is the scientific evidence that Cartesian thought does not explain everything about us either. The point of life is not to maximize our personal freedom by dogmatically harboring doubt about personal authority and paranoia about being suckered by even our most natural relational impulses. Freedom really does become another word for nothing left to lose if we consciously detach it from its instinctual foundation in relational life. We were made, in part, to be parts, to find significance in the service of wholes greater than ourselves. Facing personal extinction, we may take some comfort in the way we live on through our families, our friends, our countries, and our churches. Living on solely through one's genes or species, it would seem, is considerably less existentially comforting.

An unexpected way to unite the Darwinian and Cartesian perspectives can be found in Christian theology, as expressed in the thought of the philosopher-pope emeritus Benedict XVI. The Darwinians are right that we are relational beings; the Lockeans are right that we are personal beings. We can only be personal through being relational. And that is the point of the Christian doctrine of the Trinity. We don't lose ourselves in God, just as we don't lose ourselves in our relationships with persons made in God's image. We retain our personal identity; being personal is hardwired, so to speak, in the fundamental structure of being. And we are made to be in relationships without becoming mere parts; each of us is a relational whole by nature. It is a mistake to believe, as the Cartesians do, that we have to win our personal freedom against an impersonal nature, because we are, in fact, free persons by nature.

The Darwinian conservatives have not actually discovered the secret to human happiness. Their teaching of moderation is really one of chastened expectations, and in that respect their view is not so different from that of Plato and Aristotle. Living as healthy social animals only alleviates our misery as self-conscious and particular beings, and the aim of social and political theory is to strike the balance most people need to live as well as they can.

But to say that the Darwinian conservatives don't have the whole truth and nothing but the truth does not negate their real and welcome contribution to an understanding of who people are these days. They are right, after all, that the real beginning to being happy is renouncing the right to happiness. We Cartesian or Lockean Americans have, quite tragically and comically, been too much about pursuing happiness in all the wrong places.

Chapter 11
Originalism and Legislative Deliberation

The point of Ilya Somin's able and humane June 2015 *Liberty Law Forum* essay is to show libertarians how to deploy originalism as a doctrine to maximize "negative liberty" in America. He doesn't claim to establish that negative liberty is good, or that its maximization accords with living in the truth or with dignity. It's enough to say that it's "an important value" for many people, mainly his people. It is, as the economists say, a preference, and we all have our preferences or values.

He is candid enough to write that all theories of constitutional interpretation are value-laden. There's no such thing as surrendering one's personal preferences in figuring out, and then deferring to, the will of our Framers. For him there is in the end nothing higher than one's own will, one's own autonomy, and those not forthright enough to acknowledge that they deploy words to maximize their own values are tyrants masquerading as moralists. Being for negative liberty or self-definition all or almost all the way down is being against having to submit to willful political (or moral or religious) definition by other willful beings. Negative liberty means deferring to no personal preferences but one's own.

Somin writes to help libertarians get what they want in our country. If he lived in a European social democracy, he would not be an originalist. There, the intention of the constitution-devisers was to establish a welfare state and subordinate individual preferences to some conception of the common good embodied in governmental policy. There, Somin's goal would be to disrupt the constitutional tradition and ultimately come up with a new and better constitution. One kind of disruptive innovation he would doubtless favor, whether there or here, is judges subverting the will of the Constitution's framers through interpretive ingenuity.

As Hayek explained so well, a libertarian is really a liberal, or no Burkean respecter of custom and tradition. It just so happens that in America, the libertarians can ally with the conservatives in respecting the very classically liberal 1787 Constitution. Even Ayn Rand allowed as much.

Federalist 49 defended the decision to make constitutional change extraordinarily difficult or, as Somin puts it, "super-majoritarian." Even good government can't dispense with stability, which comes with the veneration time bestows on everything that's old and hard to change. So some Americans are moved by the classically conservative instinct that regards the Founders as great and wise men, and the history of our country as a falling away from their nobility. It's natural for conservatives to buy into a narrative of decline, and their "originalism" means recovering what we have lost. We can say that Somin deploys that veneration as an instrument in the service of his non-conservative agenda.

Libertarians these days are about recovering the "lost constitution," which means the original understanding of the limits on government when it comes to operation of the market and property rights. The country has, in fact, gotten less libertarian or classically liberal over time regarding economic regulation, and our Supreme Court has gotten less aggressive in defending negative liberty against government regulation, government redistribution of income, and property rights in general.

From this partial view, conservatives and libertarians share in being anti-Progressive. Libertarians put forth "originalism" to counter the theories of a "living constitution" that have encouraged the intrusions of the modern state. Their countering is not so much Founderism as it is an insistence that most of the change celebrated or institutionalized by "living constitution" theories has caused a contraction of negative liberty.

So when Somin evaluates theories of living constitutionalism, it is purely for their degree of usefulness for sustaining and enhancing negative liberty. Against Ronald Dworkin's idea that the constitutional text should be interpreted through the lens of reigning liberal theories, Somin objects that we can't be sure about the content of said theories. If John Rawls rules, as he still does in most of our law schools, the result might be even "welfare rights."

If, on the other hand, more of our law schools were to become like George Mason, then libertarian "law and economics" theory might actually be better than what the Framers had in mind. Somin admits, after all, that the Framers aren't as libertarian as libertarians are these days, if only because the Framers sometimes allowed politics (and democracy!) to trump economics. The trouble with living constitutionalism is that no one can be sure that whatever theory is fashionable in a given moment is their own values theorized. So originalism properly understood is better because it stabilizes interpretation in a form that libertarians can believe in.

We can begin to see now how Somin's value-laden defense of originalism differs from the natural-rights originalism of Justice Clarence Thomas. Thomas's jurisprudence of natural rights would, like Somin's, deploy the privileges or immunities clause to allow the Court to protect rights not specifically mentioned in the Constitution. But Thomas's standard is not his own partisan value-maximizing; it is the text of the Declaration of Independence as the authoritative exposition of the truthful natural-rights philosophy that guided the Framers of the Constitution. For Thomas, taking his lead from the West Coast branch of the followers of Leo Strauss, justices should either really believe—as a matter of reason—that this philosophy is true and has not been superseded by any evolution in liberal thinking, or they should act as if they believed it was true because it is the foundation of that Constitution which they are called to interpret.

Somin, in principle at least, dissents from the Declaration of Independence on "the laws of Nature and Nature's God" as being the basis of our inalienable rights, for he accepts the distinction between facts and values that is part of the science of economics. Still, he hopes to convince nonlibertarian judges to affirm his case for originalism without necessarily affirming his consistently liberal values.

It's hard to see how that strategy could possibly succeed. He finds a ready ally in Thomas on many constitutional issues, but that's because Thomas's philosophical understanding of the truth about who each of us is overlaps considerably with Somin's "negative liberty" values. And there's a different kind of overlap with the "left libertarianism" of Justice Ginsburg, who would maximize the negative freedom of women and gays. To those, however, whose values do not overlap at all with his, Somin says nothing that would draw them in the direction of originalism.

Justice Scalia is, of course, a different kind of originalist or, better described, textualist. He remembers that justices are merely lawyers and have no warrant under the Constitution either to use the law to maximize their personal values or to be philosopher-guardians. His general view is that, when in doubt, defer to what legislatures have done and avoid disrupting longstanding traditions. The Court, generally speaking, shouldn't be the source of innovation. And so Scalia's originalism is sort of the opposite of Somin's. Scalia follows the intention or public meaning of the Framers as the authoritative lawgivers and, in interpreting the law, does what he can to avoid replacing their intentions with his own. He even sees value in not replacing longstanding precedents that are very questionable. A lawyer, as Alexis de Tocqueville explained, respects settled law as such.

The West Coast Straussians sometimes call Scalia a positivist, meaning someone who thinks there's no standard higher than the will of legislators. Scalia, however, clearly believes that the natural law is higher than the positive law; higher, even, than that document of positive law ratified in 1787. But, as a judge (lawyer) interpreting the Constitution, he doesn't allow his personal values or his philosophical convictions to distort what the text actually says. Scalia's interpretive principle is pretty positivist, but positivism or conventionalism doesn't describe who he is as a whole person. That means, for one thing, that Scalia is all for natural-law arguments being introduced into legislative attempts to resolve political controversies.

Scalia's mode of interpretation doesn't lead to the conclusion that the officially positivist (if also unprecedentedly activist on the substantive due process front), pro-slavery *Dred Scott* of 1857 was rightly decided. Taney willfully misconstrued the Constitution by saying it distinctly and expressly affirmed the right of property in the Africans brought over to America to be enslaved. And what is, for Justice Thomas, the authoritative statement by a justice on race—Harlan's dissent in *Plessy v. Ferguson* (1896)—is based on the textual fact that our Constitution is "color-blind" and nowhere treats a particular person as a member of a class or caste.

More recently, the Court's insistence—shared by Thomas and Scalia—that affirmative action laws treat individuals as individuals and should be strictly limited to remediating the effects of unconstitutional legal racism, finds its foundation in Harlan's textual observation. Even, or especially, Lincoln's appeals to natural right depend on showing how the naturals-rights doctrine of the Declaration of Independence was actually embedded in particular constitutional provisions.

It's true, as Somin says, that the "free-labor ideology" of Lincoln's Republicans connected their opposition to race-based slavery with the dignified freedom of working for oneself. The Republicans were opposed, libertarians can say, to any form of governmental constraint of the labor of free persons that is inconsistent with our Constitution, and that genuine progress under the Constitution is always in the direction of free labor.

When it comes to race especially, we can call that progress in working out the implications of our Founders' intention. And the Fourteenth Amendment's main purpose was to extend the color-blind legalism of our Constitution to state law. Whether your opposition to the arbitrary cruelty of racism is a libertarian value, or respect for our Framers' intention, or stems from a belief in the inalienable natural rights we all share, you can affirm the Court's using the Constitution to strike down racist legislation.

Libertarians typically want to go further and think of the law that limited bakers' freedom of contract (see *Lochner* 1905) or that compels workers to join a labor union as a classist version of slavery. They typically slight the fact that such labor laws originate in the (arguably misguided but still sometimes successful) intention of protecting the dignity of particular workers.

Regarding free labor in general, libertarians do well to promote originalism in construing the Constitution. They certainly should say that Scalia errs by preferring allegedly settled New Deal precedents to the actual text of the Constitution, although even Somin says that the people have a legitimate interest in their attachment to erroneous precedents. For now, William Voegeli is right that if people were brought to see that their entitlements were unconstitutional, they would still regard them as indispensable to their personal security, and constitutional liberties be damned. And so Randy Barnett is right that the constitutional case against the welfare state has to be made far more in the court of public opinion than in the Supreme Court.

But for Somin, maximizing libertarian values goes beyond supporting free labor and opposing economic regulation; it extends to personal liberty or individual choices outside the workplace. The issue recently resolved, of course, is whether the Court has the warrant to announce a constitutional right to same-sex marriage. Somin was quick to affirm, from the point of view of individual liberty, the Court's decision, if not Kennedy's murky love-based argument about the entitlement of marriage. It appears to be part of Somin's value-maximizing strategy to simply ignore *Roe v. Wade* (1973) and the controversy that persists over its judicial imposition. Barnett is much more forthcoming in saying that a consistent libertarian originalist has to be loud and proud in considering both *Lochner* and *Roe* as rightly decided. Such a consistent libertarian is, then, the opposite of the consistently conservative Scalia, who considers both those bellwether cases to have been wrongly decided. Virtually everyone who celebrates libertarian progress on the personal liberty front celebrates the "judicial activism" that begins with *Griswold v. Connecticut* (1965) and that has culminated in the Court's affirmation of marriage liberty (and marriage equality).

It seems to me that anyone simply wanting to maximize negative liberty would want to join the plurality opinion in *Planned Parenthood v. Casey* (1992) in considering *Brown v. Board of Education* (1954) and *Roe* to be "watershed" decisions or super-precedents and hence exempt from the ordinary process of judicial review and possible reversal. The cause of human liberty depends, the Court claimed, on some issues being removed by the Court from political controversy, those that have to be settled to ensure that blacks and women can function freely and equally as economic and political actors. That unprecedented deference to certain precedents is hardly originalism.

But here are some differences between *Brown* and *Roe*. *Brown*, a unanimous decision, has in fact been removed from controversy, and (whatever the deficiencies of Warren's opinion) can be justified by a plausible originalism. *Roe* was not unanimous, continues to be controversial, and can't be justified by an originalism rooted in the plain intentions of the Framers. Not only that, the originalists Thomas (and Scalia) and Somin part company on the issues of abortion and same-sex marriage, and the conservatives currently serving on the Court were all appointed by Republican presidents on the political premise that true originalism is opposed to the kind of innovative activism that produced *Roe*.

That means that the justices who support Somin on the personal liberty front—being basically Democrats—tend to oppose him on the economic liberty front (see especially the ObamaCare decision). As I've said, when it comes to the liberty of women and gays, the radical individualist is the admirably uncompromising Ginsburg.

From Somin's (or Barnett's) point of view, Kennedy is the only member of the Court who wants to deploy judicial review to consistently maximize negative liberty. And when it comes to personal liberty (which is, for Kennedy, really relational autonomy), it is very difficult to say Kennedy is an originalist. It might be more accurate to say he's a kind of libertarian living-constitutionalist. He said in his rather magisterial and highly creative opinion in *Lawrence v. Texas* (2003) that the Framers deliberately gave the word "liberty" no particular content, because they knew they were blind concerning the full significance of its meaning. That meaning has unfolded over time, as each generation of Americans has found laws previously thought to be necessary and proper to have become oppressive. Liberty, in this view, is a "weapon" deployed by each generation to achieve an unprecedented maximization of freedom to define the mystery of one's own relational identity free from governmental interference.

Now, let's assume that this is a tolerably accurate account of America's political evolution, if only on the personal liberty front. And let's even assume (now we're really reaching) that our Framers didn't think they knew what liberty was with a good deal of precision. The question remains whether it makes sense to say that the Court must take the lead in declaring that the latest results in the unending war on behalf of liberty are what the Constitution demands of us all.

Kennedy, on personal liberty, is very close to agreeing with Dworkin that the Constitution is what the trendiest liberal theory now says it is. And Kennedy has even added that those who oppose that theory with a view of marriage that until recently was accepted by almost everyone—including all the great philosophers and President Obama himself—now have no reasonable basis for their opinion. Anyone who's read Kennedy's opinions can see that his intention is to write as a philosopher, going beyond the Constitution to musings about dignity and the mystery of personal identity that are in no obvious sense constitutional. And anyone who has studied philosophy can't help but notice he's not so good at it.

But that's not a problem if the point of creative originalism is to maximize the arbitrary value of personal liberty. The only issue is whether that creative originalist successfully gets away with it.

To be sure, Somin doesn't really consider his values arbitrary. He thinks they oppose cruelty and ignorance, and he would like to see the judiciary maximize its power because it is typically more enlightened than our stupid and credulous legislators. But if we agree with Justice Thomas that true liberty has to be rooted in the whole truth about human nature, there's a lot to be said for legislative deliberation and compromise, just as there's a lot to be said for the proposition of Thomas and Scalia that issues such as abortion and marriage—involving as they apparently do the nuanced balancing of competing human goods—are left by our Constitution for our legislatures to decide.

When it comes to abortion, there are some selectively libertarian defenders of a kind of judicial activism with the aim of affirming natural rights, such as Hadley Arkes. Arkes offers plenty of reasonable arguments to the effect that the Court should, at least eventually, declare all laws allowing abortion unconstitutional as a violation of the right to life. Arkes also claims (though not in his response to Somin in the present debate) that marriage is an irreducible relational institution rooted in natural purposes and the indisputable biological fact of the complementarity of the biological man and the biological woman. Anyone who thinks about human nature—as did our leading Framers—knows there are natural limits to negative liberty. One of those, of course, is that liberty can't be exercised to extinguish the biological life of others. Another might be that our Constitution can't be construed to be hostile to laws indispensable to the flourishing of members of our species in our country.

In any case, natural-rights originalists disagree on how to interpret the Constitution when it comes to abortion and marriage, precisely because the text of the Constitution can't be construed honestly to resolve the underlying moral and philosophical controversies.

Arkes's certainty that abortion is the killing of a person with rights doesn't have a clear foundation in the intention of the Framers, and so it can't, in fact, be a foundation for judicial review. But those who are certain that the life of the unborn baby doesn't trump, according to nature, the liberty of the woman to choose abortion, don't have that kind of foundation either. It's clear to me that we would have a more reasonable abortion policy if there were a "safe space" honored by our Court for popular deliberation on this issue that, whatever the Court says, will continue to be with us.

And, as John McGinnis has reminded us, liberty, as a whole, would probably be better served if defining what marriage is was left to the states. If Kennedy is right about the arc of liberty in our country, then we are the generation that's on the way to choosing same-sex marriage as a matter of public policy. But liberty to define what marriage is for oneself has to be balanced with other forms of human liberty, including the relational liberty to belong to an "organized religion." Just as, as Kennedy explains, intimate relational autonomy is degraded when its content is regulated by the state, the same is true with the relational autonomy that is the freedom of each American to be a member of a church or other form of institutional religion. Accommodating the two forms of personal, relational liberty can't be done by a Court that declares religious opinions about marriage to be rooted simply in irrational animosity.

Liberty, in truth, has to be understood, even under the law, as more than the negative liberty of isolated individuals. For liberty to be sustainable, we need some shared understanding of what our freedom from political domination is for. If Americans have reasonably competing views of what marriage (or abortion) is, and if neither the Framers of 1787 nor the authors of the Fourteenth Amendment had any thought at all about making same-sex marriage (or the pro-choice position on abortion) as a constitutional requirement, then liberty is best protected by legislative deliberation and compromising accommodation.

All in all, it's fine for Somin to write to maximize his personal preference, but we have no reason to trust him that our Constitution means simply what he says it does. He should have a respected place (thanks to our Framers' true intentions) in our complicated process of political deliberation, in which the Constitution is never simply what the Court at any particular moment says it is.

Chapter 12
Plato and the Man of Steel:
What Superman Says about Our Humanity

One reason to have a liberal education, one that's usually neglected by all those experts these days who are saying that the value of an education is measured by the money you earn after graduation, is that it's indispensable for understanding the political teachings of the better summer blockbusters in recent years, such as the very thoughtful Superman film, *Man of Steel*. Let's face it, what grown-up doesn't need a deeper teaching to divert him from all that boring action? In *Man of Steel*, battle scenes sometimes seem to drag on forever, because it just isn't so clear what it takes to kill someone from Krypton. But there's something more going on in the film, which speaks to deeper conceptions of the nature of man.

Man of Steel is all about Plato's *Republic*, something that would hit you immediately if you had actually read that great book. The filmmakers make it clear enough that they want you to read it to get their message. They show Clark Kent sitting in his car reading Plato, presumably to help him get some clue about who he is and what he's supposed to do. My message to all you young men and women is that if you want to be as good as Superman, read Plato! It goes without saying that there's nothing you can do to be as strong as Superman. Message number two, you Plato readers better be prepared to endure bullying for your intellectual virtue, as Superman himself did.

The film also has all kinds of Christian New-Agey imagery that you can grab onto if you're not much of a reader. Superman is compared in some ways to Jesus; he begins his mission at age 33, the year Jesus ended his earthly mission, for example. But that kind of comparison doesn't really hold up that well. Superman is only here to help us, not redeem us, certainly not to save us from our sins or from death. And he doesn't have any deep insight into the meaning of life or love. His life, like each of ours, is shaped by choice and chance. He has extraordinary power that falls way short of omnipotence. He's a man born to love and die, not a god. Superman's Kryptonian father predicts that the people of our planet would regard his only begotten son as a god, but that we did not do. We've never become so Nietzschean or whatever that we have come to think a mere Superman can replace our need for God himself.

The discovery of intelligent life from Krypton teaches us that we're not alone. But it also teaches us that "aliens are us." The residents of Krypton call themselves people, and their personal experiences haven't taught them anything fundamental about who we are and what we're supposed to do that we didn't already know. So the film gently mocks Carl Sagan's view that the discovery of intelligent and more technologically advanced life elsewhere in the cosmos would produce some deep transformation in our self-understanding, prove there is no God, and peacefully free us from our troubles. We were darn lucky that the Kryptonian discovery of our existence didn't mean the end of us.

The movie uses a kind of Christian "product placement" to veil its deeper anti-utopian affirmation of the Biblical understanding of who we are as free persons, or not merely parts of some "city" or deterministic nature. The film's spiritual surface draws upon the superficial spirituality of our time, but there's a lot more.

We learn that Krypton at one point was an empire, not unlike the Athenian empire or even the American empire. Science flourished, as it had to for the high civilization to develop in such a harsh environment, and all the nearby planets were colonized. Babies were made the old-fashioned way, and the life of the "city" was full of choice and chance, as free countries are.

At some point, for reasons not all that clear, Krypton turned inward, abandoned its imperial outreach, imposed population control, ended natural reproduction, and turned its science to breeding beings for the functions they will perform for their regime as workers, warriors, and leaders. We get the suggestion that they actually bred two kinds of leaders. Those, like General Zod, whose whole purpose in life was the perpetuation of Krypton as a people or regime. And those, like Superman's enlightened father, who were bred to be something like philosopher-kings who still cared for their people. The difference between the warrior Zod and the philosopher Jor-El is reflected in the color of the uniforms. According to *Republic*'s so-called "myth of the metals," gold distinguishes the soul of the top leaders, and silver that of the guardians who are more about fighting battles than making policy. In the *Republic*, the myth or noble lie isn't literally true, although it does justify a genuine merit system based on examining children for their natural talents. On Krypton, the mixture of elements that characterizes the manufactured souls is more literally true.

The scheme, the use of scientific wisdom to sustain the political order on Krypton, is close in all the details mentioned to the one found in the "city in speech" Socrates constructs with his interlocutors in the *Republic*. The key difference is that the Kryptonians actually had the technology to impose control, or abolish choice and chance, on reproduction by taking people (Kryptonians) out of the picture altogether.

One difference between our time and all the preceding ones is a reasonable person could believe today that imposing such control by moving reproduction outside the womb might actually be possible. The attempt to replace nature completely with technical control, we learn, destabilized the core of Krypton, and the result was decline and eventual destruction. In the *Republic*, the breakdown of the perfect city is caused by scientific miscalculation. On Krypton, any miscalculation, we can think, should have been corrected by the philosopher-kings, but, not surprisingly, their wisdom turns out to be imperfect and so unreliable.

Superman's philosopher-leader dad, Jor-El, realizes, too late, that the only hope for Krypton is a return to nature, to choice and chance, beginning with the risky business of having a natural baby. His wife gives birth in secret, and the parents are immediately filled with love for their own child, as opposed to a child of Krypton. That child is a return to hope; the S that comes to stand for Superman is actually Kryptonian for hope.

Jor-El now cares for both his people and his particular person, and he plans for both their futures. He sends his son in the direction of a promising planet along with the "codex"—or the genetic material of a billion future Kryptonians—embedded in his body with hope for them all.

General Zod leads a rebellion against this "heresy" and on behalf of the eugenics-based people. He's defeated and sentenced to indefinite rehabilitation. But Krypton is soon destroyed, and Zod manages to escape into the cosmos with his genetic mission of somehow sustaining the Kryptonian people into the future. His hope is first in the colonies, but they all died out in the absence of Kryptonian direction. But he also has hope in the continued existence of the "codex" that left his planet with Jor-El's son.

Zod's is a purpose-driven life, and his fanaticism flows from the fact of his lack of freedom, of his inability to choose who he is. He can't help but do whatever is required to defend his people, and he's probably not wrong to think that their future depends on his conquest of Earth. It goes without saying that nobody in the movie's audience, which includes no one from Krypton, cares about his people's future. And so nobody really "gets" the nobility of his mission. The Kryptonians of the future that he aimed to liberate from their encoded slavery in Kal's body would have, of course, built monuments to his magnanimity.

A fundamental issue raised by the film is whether a being artificially made to be only a part of a political community could be a person in full. We see that Zod really isn't, despite his fearless and skillful devotion. Arguably Kal's biological father is, but he was one of the few bred with the freedom required to make a leader's prudential decisions. We're not given the comfortable lesson that in each particular case irreducible individuality or personality triumphs over genetic manipulation.

The Greek and Roman efforts to make citizens through education sometimes failed, and it's the not-so-secret teaching of the *Republic* that it's contrary to nature, or both undesirable and impossible, to eradicate personal choice through some comprehensive and highly intrusive process of political socialization, one that abolishes privacy, the family and chains even sexual behavior to the requirements of the just city. But the founders of "the city in speech" in the *Republic* couldn't even imagine an artificial replacement of natural birth. In the case of Krypton, genetic control, not merely educational manipulation, seems to have been successful in producing beings who reliably performed the functions for which they were made. To eradicate chance or unpredictable behavior, sexual behavior had to be detached from reproduction; all sex, in a way, became safe sex.

Although artificial reproduction can produce beings who are merely "parts," we still learn that a regime that aims to make itself that closed or restricted or detached from natural spontaneity is contrary to nature. Zod's fiercely loyal female subcommander tells Kal-El (Superman) that "evolution always wins" to explain why his dad's last-ditch experiment in personal freedom will fail. But of course the irony is that no regime has ever been more opposed to nature than Krypton.

Krypton's inevitable decline and fall is a victory of natural evolution over the effort to provide a conscious and volitional replacement for it. It's not true that human liberty is defeated by evolution; the truth is that we are "hardwired" for choice and chance and can't flourish without them.

We're hardwired to be free, but we're also hardwired to be relational beings. *Man of Steel* is nothing if not a celebration of fathers. Maybe the most repulsive feature of the *Republic*'s "city in speech," for us, is the absence of parenthood. Devices are invented so mothers won't recognize their biological children. Marriage is reduced to coupling, a quickie, arranged scientifically to improve the quality of the citizenry. And fatherhood disappears altogether; men don't know and aren't attached to their biological kids in particular.

You don't have to be a feminist to notice that the discussion of the communism of women and children in the *Republic* is so destructive of human love and human "relationships" as they actually exist because all the interlocutors are men. A woman's voice would have introduced some realism about a mother's love and the need for fathers. And we can assume that a woman would have let those men have it for not thinking of themselves as having paternal responsibilities. Men, on their own, are tyrannical and ridiculous in privileging public life over the pleasures and responsibilities of the intimate life of the family. A subtext of the *Republic* is that men insult intimate life because of their erotic inferiority by nature. They can't actually have babies, and their sexual lives are more limited by time.

Krypton's eugenics scheme perfects the deconstruction of the family and diminishing erotic or relational life. Women no longer have kids, and so they no longer have to be educated to care for their own. There's no need for marriage at all, although it seems to still exist.

The single most moving moment in the film is the relational transformation that occurs when Jor-El and his wife are bonded by their shared love of their own child. That's nothing less than the rediscovery of the natural foundation of the love that properly distinguishes self-conscious persons. Love of "the city" is nothing compared to love of one's own child. And contrary to what philosophers sometimes think, and what the *Republic* seems to suggest, Aristotle reminds us that the most relational human bond is between husband and wife sharing responsibility for the goods, mainly the kids, they share in common.

The *Republic* shows that men more than women need this lesson about being a parent. And who can deny that today men find it harder than women to think of themselves as responsible parents? That explains, of course, both why we have so many single moms and why men are faring so badly. Maybe we need a female philosopher to write a supplement to Plato's dialogue about the indispensability of fatherhood. One reason, after all, that Socrates got away with talking his interlocutors into so much laughable nonsense about deconstructing the nuclear family was the absence of the woman's voice.

It's deeply instructive that *Man of Steel* displays for us wonderfully admirable fathers, even as it was released on Father's Day. Superman has two dads! And he's darn lucky that he does. He has his biological father Zor-El, and his foster-father Jonathan Kent, an ordinary rural guy from Kansas. Two of the three heroic "role models" in the film act mainly as dads, and the third, Superman himself, is who he is largely because of what he was given by those two dads. We're reminded that fatherhood is less directly biological than motherhood, but that makes being a father a freer and arguably more sacrificial choice. The foster father in this story is, in fact, more of a father than the biological one. Superman, ironically, only knows his biological father as disembodied or displaced consciousness, or not as a father in full. From the philosopher Jor-El, he gets his wisdom and his intellectual orientation toward the world. It's because of this father, after all, that he can understand Plato and apply what he's read to saving us from what seems to be those monstrously amoral products of Kryptonian eugenics. He actually gets from Jor-El all that's natural about who he is.

According to Aristotle (who was refining Plato just a bit), by nature we're incomplete. We become who we are by acquiring moral virtue, the habits and opinions that are the foundation of the character that allows each of us to act freely and responsibly. Moral virtue is neither natural nor contrary to nature; we're hardwired to need to be completed by it.

The Kryptonians, having had their natures altered with "prosocial" behavior in mind, need that completion less or are more oriented to a certain kind of completion. But Kal-El/Clark Kent, free of eugenic enhancement or direction, could have been completed in a wide variety of ways. He was completed, in fact, by being raised by a trustworthy, steadfast, loving American man and his wife from Kansas. Jonathan didn't raise Clark to be just like him; he raised him, without really understanding him, with all those natural superpowers in mind. He knew his son had to remain, in part, an alien, and that his was to be a singularly mission-driven life.

Still, there's no denying that the main source of Superman's moral virtue is his foster father. Given those superpowers, Superman could have made his own life and our lives hell without the character, developed in him by his Kansas dad, which allows him to control his desires with his singular mission in mind, one version among many of the singular destiny that constitutes every personal life. It's because Superman is really from Kansas that we can trust he's not our enemy.

We can't forget, of course, that not only does Superman have two dads, he has two moms. We're shown a biological father and a foster-father, but not a single father. Both marriages are good, and both wives and moms are tough and loving. Fatherhood is highlighted, to repeat, maybe only because fatherhood is slighted today, but it's not presented outside of its proper relational context. Dads can't be moms. That's a natural fact. But the film stays true to the *Republic* by making a good deal out of another natural fact. It's a male prejudice to believe that women can't be fine warriors. Maybe the toughest character from our planet is the gutsy Lois Lane, and no male Kryptonian revels in battle the way Zod's subcommander Farora-Ul does.

Let me conclude by calling attention to a key specifically Christian dimension of *Man of Steel*. The "city in speech" in the *Republic* comes into existence in response to the "open" decadence of imperial, democratic Athens. Part of "the noble lie" is telling citizens the lie that they all came from the same mother earth. It's a way of convincing them that being part of a particular city is natural. And the distinction between "us," one's fellow citizens, and "them" is a natural one. That means it's only just to treat people from other places in political terms, as potential enemies that threaten one's own domestic order. It's corruption to be open to their decadence. Krypton actually made the distinction between "us" and "them," in a way, natural through genetic manipulation. And so the Kryptonians had every reason to close themselves off from other, alien peoples, and to regard those genuinely different people as threats.

With the destruction of their home planet, the remaining Kryptonian warriors choose to take "us" versus "them" on the road. They had to find another planetary home, and that meant destroying the alien people already there. Coexistence was impossible, because the differences in their ways of life weren't only political or conventional. The Kryptonian warriors weren't made for anyone but their own people, even at the expense of others. They were hardwired to be political, as opposed to being cosmopolitan.

So Jor-El maybe was naïve, in his enlightened sophistication, in thinking that his son could be the bridge between the people of Earth and the people of Krypton. Or, arguably, maybe he could have been had philosophers such as his father retained political control of his people, and so the return to natural reproduction had been institutionalized. Superman, too, was initially naïve, the way Americans are, in suggesting that the earth could be shared by the two peoples. But he soon enough figures out that's not possible. And he has no choice but to become as "us" versus "them" as General Zod. "Krypton had its chance," he shouts, and he's not going to give it another. Superman's "us" is us, of course, because his birth was natural and among us is where he was raised.

In the absence of artificial reproduction, the people of Earth and Krypton are amazingly similar. The differences in physical powers and technological development are trivial. In that respect, the "us" versus "them" is unnatural; it's based on a life-destroying personal mistake about who we all are. And it's not that we on earth haven't been and won't be tempted by the same kind of error. (Read the *Republic* and *A Brave New World* and any transhumanist manifesto.)

We get the strong impression that the personal identities of

Americans (and everyone on Earth) and Kryptonians are so alike that they must have had a common origin, even a common Creator. Aliens are us, it turns out. So we have a cosmopolitan teaching that doesn't abolish political and other relational, personal distinctions, beginning with the family, but just puts them in their proper place. Well, that's what St. Augustine does in the *City of God* and Plato seems not to do in the *Republic*. That means there's little wrong, and a lot right, with the city of man being a sophisticated, even somewhat imperial, democracy with an outreach to people everywhere. There's nothing wrong, that is, if such a country has a place for Kansas.

Chapter 13
Southern Discomfort

Tracy Thompson, a very savvy Southern journalist, has written *The New Mind of the South*, a title that echoes W. J. Cash's classic *The Mind of the South* (1941). Cash's graceful and memorable book was distinguished by its audacity in presenting the South's mind as a single and relatively unchanging entity. It was published two years after historian Perry Miller's equally unprecedented *The New England Mind*. Those two "minds," one aristocratic, romantic, individualistic, hedonistic, and socially irresponsible and the other intensely egalitarian, reformist, religious, idealistically repressive, and public-spirited, are the two extreme forms of American self-consciousness.

Americans at their best draw from them both. The best criticism of Cash's book is that it was not about the mind of the South at all. He quoted Henry Adams with approval that "strictly, the Southerner had no mind, he had temperament." So he ignored the best Southern minds, from Thomas Jefferson and John C. Calhoun to William Faulkner and many others, as irrelevant exceptions to the temperamental rule of disdain for real thought, and of being easily seduced by Romantic and violent rhetoric. By contrast, the Southern writers who, in 1930, published *I'll Take My Stand*, an apology for the South and the agrarian tradition, saw in the Southern love of leisure an inclination to find time and space for intellectual achievement and real culture. So Cash's view of Southern continuity was often really a condescending view of the incapacity to change, including the South's passionate aversion to real political deliberation. One piece of evidence that Cash at least exaggerated Southern irresponsibility is Thompson's observation that, despite it all, the South has changed quite radically and quite consciously over the last several generations, and the mind of the South today is much newer than Cash would have imagined. Amid all the change, Thompson wonders, what has been preserved and what is worth preserving about Southern intellectual identity and imagination?

Thompson grew up in Georgia and now lives outside of Washington, D.C., and her book ranges easily from memoir to perceptive reporting, with plenty of moral reflection thrown in. She writes against "the Southern genius for living in an imagined past" or its penchant for being ridiculously sentimental in bemoaning the death of chivalry. She sees the antebellum South's admiration of Greek and Roman culture, reflected in architecture especially, as nothing but a way of justifying slavery. She employs some excellent pop sociology in the service of purging the Southern imagination of racism, aristocracy, and misguided individualism. She does equally well in describing the "slow-motion catastrophe" that continues to destroy the economic and traditional infrastructure that supports civilized decency in the rural South. If the "mind of the South" is basically all about being immersed in the agrarian way of life and having an attachment to particular small towns, then it really doesn't seem to have much of a future. But she denies, not without reason, that "clinging to some particular tract of real estate" is at the foundation of Southern identity.

It is, instead, a kind of selective nostalgia for a shared Southern past. In that respect, being Southern is now not about "agrarian culture," but "agrarian values" detached from that culture. Nostalgia, she notices, is what moves people who have been uprooted and disoriented; there is no Amish nostalgia. From that point of view, Southern values, found, for example, in *I'll Take My Stand,* are "a radical challenge to the American worship of technology, progress, and personal fulfillment." These conservative values came from a "complex web of community" that was short on "breadth," but strong on "supplying an overall sense of order and belonging." Though these values are, in truth, "a feature of agrarian life in all societies," they persisted in the South longer than in the rest of the country. Thompson now sees hope that they can be translated to an urban context. These values, after all, also display the ecological concerns of post-materialistic, sophisticated youth, who want to reach a "truce with nature" and free their lives from "a vicious cycle of production and consumption." And it's those "agrarian values" that supply the key part of her criticism of the "aggressively pro-business class" that now dominates the South.

She also embraces one aspect of Southern aversion to public life or big government. The Southerner finds his place, his social life, at home. And it's the reconstruction of home as "the most ancient foundation of community" that's the promise of the South. So the peculiar tradition of Southern individualism is one reason why the "business first" mentality has produced so much recent prosperity; the individualism was liberated from its agrarian context and tribal and racial prejudices. But another result of this individualism is "suburban sprawl," which is no fit home for anyone. Thompson hopes for a new public approach "to land planning and conservation that draws on concepts of community familiar to an older, agrarian South." One can't help noticing how un-Southern it is to make "home" a public concern, but the virtue of selective nostalgia is the ability to appropriate parts of the past to justify the concerns of the present. One good thing Thompson has to say about the antebellum South is that rich and poor, blacks and whites lived in "close proximity." One good thing about Southern individualism and lack of public spirit is the absence of zoning. Here, in Floyd County, Georgia, it really is true that mansions and trailers are often found side by side in rural areas. Today, however, the suburban South is increasingly full of gated communities, and the rich and smart have fled from rural areas. It's "global capitalism," not political choice, or race, she emphasizes, that's at the foundation of the new residential segregation in the South. The enemy of home, living as a person whose identity comes from being at home with an extended family embedded in a particular place, is now, more than ever, capitalism. Nobody's bemoaning the effect of "suburban sameness," of commodification and homogenization "on the character of, say, Des Moines." It's the South that stands against the depersonalization that comes with the erosion of community, place, and belonging.

With all due respect to Thompson's observational and rhetorical skills, her defense of public-spirited urban planning and environmental sensitivity seems more liberal or progressive than particularly Southern. The South isn't really lost; the struggle continues. To be Southern is somehow to be both an American patriot and a rebel, a dissident. Taking a rebel's stand as an honorable, and, if necessary, violent, individual is distinctively Southern. So, as Thompson says, it's the "obstinate insistence in maintaining a dual citizenship in a nation and a region" that makes a Southerner a Southerner. A Southerner has two political, as opposed to merely cultural, identities.

We can say, following Alexis de Tocqueville, that the South is distinguished by being a huge exception to the generalization that ours is a middle-class country. The American, in general, is a free being who works. But the Southern master prided himself on his leisure, on the freedom given to him by the work of the slaves. And the African slaves, of course, lacked the freedom to work for themselves. Insofar as the South has a distinctive "mind," its foundation is the experience of the aristocratic master and the oppressed slave (oppression, of course, that continued under Jim Crow laws and segregation). That "mind," Thompson is correct enough to say, is found in people whose bottom line isn't money. The aristocrat believes he is too good to give money a second thought, and the slave has to live with having no hope of ever earning any significant amount for himself.

From the perspective of the Declaration of Independence, those are experiences to be gotten over. They certainly have nothing to teach us about either prosperity or justice. Air-conditioning and integration, it's often said, have made the South the most livable part of the country. Atlanta became "the city too busy to hate," too busy making money to have time to be guided by the South's prejudiced past. Thompson criticizes Atlanta for its forgetfulness, but isn't that what is required for members of both races to come together as members of the middle class? Certainly she mainly criticizes the whites of Atlanta for forgetting to be ashamed of who they were, and middle-class blacks for being too satisfied with who they are.

Tocqueville in *Democracy in America* means to arouse in us a kind of selective nostalgia for aristocracy. He tells us that the Southern masters had the vices and virtues of any aristocracy. Despite their monstrous injustice, they had the virtue of proudly and generously reminding us that we are more than beings with interests. Neither Tocqueville nor anyone else predicted the way the Civil War would play out, but he did predict, in effect, that one result of the abolition of slavery would be the insistence on segregation. Thompson is aptly too Southern, on the other hand, to not be deeply critical of the vulgarity and other materialistic excesses of middle-class life. And there is a way to view Thompson's sociology from a more political, philosophical, American perspective on the South's defense of human particularity, of the individual, place, home, family, and the personal God.

To what extent does it make sense to speak of "the mind of the South" as something distinctive, and so better and worse, than "the American mind," in our country? To begin with, the South isn't primarily a cultural phenomenon. It has political boundaries, if not exactly a single political boundary. The South is composed of those states whose laws sanctioned race-based slavery in the years prior to the Civil War. Secession occurred on a state-by-state basis. And the states were received back into the United States on a state-by-state basis, if not on their own terms. The South is not that "region" of the country that once called itself the Confederacy, though it's true, of course, that the second political fact that gave "the South" an identity, a mind, was the Confederacy and its defeat. That defeat was military, but not so much intellectual or imaginative. The "lost cause" isn't really lost; the struggle continues. Thompson aptly quotes Tocqueville to the effect that the legal eradication of race-based slavery will be forever insufficient to remove all traces of its existence.

Voting in the South can still be explained to some large extent as racial identity politics; the overwhelming majority of whites (in most places most of the time) vote Republican, and almost all African Americans vote Democratic. That's despite the many points of personal identity that middle-class, evangelical, and Southern blacks and whites share in common. Right at the Civil War's end, the unjustly neglected Yankee American Catholic Orestes Brownson laid out his version of the contribution of the South to the future of the American mind. The Northern or Puritanical excess, he thought, was in the direction of an abstractly abolitionist humanitarianism, one tending toward the pantheistic deconstruction of all the distinctions that constitute the political, familial, and genuinely religious nature of human beings. The Southern excess was in the direction of a selfish, often apolitical, secessionist, tribal particularism at odds with the truth about the equality of all persons under God. So the individualism of the Southerner is multidimensional and polymorphous; its anti-abolitionism, Brownson writes, is on behalf of securing all particular human places from humanitarian projects to abolish them.

It goes without saying that identifying the abolition of slavery with other forms of pantheistic deconstruction humored the pride and served the self-interest of the Southerner. But Brownson was deeply anti-slavery and still saw his proudly secessionist point. The Northern and Southern excesses are already present in Tocqueville's account of America's two foundings, in New England and in Virginia. New England was settled by educated, middle-class family men, who brought their families with them, in the service of making a religiously inspired egalitarian political idea real. Their achievements on behalf of democratic institutions, universal political participation, provisions for the poor, and universal public education were, Tocqueville reports, both unprecedented and unprejudiced. Much of Thompson's criticism of the South's lack of devotion to egalitarian political reform is Puritanical, which is to say it's far from completely wrong. The South really is weak when it comes to public education and indispensable social services.

The Puritans were animated by an egalitarianism without condescension based on the insight that every person is not merely a being with interests, but a being with a unique and irreplaceable soul. The downside of Puritanical idealism was a kind of intrusive idealism that makes every sin into a crime and tramples politically on liberty of conscience. America's high-minded egalitarian idealism from the time of the abolitionists until now is indebted to the Puritanical mind. All our puritanical, prohibitionist, and progressive excesses, all our politicized moralism that opposes itself to personal freedom and individual rights also are indebted to the Puritanical mind. Egalitarianism without condescension readily morphs into condescension toward ordinary private lives. No politicized Pilgrim can admire those who are happy merely being at home.

The founders of Virginia, by contrast, were selfish men on the make, without families or class or educated enlightenment, out to get rich quick. They were lovers of individual liberty, to be sure, but not the political liberty of the Puritanical participatory idealism. So it's not surprising that race-based slavery took root there, a get-rich plan that worked with tobacco. Virginia became dominated by an aristocracy based on slavery, one that included, of course, George Washington, Thomas Jefferson, and James Madison. Tocqueville reports that it was a lucky break that our leading founders were aristocrats, who limited the intrusive, democratic power of government with individual liberty in mind. Jefferson, of course, held that all human beings had rights but that didn't inspire in him the egalitarian idealism of the Puritans. He hated, in fact, all forms of Calvinist political moralism, and he supported liberty of conscience and liberty of minds to oppose it. Jefferson's tolerance of "viewpoint diversity" at his University of Virginia didn't extend to Calvinist instructors or instruction in Calvinist theology.

So even Jefferson's draft of the Declaration of Independence, we might want to say, was inspired by the perhaps exaggerated individualism of Virginia. But that draft was improved, of course, by the residually Puritanical members of Congress, who reconfigured "Nature's God" as the providential and judgmental God of the Bible. The Declaration harmonized, so to speak, Virginia's proud and selfish particularity with the personal universalism of New England Christianity. And so the Declaration goes beyond John Locke in its display of a people's political responsibility under God. Similarly, Abraham Lincoln's affirmation of our political Fathers' devotion to natural rights as an anti-slavery creed would have been, by itself, insufficient to end slavery in our country without the neo-Puritanical egalitarianism of the abolitionists. And Lincoln's dedication of a nation to the egalitarian proposition was meant to bring together what's best about the Puritans and what's best about Mr. Jefferson. The Civil War turned out to be victory for New England (and radical Republicans) over Virginia, a victory too temporary and incomplete, however, to free Southern particularity from its distortion by racism. But the good news is that it also failed to destroy what's good about Southern particularity. After the war, the aristocrats returned to power for a while, but they were displaced, even in their own minds, by manipulative, racist, populist demagogues who were, in turn, often manipulated by Northern oligarchs.

Walker Percy, in his remarkable "Stoicism in the South," describes the Stoic Southern mind of these aristocrats, the mind formed by devotion to the classical virtues of magnanimity and generosity, by being a member of a class distinguished by virtue both moral and intellectual, by knowing, as a result, who you are and what you're supposed to be as a free man responsible for yourself and others. A Stoic does right by others not out of love or charity, but so as not to compromise himself by being ungracious to others. The Southern Stoic, Percy claims in quite the Aristotelian fashion, displayed a kind of rare natural perfection in our hemisphere. Southern literature at its best is a critical account of the mind of the semi-dispossessed aristocrat. Faulkner and Walker Percy, for example, let us see the self-deception at the core of racist paternalism, as well as the neglect for the truth about natural rights taught by Jefferson. But they also let us see how empty middle-class life is from an aristocratic view, and how clueless those who so methodically devote themselves to the pursuit of happiness are about what human happiness is. True individualism, from this view, regards rights not as rooted in calculated interests but as points of honor to be exercised honorably.

Among the instances in which Southern Stoic virtue has elevated the American mind, the most obvious is Harper Lee's character Atticus (note the name) Finch in *To Kill a Mockingbird*. Atticus's virtue had nothing to do with Christian charity or the liberal understanding of rights. He was courageously and paternalistically taking magnanimous responsibility for those his society deemed inferior, for those who couldn't defend themselves against the vicious mob that threatened the rule of law in the decadent South. And then there are the Stoic characters of the novelist Tom Wolfe. There's one who becomes "a man in full" by reading Epictetus, and so knows what to do as a rational man completely isolated in a maximum security prison. There's also the star basketball player in *I Am Charlotte Simmons* who learns how to treat women and regains his manly self-confidence through absorbing—making his own—his professor's very Stoic reading of Aristotle.

In Wolfe's novels, the foundation of coming to live according to this version of natural perfection has nothing necessarily to do with being raised with Southern "class," but he shows us that, in the classically Southern version, becoming a member of the class of rational, responsible, relational men is a possibility available to us all. Wolfe, by reminding us that it's barely possible but highly countercultural to live as a natural aristocrat in our clueless and trashy time, when our institutions of higher education are the most clueless and most trashy parts of

American life, frames a narrative of American moral and intellectual decline. His nostalgia for the past is meant to be selective, and it's meant, of course, to inspire personal action in the present. The purely Southern mind, like all aristocratic narratives, is a reflection on our movement away from what was best about the past. It's a narrative of decline and fall from aristocracy to democratic vulgarity; it's strong on character and slights egalitarian justice. The Southern mind is anti-progressive or takes on claims about universal "History" through particular historical memories about great men and their flourishing in particular places.

Cash's *The Mind of the South* has often been read by Northern liberals as evidence of Southern gullibility and prejudice, as echoing the views of literary hero H. L. Mencken. And Cash does incisively present plenty of evidence along those lines. But his critical analysis is from a Southern and aristocratic perspective. Consider the wonderfully eloquent conclusion to his book, which is often viewed, with good reason, as the whole Southern mind in brief:

> Proud, brave, honorable by its lights, courteous, personally generous, loyal, swift to act, often too swift, but signally effective, sometimes terrible, in its action— such was the South at its best. And such at its best it remains today, despite the great falling away in some of its virtues. Violence, intolerance, aversion and suspicion toward new ideas, an incapacity for analysis, an inclination to act from feeling rather than from thought, an exaggerated individualism and a too narrow concept of social responsibility, attachment to fictions and false values, above all too great attachment to racial values and a tendency to justify cruelty and injustice in the name of those values, sentimentality and a lack of realism—these have been its characteristic vices in the past. And, despite changes for the better, they remain its characteristic vices today.

Cash agrees with Tocqueville that what distinguishes the temperament of the South has to do with the virtues and vices of any aristocracy. That means slighting the bourgeois virtues, which are realistic, unsentimental, averse to cruelty, just, and tolerant. The "exaggerated individualism" is what we see in the South in the absence of Stoic responsibility. But there's also something legitimately Puritanical in the just criticism of the Southern states, especially today, for not taking social or political responsibility—not taking good government—seriously enough. And the preference for feeling over thought, "the incapacity for analysis," is what you have in the absence of both aristocratic education and middle-class discipline. Cash is, however, wrong to think analysis and calculation are the whole of thought or spiritual life. So the newly prosperous South is in some ways an improved South, but not improved in every respect. And we can't forget, of course, that urban/suburban prosperity has been at the expense of what has always been good about the rural South.

Cash did follow Mencken, and Southern Stoics such as the poet William Alexander Percy, in having a very poor opinion of the uneducated individualism and raw emotion of Southern religion. It was, as Will Percy said, for "white trash" and for "Negroes" incapable of ruling themselves. Neo-Puritanical liberal Protestants justly criticize Southern fundamentalism's disconnection of religion from any sense of social responsibility. And the last Puritanical invasion of the South might be considered the Civil Rights movement, with Martin Luther King, Jr., for example, having been educated in a liberal understanding of the connection between Christianity and social justice. Cash doesn't try to do justice to Southern African American Christianity, and the place of churches and preachers in leading local communities.

The "Negro spiritual" always had the double meaning of longing for both spiritual and political salvation. Puritanical faith lost that double meaning over the years, and religion became associated with solely a sophisticated devotion to social justice. Lost was the "otherworldly" understanding of Christianity as being about the drama of salvation of particular souls. Liberal Protestantism became nothing more than a branch of progressivism, and a particularly condescending and imprudent one.

The exaggerated individualism and deep emotionalism of Southern religion has the advantage of focusing on the singular destiny of each of us. It's about personal, not political, salvation. The focus on a salvation that depends on faith and not works is a kind of self-obsession, one particularly repulsive to thoughtful and meritocratic Stoics. But it's one that has kept the focus on the particular connection between the personal creature and the personal Savior, and so it's an antidote to the kind of self-obsession that comes with believing that one's fate is solely in one's hands. It's also an antidote to materialistic self-obsession in emphasizing that the key personal quality is love or charity. Unlike the proudly particularistic Stoic, the Southern Christian believes that we're all uniquely and irreplaceably equal under God. And this belief is most fully lived out in the lowest of Southern churches, the holiness church and the Assembly of God (see the Robert Duvall film, *The Apostle*).

One answer to the Puritanical, or progressive, criticism of the South for being weak on public welfare is that it compensates personally by being strong on private charity. Southerners are often astoundingly indifferent to the quality of their public schools, but they lavish loving attention on "Sunday school" and increasingly on Christ-centered schooling at home. So the Southern mind is singularly alive to the personal truth of Christianity. It's home to the religion that Tocqueville hoped would be the foundation to our common morality and a brake on egalitarian hopes for what can be accomplished through social reform.

Thompson and Cash both assume that the progress of business and urban sophistication in the South will eventually mean the withering away of fundamentalist or evangelical belief. They're both biased by the certainty that no enlightened person could believe Christianity is literally true. Thompson predicts the "old fusion of evangelical religion and Southern culture" has about run its course, which is not a prediction that does justice to the way displaced persons find homes in suburban, untraditional, and aesthetically challenged mega-churches. Still she is right to add that one of the pathologies of the increasingly precarious existence of the lower middle class in the rural South is the disconnection of persons and broken families from "church homes." And she is right to question the effects of media-driven sophistication on the future of evangelical belief in general. Thompson does overlook the rather rapid growth in the membership of "orthodox" churches in the South— Catholics, Anglicans (or dissident Episcopalians) and even various "national" (for example, Russian) Orthodox churches.

For me, a key moment in the development of the Southern mind was Walker Percy's and Flannery O'Connor's discovery of a kind of American Thomism, through a combination of the Stoic criticism of middle-class materialism, and the Christian criticism of Stoicism (and partial affirmation of the justice of middle-class life). I'm in a position to see a good number of evangelicals experiencing basically intellectual conversions, based on the truth as they see it. This kind of conversion remains, of course, mostly a fairly elite phenomenon. Still, it's possible to see in the South some evidence to support Tocqueville's prediction that the Protestant, evangelical position is an unstable mixture of emotional individualism and personal authority, and so eventually most Americans will become either Catholics, or orthodox authoritarian high-theological in the mode of Catholics, or pantheists (see Ross Douthat's 2012 book *Bad Religion*).

Cash is especially good in seeing how the proud aristocratic manners and morals of the South were, in fact, remarkably democratized. Part of the Southern mind is the mixture of Stoicism, Protestantism, and liberty-loving, place-loving patriotism found in country music. The struggle of democratic gentlemen to have a real future is displayed in the TV classic *Friday Night Lights* and Jeff Nichols's remarkable film *Mud*. Add that the theme of the democratized—and post-racist and post-classist—Southern gentleman first surfaced in Charles Portis's classic Arkansan novel *True Grit*, and that democratization extended to women too, with the most uncannily clever, truthful, and courageous character being a girl. That struggle is being quite self-consciously carried on today by Texan Matthew McConnaughey in various roles. We can say that the deepest explorations of what's best about Southern virtue these days can be captured in the emerging discipline of "Texarkansan Studies." The most recent outstanding contribution to this exploration is surely Clint Eastwood's *American Sniper*.

I went with my wife to an afternoon showing of *American Sniper* in Rome, Georgia. We were very lucky get the last seats (and, for once, we were pretty early). At the film's end, everyone departed with the kind of hushed reverence that's higher praise than applause. It was a very Southern appreciation of the portrayal of the best of who we are. Bradley Cooper had spent meticulous months perfecting every mannerism of an ordinary "manly man" from Texas. He was so successful in nailing the accent and the "look" that most everyone in the South can say "I know that guy."

The film gives us the heroic, but, course, far from perfect—life of the protector, the American Platonic warrior/guardian. His father tells him there are three kind of people: sheep, wolves, and sheepdogs. And the sheepdog's purpose is to protect sheep from wolves. The warrior uses his natural aggressiveness, his personal strength (both physical and emotional), and his acquired skill to protect his own from those who would threaten them. The American Sniper's dedication is to "God, country, and family," but it extends readily to protecting his "brother" warriors in the Marine Corps.

The American Sniper is the "citizen-soldier" of country music, but he's not some one-dimensional Spartan or some relationally challenged misfit from one of Eastwood's earlier films. He smart and witty, never loses his head in battle, knows how to love, and has much of the Christian-Stoic heritage of manners and morals without the higher education, status, racism and other prejudices of a traditional Southern aristocrat. He is, in considerable measure, a natural aristocrat, although, of course no philosopher-king. The film reminds us that what Walker Percy called the comparatively honorable and violent South has always given us a disproportionate number of our warrior/protectors. Where we would be without them? It's easy to say that since the days of the Confederacy Southern men have been suckers serving questionable causes, but that would be the height of ingratitude. And God, country, family, and one's brother warriors aren't such questionable causes, even if the means—such as the misbegotten second Iraq War—chosen to defend them sometimes are.

It's very true that I've slighted the contribution of African Americans to the Southern mind. But it's not that different from the contribution of the Southern Stoic-Christian generally. The manners and morals of Southern African Americans have always been a highly reserved and deeply proud bulwark in defense of their dignity in the face of oppression. And it was the heroic virtue of the leaders of the Civil Rights movement—who combined classical courage with Christian love—that magnanimously saved the South from the "original sin" of slavery and every form of legalized racism. It was the fearful white moderate, who knew what was right but preferred order to justice, who had to be turned around to do what was right by the stunning nobility of those willing to risk everything to secure their natural and God-given freedom. According to Walker Percy, it was the success of the Civil Rights movement that "let the South off the hook," allowing Southern virtue to be displayed for what it is, when undeformed by injustice.

Chapter 14
Why Republicans Should Watch More TV

As I write this, Republicans are poised to take the semi-deserved brunt of public anger after the maddening fiscal cliff showdown, a further hit to a brand already tarnished by the 2012 election results. To all the political theorists, intellectuals, and social scientists cooking up strategies to revive the party, I say "watch more TV."

I don't mean, of course, the garish reality shows and talent competitions that increasingly dominate the airwaves. The best and most instructive shows are the various multi-year series on cable, which have benefited from technology that allows episodes to easily be viewed repeatedly and whole seasons in a condensed period. And, the distance between the "movie theater" and home viewing is narrowing all the time. The best of the TV shows are now on the whole superior even to many Oscar-winning films. Many of the best actresses and actors are now working in them.

Beyond their artistic value, these highly intelligent and savvy shows provide some of the most penetrating social and political commentary found today. Three of them in particular can guide reflection about the meaning of the 2012 election results: *Girls*, a comedy about the sex lives of Brooklyn's twenty-somethings, *Big Love*, which follows a beleaguered polygamist and his three wives, and *Friday Night Lights* (a show based on Buzz Bissinger's book of the same name), about an admirable coach and his noble players in a west Texas town with nothing much going for it but high-school football.

Why those three? Well, to begin with, the creator, star, and director of *Girls*, Lena Dunham, made a controversial campaign spot for the president. It was aimed at privileged single women, one that encouraged girls to have their first time (voting) with Obama. *Big Love* anticipated some of the dilemmas associated with the Mormon moment in American political life with Romney. And, Romney tried to appropriate some of the wholesome, robust small town virtues of *Friday Night Lights* when he deployed (and sort of mangled) Coach Eric Taylor's "Clear Eyes, Full Hearts, Can't Lose" slogan for his campaign.

That Lena Dunham commercial might have made a real contribution to enhancing the president's turnout, for all I know. Certainly, it was consistent with the Democratic convention's insistent appeal to women's rights, especially the rights of single women. But there's at least one irony: Dunham is a genuine defender of women's right to choose. Her characters, however, so rarely actually choose well. So, we conservatives are tempted to say we have no reason to believe their voting behavior is better than, for example, their sexual behavior.

The girls on *Girls*, mostly graduates of elite liberal arts schools, have no idea who they are and what they're supposed to do. Despite their privileged backgrounds, they have almost no manners and no morals. The Dunham character, Hannah Horvath, is the most confused of them all. She does manage to say thank you for the rare, ambiguous compliment that comes her way. But she's also just about never moved by generosity or charity or even ordinary self-restraint, and neither are the others. Hannah is a film studies major who didn't learn much in college (that's generally true of majors ending in "studies"); she comes to the big city to write, but she lacks the education, talent, and discipline. Like most of her friends, she has no marketable skills, no work ethic, and a rich sense of entitlement. So she sponges off her parents until they abruptly cut her off.

The quality of relational life on the show is often abysmal with the resulting visit to the abortion clinic, STDs, various pathetic hook-ups, and whiny pretend marriages. It turns out that these girls, like us all, want meaningful work and authentic love, but they have very little idea how to find them. We just know those girls would be happier if they could live for something greater than themselves, for some principle or family or their country or even God.

There are reasons for conservatives to recoil from or refuse to watch *Girls*. We could begin, of course, with the fact that we see way too much of Hannah way too often. From a merely artistic view, the show is oblivious to the sound principle that when it comes to nudity on screen, less is more. We could go on to get all indignant about other disgusting incidents so casually depicted. As Ross Douthat wrote, however, in "Daughters of the Revolution," the show's critique of contemporary (white, upper middle-class, New York) sexual mores is explicit rather than esoteric, in neon letters rather than between the lines. Things that are really revolting from a moral or relational point of view are portrayed quite negatively. And whether it's Dunham's intent, the show's message is that these girls *suffer* from lack of character, that they are, to a point, victims of an easygoing world of privilege that deprives them of the experiences that allow them to develop character. And if you want a basically conservative (or even libertarian) indictment of what passes for liberal education these days, watch *Girls*.

Dunham herself would reject the solution of returning to the repression of traditional religion and morality. But, true conservatives agree, after all, that we are unable to simply go back ever. And social scientists on both sides have to admire a show that so precisely defines social and relational problems while suggesting that there are no easy solutions.

The other HBO series, *Big Love*, is still relevant years after it ended. The show's central family of dissident Mormons grapples with the challenges of polygamy in the age of feminist egalitarianism. We learn how hard polygamy is on the husband (each wife has her own house!) if his wives really expect equal treatment. We see him popping Viagra desperately, because it's really not possible by nature to love all your wives equally all the time. We also see him having to sneak around for a while with his first wife at the expense of the others as if it were an affair. We also wonder whether polygamy, in his case, flows from his authentically interpreted religious principle or from his weakness for younger women. It's strange to see wives accepting the fact that their husband is dating again. And we're shown that a downside of polygamy is that your oldest son might become almost fatally attracted to your youngest wife. Said son can also get dumped by a very promising girlfriend when he tells her she'll only be his first wife. The more prudent approach, followed by his dad, is to break the news to her well after they're married.

On the other hand, there's no denying how much this family's father is willing to sacrifice to keep everyone together, more than any of his more ambivalent or relatively self-obsessed wives, and he thinks of his family in terms of eternity. *Big Love* is about a new kind of polygamy far different from the sinister form that put Warren Jeffs on trial struggling to emerge from the shadows and gain acceptance. *Big Love*'s Bill is a good guy and a respected community leader with a problem with the law we're led to think he doesn't deserve to have.

Not incidentally, the creators of *Big Love* are gay and interested in promoting the cause of same-sex marriage. The pathologies connected with being gay and being a polygamist both come, they suggest, from the shame of being in the closet. The kids struggle pretty desperately on *Big Love*, but maybe they wouldn't if their loving family could live loudly and proudly in the open. The show presents homosexual Mormons also stuck with denying or hiding the truth about themselves, and even being driven to suicide.

Big Love was a politically cutting-edge show in suggesting that marriage ought to include homosexual couples as well as polygamous groups. In the late nineteenth century the Republican Party forced Utah and so the Mormon Church to abandon polygamy as a condition for becoming a state. The Supreme Court, in an opinion that arguably allowed Christian religious prejudice to trump the Mormons' free exercise of religion, an opinion that has no value as a precedent today, refused to intervene. The nineteenth-century Republicans understood polygamy to be a relic of barbarism. This does not answer the question "what about genuinely consensual and richly feminist polygamy, a kind of polygamy compatible with the wives' autonomy and fulfillment?" Once we've accepted two moms, why not three?

Big Love seems, at first, ineffective as propaganda for same-sex marriage. Opponents often argue that if same-sex marriage is a right, then so is polygamous marriage. Most proponents assure us that there's no such slippery slope from one to the other, largely because support for their cause would dwindle if the prospect of polygamy was a real issue. But the show's creators, by identifying marriage equality as including the highly relational, genuinely religious, sophisticated, prosperous, fecund, and self-sacrificing polygamists, insist that in our time marriage can take many forms. To revise the public understanding of marriage is not to empty the institution of significance or responsibility.

Big Love was also cutting-edge in evoking the deep suspicions many Americans have about the incompatibility between Mormon life and our increasingly libertarian idea of personal freedom. The public response to the show's characters may point to why Romney's Mormonism made his electoral challenge somewhat more difficult. He has been quite a successful businessman but also a devoted father, leader of his church, and exceptionally charitable and generous with his time. But he thought being a Mormon limited how much he could dare show us who he is.

Most Americans, it goes without saying, are repulsed by the unproductive, narcissistic, and amorally extended adolescence of the girls on *Girls*. So, as the Obama campaign pandered to that show's demographic, the Romney campaign, now and again, countered by identifying itself with a more edifying cable series, *Friday Night Lights*. (*FNL* actually began as network show and remained comparatively restrained but not unrealistically prudish in its use of language, sexual situations, and so forth when it was forced to migrate to cable and back again to the network.) Taking place in West Texas, the show espouses a very Southern understanding of what's important about life: family, hometown roots, a worthwhile vocation, gritty virtue, and God.

Friday Night Lights centers on the team's coach Eric Taylor who is an altogether admirable and talented leader of men. For the young athletes schooled by his leadership, a key formative experience of their lives—in some cases, the only great experience of their lives—will be how they perform as part of the team. And, the team is, of course, in many ways, the heart of the town. They are the *Panthers*, the only thing that genuinely invigorates the often disappointing and dreary lives of most of the town's citizens.

Romney sometimes psyched up his crowds with a spin on the inspirational words with which Coach Taylor concludes each of his pre-game talks: "Clear Eyes, Full Hearts, Can't Lose." There's nothing pious about the coach's words—they're the code of the warrior, the Southern Stoic, the classical man of moral virtue. The coach, of course, respects religion and sometimes joins his players in prayer, but that's what any gentleman would do. Coach Taylor is a "natural aristocrat" and so almost completely free of conventional prejudices of race, class, and gender; his character and talents, we learn in the final show, would be recognized anywhere. The same is true of his remarkable wife Tammy, whom the coach recognizes as his equal in every crucial way.

One sign of Romney's tone-deafness is the way he changed Coach Taylor's words: "Clear Eyes, Full Hearts, America Can't Lose." Not only is the cadence of the original screwed up, but Romney never called for Americans to sacrifice for their team as citizens. Worse, he seemed ignorant of the significance of what the coach says and does, the ways his example might actually inspire most Americans. He probably never even saw the show, but it's not too late for other Republicans to gain some wisdom from it to help secure future victories.

Friday Night Lights, like *Girls*, is about how hard it is to find meaningful work and love these days in our country, but it focuses on a quite different, more economically and educationally unfortunate, and arguably more compelling demographic. Shrinking small-town America, and the sinking lower-middle class, we learn from Charles Murray's book *Coming Apart*, are viewed with a mixture of indifference and condescension by our increasingly libertarian meritocratic elite. Romney seemed sometimes to share that condescension, particularly with his notorious comment that his job is not to worry about the 47% of Americans who don't pay taxes. From the point of view of *FNL*'s small town Dillon, Texas, both political parties are too oligarchic, equally remote from the town's economic and cultural concerns, particularly those related to family life.

Much of the show is about very disadvantaged players often heroically struggling to improve their dysfunctional families, most of which are fatherless in some way. They know far better than the grown-up kids of *Girls* that familial responsibility is the foundation of a good life, no matter how much the ideal eludes them. Consider the artistic, underdog quarterback Matt Saracen, with an estranged mother and a father in Iraq, knocking himself out to care all alone for his grandmother with Alzheimer's. Or the two Riggins brothers, also without parents, seeing each other through life's trials despite their frequent flare-ups. Tim Riggins even serves what ought to have been his brother's prison term so that his nephew can have what they didn't, a father.

The point of these narratives is that the so-called 47% is hardly wallowing contentedly in the thrall of government dependency; we are not a nation divided into makers and takers, as some have put it.

Friday Night Lights is all about real men and women living admirably and having to struggle much harder than they should to sustain meaningful work and stable families. If these young men are nonetheless better off than their counterparts on *Girls* in some crucial ways, it's partly because they have been slapped pretty hard by the adversity that builds character. And thanks to football, a strong and persistent Southern sense of family, and, yes, even religion, they have been, despite it all, better raised.

In its present disarray, Republicans should be looking for a leader who is clear-eyed about the threats to a dignified life shaped by love, work and community portrayed in both *Girls* and in *Friday Night Lights*. That means the Republicans have to become less oligarchic and less libertarian and more genuinely meritocratic than they have been in recent years. They have to somehow become less callous and condescending and speak in terms of magnanimity, the significance of families, and the dignity of real work. The Romney campaign, after all, was all about entrepreneurs and "job creators," not the dignity of worthwhile work well done or why meaningful work matters to most people. The party's leadership should have a proper appreciation of the virtue and aspirations of ordinary Americans in the increasingly vulnerable middle class.

If you think about it, the conservative impulse in our country is to counter threats to middle-class virtue. That means opposing the degraded and clueless thought and behavior displayed on *Girls*. And it means opposing government programs that undermine personal responsibility. Those programs don't include our relatively minimal entitlements such as Social Security and Medicare that function to hold families together. There's a theory, traced usually to the distinguished sociologist Gunnar Myrdal, that the welfare state would keep individuals from either having children or caring for the elderly, because they could afford to live well on the government's dime without those entanglements. But Social Security hardly pays the elderly enough to fend well all alone, and it more often helps to allow children to stay connected with the old and frail parents.

Until very recently, the main cause of our birth dearth was low fertility among those who don't need or benefit that much from government programs. Most of the young people represented by *Friday Night Lights* are very open to kids, and some of them are having them very young. If you want to find lots of kids in our country, hang out with small-town members of the lower (or at least not upper) middle class. There's evidence that the birth dearth has spread in the direction of even that portion of the middle class in the last few years, probably because of their rapidly deteriorating economic condition, which also means fewer children have the benefit of married parents. If that's so, the remedy isn't, of course, condescending welfare or make-work programs. It is, in part, the return to prosperity promised by Republican deregulatory and supply side economic reforms, but it's also, in part, programs aimed at supporting the relational dignity of struggling parents.

Chapter 15
Tocqueville and Keeping
Our Countercultural Churches

To begin with a simple point, one basic insight of Alexis de Tocqueville is that things are always getting better and worse. And so it would hardly be surprising that Tocqueville could be used to defend the advantages of religious establishment. He, more generally, is unrivaled in arousing a kind of selective nostalgia that helps us remember the advantages of aristocracy. He says, in *Democracy in America*'s conclusion, that aristocracy is better in cultivating great individuality, and, as a partisan of greatness himself, he's chilled when he thinks about how little room there will be for men such as himself in a democracy. Democracy, however, is more just. Tocqueville takes the Creator's view, and not his own, by preferring democratic justice to aristocratic greatness. His tasks are to make democracy as compatible with greatness as possible and to see greatness in democracy.

Tocqueville says modern democracy is, in fact, Christian in inspiration. What Aristotle and Plato taught was, in the crucial respect, untrue:

> The most profound and vast geniuses of Rome and Greece were never able to arrive at the idea, so general but at the same time so simple, of the similarity of men and of the equal right of freedom that each bears from birth; and they did the utmost to prove that slavery was natural and would always exist . . .
>
> All the great writers of antiquity were part of the aristocracy of masters, . . . and it was necessary that Jesus Christ come to earth to make it understood that all members of the human species are naturally alike and equal.

There's a lot here opposed to the Aristotelian idea that it's the function of the state (or city) to inculcate a higher or spiritual and aristocratic understanding of moral virtue in people. The classical view was that all human beings—except perhaps the rare philosopher—are stuck in the natural slavery of the "cave" or the political order. But the truth taught by Jesus—the truth about persons—is that all creatures made in God's image have "the equal right of freedom" from some comprehensive civil theology or even from some established or politicized church.

Tocqueville almost begins *Democracy in America* with a judicious appraisal of a Christian heresy that was the basis of the first American founding. The Puritans, he explained, were educated political idealists who founded a real and unprecedented democratic country that was less distorted by political prejudice than even Plato's city in speech. They were all about egalitarian political participation and the education of everyone as beings with souls. Their egalitarian idealism was admirable and remains an indispensable feature in elevating our democracy above individualistic self-concern. But the Puritans erred by criminalizing every sin, using Exodus, Leviticus, and Deuteronomy as the foundation for civil legislation, and for intrusively offending the right to freedom of conscience. There's nothing about the teaching of Jesus, Tocqueville claims, that could justify making political life that comprehensive for religious reasons.

Not only that, religion can be effective in America only insofar as it stands apart from the general tendency of democratic development. The Americans, Tocqueville explains, are Cartesians without ever having read a word of Descartes. That's because the democratic method is grounded in the same principle as the Cartesian one—"doubt." It's the doubt of personal authority that frees the democratic mind for self-determination. It's an offense against my egalitarian freedom to allow priests, parents, politicians, and so forth to rule me by privileging what they think. But the problem with this assertion of personal pride is that it points in a direction of a more overwhelming personal weakness. It's true that no one is better than me, but I'm no better than anyone else. That means I have no point of view by which to resist public opinion or the other impersonal forces, such as pop science, history, technology, and so forth that surround me. So American freedom leads, finally, to the apathetic passivity of what Tocqueville calls the heart disease of individualism, of being emotionally locked up in the tiny world of one's puny individual self.

But the Americans, Tocqueville reports, exempt religion from their habitual doubt. Their view is that they need some dogma to exercise their political freedom well, to have the confidence to think and act well. That creates space for religion to perpetuate what's true about aristocracy. Human beings are distinguished by their souls, and each of us by taking his or her immortal personal moral destiny seriously. That's what Americans, Tocqueville reports, hear in church on Sunday. It was in Tocqueville's time as it is in ours that the observantly religious Americans have a countercultural confidence that insulates them from democracy's degrading excesses. It's our religiously observant Americans, after all, who can extend their hearts enough to have babies enough that the global "birth dearth" displays itself much more gently in our country.

The democratic truth is that we're all created equal, but truth, by itself, easily morphs into apathetic passivity and material self-indulgence. The aristocratic truth is that to be human is to have a singular greatness (and misery) not shared with the other animals. The Christian truth is that all men were equally created to display the greatness of unique and irreplaceable individuality, and part of that greatness is the truth about who we are that we can joyfully and responsibly share in common. The danger in democracy is that Christian churches lose their capacity to be genuinely countercultural, or teach the truth that will be neglected "on the street" in middle-class democracy. And so the separation of church and state is to keep the church from being corrupted by excessive concern with endlessly egalitarian justice and the logic of the market. The separation benefits the integrity of the church by limiting the claims for truth and morality of the democratic "social state," which includes the democratic political state.

So it's both futile and even un-Christian to think that there could be, in the modern world, a state that favors or properly appreciates the church. Orestes Brownson, the greatest American Catholic thinker ever, said all the church should need and want from America is freedom to pursue its evangelical mission. That means, of course, that Americans should understand political freedom to be freedom for the church, for an organized body of thought and action. And we can see that the church flourished in America in the relative absence of politicized intrusion or corruption for a very long time.

The danger now, as always, is that the individualistic yet highly judgmental democracy, our creeping and creepy mixture of progressivism and libertarianism, will seek to impose its standards on our countercultural churches. Tocqueville was aware, although maybe not aware enough, of that danger. Who can deny that the danger is greater now than ever? Today's issues, Tocqueville would probably say, have their origins in the surrender of our contemplative Sundays to commerce and "seventh-day recreationalists."

But anyone who thinks today's remedy would be an established church would do well to remember how the establishments in Spain, Ireland, and Quebec worked out, and especially about the hyper-secularist and sometimes nihilistic counter-movements in the name of democracy they generated. Those attempts to wield fundamental political influence produced clericalism and a kind of intrusiveness we Americans associate with the Puritans. The film *Philomena* is distorted by a kind of fanatical anti-Catholic ire, but peel away that unfairly self-righteous anger and we still see evidence of a Puritanical Irish church and society not particularly solicitous of the equal rights of persons—including mothers, wed or unwed—to liberty.

Chapter 16
Honor, Love, and Being a Father in Full

The first thing to be noticed is that Father's Day was an afterthought. Mother's Day came first. Maybe the thought was that mothers needed a day, because it's so easy to forget how much we owe to what mothers as mothers do. Such special days we usually reserve for saints and heroes, to those who have done great deeds and displayed heroic virtue. And not so long ago most of that honor was given to men. But, in fact, nobody's deeds and virtues have been more important to me than those of my mother. Mother's Day isn't for mothers in general. It's for my mother. Surely Father's Day must be viewed in the same relational, highly particularistic spirit. George Washington, the father of our country, hasn't really done as much for me as my father, the man who raised me. Everyone owes George Washington a debt of gratitude, but most everyone owes more to his or her dad, who usually didn't do much of anything for more than 99% of all Americans.

Fatherhood, of course, seems to have fallen on hard times. There's many an expert calling upon us to remember the Fathers. As far as I can tell, most of that effort is directed toward men. Men, don't forget that you're happier when you become and act like a father, and don't forget that women and children still really need you, despite some evidence to the contrary. Studies still show that women, and especially mothers really benefit from a good, reliable husband, but it's not that tough for a woman these days to live without such a man if she must. Studies also show that men live longer and are altogether less screwed up if they have any wife, good or not. And most of them need to be a real father just as much, whether they realize it or not. One of the most alarming statistics I know about is the skyrocketing number of men over 65 who are unmarried and without any real connection to children or any other members of their family. Talk about loneliness! Talk about wards of the state once that dementia or some other form of debilitation kicks in! Our health care system is semi-affordable only because of the still huge amount of voluntary caregiving by women to those they love.

What about lonely old single women? The problem just isn't as big. Divorced and widowed women are considerably more likely to remain close to the kids than comparable men. And women, let's tell the truth, are just more relational, more able to make close friends at all points in life, than men. Now it's true that old women have a tougher time finding a new husband or a new sexual companion than old men. But they're typically more honest with themselves about who they are and what they need to live well. My "takeaway" from reading Tocqueville on the family for the first time decades ago was all about how unerotic and vainly individualistic American men are in comparison to American women. And even the American women Tocqueville described aren't as pleasingly erotic as they might have been. They have to spend so much time calculating about how to manipulate men to help them make a relational home.

It's American women, Tocqueville explained, who make American freedom the source of a new and in some ways fairly unprecedented practice of the virtue of chastity. Aristocratic and many traditional marriages were typically arranged for reasons having little to do with erotic love. That means it was hard to blame married men, at least, for giving in to the call of nature and fooling around. But in a democracy, the good news is that you're free to marry whom you please; the institution of marriage has been largely detached from issues of property. American men pretty much calculate, usually badly, about how best to get to have sex, and the American woman about locating sex within marriage. So she tells the man who proclaims his love that they can marry, and that, of course, she's not about to lose her mind to a man whose words of love are just words. So, for his own good as well as her own, she directs his eros in its properly enduring and relational direction. She guards chastity, gratefully accepting the help of religion, as the foundation of democratic marriage and family. There is a close connection between the decline in chastity and decline in men thinking of themselves as responsible fathers, which should surely be clearer to today's women than it is.

veryone knows when a woman "hook ups" or "moves in" with a man she's much more likely than the man to be thinking in a family way. She appears not to be calculating as well as she used to about the best means to achieve that end.

Contraception, of course, has complicated the female calculus, liberating her in a way for both sexual enjoyment and from the necessity of motherhood. The problem is, it has liberated men in much the same way. Contraception works against the connections between love and marriage and parenthood that democracy seems to have solidified and has apparently weakened to the point of near-impotence the American woman's defense of chastity.

It shouldn't be surprising that in a democracy in particular the experience of fatherhood requires the active assistance of women. In aristocracies, fatherhood was properly patriarchal; it was a political institution. The father proudly commanded the family, and his children and often even his wife lived in a rather reserved distance from him. The authority of the father was uncontested, and his honor wasn't narrowly parental. The aristocratic family, obviously, was good for social order, but, Tocqueville adds, it wasn't so good for paternal love.

Tocqueville highlights the new birth of love of father and son in a democracy. They're stuck in the same small house, and there aren't any emotional barriers to get in the way of natural affection. And so father and son move closer and closer to a bromance, the "I love you man" of relationships. We see in our time that the last remaining barrier to a father's love, the idea of the division of labor between parents, has largely crumbled. And, of course, we now, for better and worse, educate girls, even at home, pretty much the way we educate boys. Since the time of Tocqueville, fathers have grown closer to their daughters too.

Before we criticize our democracy too much, we have to look around and see contradictory trends: more deadbeat dads, more single moms, but more loving fathers sharing, not quite, of course, equally, in the joys of the daily duties of parenting. Studies show that men and women who are actually married with children today don't feel all that trapped or oppressed, have found ways to share in some way or another the duties of both economic productivity and lovingly caring for the kids, and are generally the happiest of Americans. I could go on and note some other new trends, including the high-tech breakthroughs that have made it easier to work from home, to be both a productive and a stay-at-home dad (or mom). It's also easier, of course, to school from home. For many Americans, it's not a huge challenge to choose to be a father in full these days, especially for observant members of relatively orthodox churches.

There's undeniably an increasingly pronounced class division here. Even without religious support, something like the traditional family is making a comeback among our rich and sophisticated "cognitive elite." Those elitists talk "do your own thing" as if they were still in the 1960s, but act more like the nuclear family of the 1950s. Meanwhile, the lower part of our middle class continues to talk "traditional values," while not having the wherewithal to live them. There's the scarcity of decent jobs, the disappearance of the "family wage" with the collapse of unions and employee and employer loyalty, and the detachment from the support of churches. For both economic and more broadly cultural reasons, the relational lives of most of our bottom 50% are getting more pathological.

Still, I'm sticking with the generalization that these aren't bad times at all for fathers, for married men with children. And traveling in prosperous, highly educated, and religious circles in the South, I sure see a lot of admirable and "self-fulfilled" fathers, who are often closer to their kids than their fathers were to them. One problem for men, however, is fewer of them are thinking of themselves as fathers. It's often been noted that the one relational tie that can't be deconstructed by democratic individualism is the tie of mother to child, whereas the tie of the father to child is much more vulnerable. So the family form that's surely more prominent now than ever is the single mom with a single kid.

The burden, in general, of being raised by single moms or in homes with deadbeat dads seems to fall harder on boys. Girls raised by single moms end up pregnant out of wedlock more often, but boys without a responsible father as a role model fare even worse. Consider that the decline of the experience of fatherhood goes a long way to explaining why men are disappearing from our colleges, and why our professions are slowly but surely becoming dominated by women. Young men are thinking less about preparing themselves for marriage and the family; their adolescence is extending further and further. Women think they can no longer do what's required to make men reliable husbands and fathers. And so they act accordingly. I often ask my class what a woman should be called who can't earn her own living, who says she'll depend on her husband for support. The answer, of course: a fool. That's not to say there aren't steadfast fathers. It's just that it's a mistake to bet one's life on one.

The trouble is, of course, that too many Americans believe that being free means regarding all the relational encumbrances of life that flow from love as "lifestyle options." Women have been taught by the Supreme Court that they're free to define the mystery of their personal identity as they please, and that's one reason, to be sure, for our birth dearth. But women actually believe that less than men. And mothers, surely, almost never.

So the decay of institutional support for relational life, based in some large part in the sophisticated acceptance of anti-relational or "autonomous" ideologies, gives men the sexual liberation they often think they want but also personal liberation that disorients and debilitates them. Remember what distinguishes the experience of being a mom from being a dad, maternity and paternity. The child is never part of the body of the father; his contribution to the new life is momentary and even forgettable. Motherhood is a more natural experience. Fatherhood is much more a matter of choice and acceptance, a choice to be who you really are as a free and relational being. A woman can't not acknowledge her child as hers (well, let's skip over abortion here); fatherhood is more an act of relational liberty, a free act of love. It's easier by far not to be a father than not to be a mother, and it's easier to mix fatherhood up with all sorts of considerations that don't have much to do with love of a particular child. That's why men need lots of help they can't provide for themselves to be who they should be as relational beings.

Men, including but not only biological "fathers," have to be lovingly taught with both words and deeds that it's good for them to be fathers in full. And we sometimes have to be reminded of the Biblical breakthrough that demands that fathers and mothers be honored equally. When fatherhood was "patriarchal" or a lot bigger deal than taking loving responsibility for a particular child, fathers were honored too much. In a high-tech, non-relational time, fathers almost seem superfluous, and the cultivation of fatherhood is too often no longer worth the mother's time and trouble. Fathers these days—consider how they're portrayed in popular culture from the *Simpsons* to *Mad Men*—aren't honored enough. Men, because they don't really think of themselves as fathers, are too often not acting honorably at all. The personal, Christian contribution, one based on the Biblical commandment, was to replace "paternal" with "parental" authority, equal authority and honor for both the man and the woman who assume loving responsibility for the care of their children. That fatherhood is not as "biological" as motherhood might be understood as an advantage for our time, when single men should come to see (be led to see) it's good for them to assume loving shared responsibility in marriage for the children of all those single moms.

Chapter 17
Atticus Finch's American Stoicism

It's hard not to think of the printing of two million copies of Harper Lee's "new book" as a capitalist macroaggression against America. Many readers consider it a sequel, although it's really a rough, and in some ways, misbegotten draft of *To Kill a Mockingbird*, the work that stands as the one and only account of heroic virtue shared by all Americans. When I go to my college classes, I (fake) struggle to find a piece of cultural literacy that all of us in the classroom share. The result is always the same.

Given the place that this 1960 book—allied with its 1962 movie version—has assumed in our country, we should defer to Ms. Lee's decision about how to think of Atticus Finch. It's telling, after all, that she never reworked the draft for publication. On her agenda of possible future novels, we know from a letter, was one "laying into" her home of Monroeville, Alabama in 1958—when the anti-integrationist fanaticism in which her father (A. C. Lee) and her town participated would have been at its height. But she never wrote that novel (or any other). She did well to let Atticus be who he had become.

That's not to say the portrayal of anti-integrationist Atticus in the 1950s contradicts the one we know so well from the time of the Great Depression, a noble defender of the rule of law against the racist mob. At a conference on the Southern novelist Walker Percy just over a month ago, I predicted that the Atticus of the "sequel" would likely be an anti-integrationist. Percy, taking note of the character's classical name, described Atticus as the most celebrated of the Southern Stoics. The Louisianan writer had learned from the man who'd raised him—the philosopher-poet William Alexander Percy, author of *Lanterns on the Levee*, that the leaders of the South, antebellum and post-bellum, considered themselves disciples of the Greek and Roman philosophers.

Tending to favor in particular the Stoic Marcus Aurelius (the philosopher-emperor) and Epictetus, they thought of themselves as members of a ruling class of rational men, a class that included the best men of the South—and the best of men across time and space. According to Will Percy, Pericles and Robert E. Lee would have recognized each other as kindred spirits.

Privileges coming from nature and social place are accompanied by responsibilities. And those responsibilities are fulfilled through the practice of the high virtues by men of means, magnanimity and generosity. Upholding one's responsibilities presupposes courage, moreover, or rising above fearful materialistic calculation. Will Percy, pretty much like Harper Lee's Atticus, stared down a racist lynch mob attempting to take the law into its own hands. And again like Atticus, he thought of himself as using what he had been given to elevate the community for which he had assumed responsibility. The motivation of these Stoics was fulfilling one's duty to be an unflinching rational fortress of virtue. As Atticus told Scout, "before I can live with other folks, I have to live with myself." Those Stoics knew, and know, who they are and what they're supposed to do. They think of themselves as always acting accordingly, even at the cost of deep loneliness or death.

Will Percy was, like Atticus Finch, a lawyer. The character and the man defended the form of the law, and the protection it afforded all men and women, against the irrational animosity that sometimes rouses up ordinary people in a democracy. They showed us that Alexis de Tocqueville was right in saying that lawyers are—at least sometimes—to be cherished as the closest thing we have in America to an aristocracy, a class rationally and temperamentally attached to a standard higher than mere popular inclinations. Their standard is not sectional but matches that of their country. It is the principle that all men are equal before the law.

Now, your Southern Stoics aren't aristocrats because they are lawyers. Often they are lawyers because they are aristocrats. Their honorable manners and morals in fact originated in the Southern aristocracy based on race-based slavery. In thinking about that complication, we return to the astute and balanced observation of the Frenchman who visited in the 1830s. Tocqueville saw the Southern masters as having the virtues and vices characteristic of any aristocracy, and it's those virtues that will always merit our attention as qualities lacking and still much needed in our largely middle-class country.

Those virtues persisted and became less ambiguously noble with the disappearance of slavery. Not only that, as we see in so much of Southern literature, those virtues became part of the consciousness of being a "dispossessed aristocrat." The Southern literary imagination before the war, Walker Percy explains, was consumed by defending slavery. After the war, it became both critical and appreciative of the display of the distinctively Southern ways of life, as formed and deformed by the "original sin" of slavery.

Atticus, despite being a local political leader and man of breeding and learning, doesn't have much money or property at all. Most of his daily rounds and his personal associations are pretty democratic or ordinarily middle class. Still he defines himself against what's "common" in terms of the classical moral virtues of the Greeks and Romans. And so his community recognizes him as a ruling class of one by returning him to the legislature time and again without question or opposition.

Harper Lee's classic book and especially its movie version teach us about the cruel and ignorant vulgarity of racism. She engenders not just contempt but also some pity for the low-grade "white trash" characters who live in the thrall of cruel and ignorant illusions about African Americans. *To Kill a Mockingbird*, however, is mostly a tale of a magnanimous man, of a man whose virtue can only be seen in full when it is required to try to save a wrongly accused man and to arouse his community to a sense of duty that might protect the people from themselves. More than trying to save a particular man, he tries to save the truth and virtue on which the fictional Maycomb's civilization depends. It's also a tale of a very lonely man—a widower whose companionship is his children and his books, the delight in which he shares with Scout every night—who has the class not to whine that most of those in his life are beneath him.

In his essay "Stoicism in the South," Walker Percy writes that these Stoics were a genuine manifestation of a kind of natural human excellence right here in our country. They were, he adds, only secondarily Christian. This is true of Will Percy and Atticus, who make mention of the virtues of Jesus only when they overlap with those of the philosopher-emperor. They and their children attended church (for Atticus, the Methodist church) and worshipped God with their local community. But they did not seem to pray. As Scout observes about Atticus, he "liked to be by himself in church."

Percy wrote his essay to explain the failure of Southern leadership to respond responsibly to the challenges of getting rid of segregation in the wake of *Brown v. Board of Education*. They, for a while, joined the vulgarly racists populists in resisting integration as an imposition from outside that challenged the established social order. The Stoics heroically defended the black person who could not defend himself—but did so paternalistically. What they could not bear was the "insolence" by which blacks came to demand that their rights be protected by a legal transformation that had nothing to do with Stoic virtue. What the Southern Stoics lacked, Percy claimed, was belief in the truthful insights of Christians about the equality of all men under God and the loving virtue of charity.

As Tocqueville said, a failing of aristocracies in general is the complacent expectation that things will always be about the same as they are now, and that slavery or inegalitarian servitude of some kind will always be with us. So the Southern Stoics, partly in their misplaced magnanimity or proud self-admiration, missed the justice in the Civil Rights movement's clamor for liberation. And, for a while, they didn't choose the rule of law over irrational populist inclination, the kind expressed at the meetings of the White Citizens Council that the Atticus of *Watchman* justifies as the extremism that curbs the extremists on the other side.

For any student of Walker Percy and Southern Stoicism, it shouldn't be surprising that Atticus was a magnanimous defender of the black person's rights under the law in the 1930s and yet endorsed illegal responses to the defense of that person's rights in the 1950s. All this might be a teachable moment in the greatness and limitations of aristocratic leadership. It might also stimulate thought on the place of classical philosophy in America, as well as the relationships between pagan and Christian virtue and coming to terms with the truthful claims of both magnanimity and justice.

That conclusion, however, depends on the assumption that the Atticus of the two books is really the same person. Both are written by one author. But *Go Set a Watchman* was discarded by the author, at the suggestion of her editor. The draft was written in the third person, but it is basically from the point of view of Jean Louise Finch returning to her hometown after spending years in New York as an artist. So it's a pretty standard story of a sophisticated young woman in rebellion against the provincialism and narrow-mindedness of the people she grew up with, beginning with her formerly idolized father.

The editor's suggestion was to rewrite the book from the point of view of a strikingly perceptive little girl who loves and admires her dad above all. That, of course, places the time of the book back when he was at his best. It was a shift that transformed *To Kill a Mockingbird* into a children's book (or what today is called "young adult fiction"), and the South's most penetrating writer, Flannery O'Connor, famously dissed it as such. But it's one hell of a children's book. The author took on the responsibility of thinking through what children should know about the virtue of a great man. It also means that any criticisms of the Stoic lawyer that creep in (and some do) have to be subtly indirect.

For Atticus, if you think about it, falls short of perfection. While he is to be admired for defying local convention in defending an African American man against the accusations of whites, maybe he goes too far. He is way too hard on the poor white woman who alleges rape and her family who lie to save their dignity. The poor whites are reduced to animalistic stereotype by Atticus's formidable rhetorical skill; a skill that didn't even seem to be aimed at winning an acquittal from a random selection of ordinary white men, who didn't want to think of any white as worthy of pity—as inferiors—in a relationship with African Americans. Atticus makes them seem much worse than they really are, as he acknowledges privately elsewhere.

Now Atticus does tell his son Jem that whenever a white man cheats a black man, "no matter who he is, how rich he is, or how fine a family he comes from, that white man is trash . . . . There's nothing more sickening to me than a low-grade white man who'll take advantage of a Negro's ignorance." The standard of being low-grade trash is all about behavior regardless of social circumstances, and so it's not the case that all poor whites are trash. And he speaks to the jurors as if they are better than trash. But the overwhelming impression is the identification of trashiness with poverty, just as the general impression is that poor

African Americans are innocently ignorant—easy to cheat—and so need to be protected from trashy white men who take advantage of them.

Here we see why even the Atticus of *To Kill a Mockingbird* would not look forward to a world in which African Americans would no longer need the protection of men such as himself because they could deal with trashy, low-grade whites on their own. It's one thing to acknowledge that African Americans have equal rights under the law, it's another to see them asserting them on their own.

And one piece of evidence that the lawyer believes that his client, Tom, is less than who he really is, is that Atticus too readily identifies Tom's plight with that of Boo Radley, a man deserving of being excused from the rule of law. That's somewhat condescending. But as Walker Percy remarks about the man who raised him, the somewhat condescending concerns that move the magnanimous man are better than the lack of concern for others' well-being that characterizes our apathetic individualists these days.

There's no way children would notice Atticus's shortcomings. Far more important that they come to see how wrong it is when people put their selfish desires and reputation before truth and justice. And, through the eyes of Scout, Atticus actually morphs into a better man than Ms. Lee originally imagined A. C. Lee to be.

The film, an emotionally intelligent adaptation by the great Horton Foote, is arguably more insistently edifying than the book. It's less about the day-to-day details of small town life and focuses more on the drama of the trial. Unfortunately, but perhaps necessarily, it truncates Atticus's closing argument before the jury, removing his marvelously precise account of what equality before the law is not, and also leaves out his invocation of Thomas Jefferson, who "once said all men are created equal."

We all know where Mr. Jefferson said that, and so there's no need for Atticus to mention the place. Atticus does say that "certain people use that phrase out of context," mentioning "Yankees and the distaff side of the Executive branch in Washington." And other people misuse it to justify the promotion of "the idle and stupid along with the industrious." Those "educators will gravely tell you" that "because all men are created equal . . . the children left behind suffer terrible feelings of inferiority." It almost seems an anachronistic reference to *Brown*—at the time, a six-year-old decision—that roots racial inequality in feelings of inferiority. But what Harper Lee's character means is that, contrary to the Yankees' humanitarian social science, some people ought to feel inferior.

Atticus's general message is that pity, although sometimes a truthful emotion, often blinds us to the truth associated with justice. It's not even against Jefferson's principle, he goes on, to acknowledge that "some people have more opportunity because they're born with it," as Atticus himself was, as long as they use it well. It's just a fact that "some people are born gifted beyond the normal scope of men," and that's not the business of the government.

It takes a man of aristocratic character, you might say, to be able to speak so eloquently to Americans about what equality is not, although there's not a word Atticus says with which Mr. Lincoln would have disagreed. The Stoic and the Republican are equally against the promiscuous levelling of the Progressives' welfare state.

For Atticus, "there is one human institution that makes the pauper the equal of a Rockefeller, the stupid man the equal of an Einstein, and an ignorant man equal of any college president. That institution . . . is a court." It's the courts that "are the great levelers, and it's in our courts that all men are created equal." All men are equal before the law, which means they aren't equal—and shouldn't be regarded so—in most of the arenas of life. The leveling that is the law has nothing to do with natural differences or personal gifts.

That is not, of course, a Christian teaching. And Walker Percy (not to mention Martin Luther King, Jr.) might be right that living out the proposition that "all men are created equal" requires a Christian dimension that Atticus can't provide. The Christian dimension of Atticus's message to the jurors is that we're all sinners—liars and cheaters lusting in our hearts. But his point is that we all—black and white—equally need the restraint of the law, not that we're all equally worthy of love.

Still, it's not the case that the courts are somehow better than the people. "A court is only as sound as a jury, and a jury is only as sound as the men who make it up," says Atticus. The courts only fulfill their promise as levelers if jurors follow Atticus' injunction: "In the name of God, do your duty."

The rule of law isn't anti-democratic because, in our country, it depends on the virtue of the people. The rule of law, we can say, depends on a touch or more of the Stoic rubbing off on us all. Now, of course, on that day in fictional Maycomb the jurors didn't do their duty. Nor did Atticus expect they would. The book teaches children what they need to know and admire to grow up to be someone who does his duty despite what others may do.

We can see what Harper Lee tried to accomplish for her country—and not the South in particular—through the drama of Tom Robinson's trial. So what we learn from *Go Set a Watchman* is irrelevant for understanding the Atticus of *To Kill a Mockingbird*, who is a different and better man. Well, not entirely different, but better along the lines of his distinctive virtues. Atticus Finch, Harper Lee's gift to her country, is less a Southern than an American Stoic, one democratized by the egalitarian teaching of Mr. Jefferson.

The "teachable moment" here is that democracy needs men and women of rare and elevated virtues. We depend on them to elevate us all for being responsible for the rule of law.

Index